Constitutional Politics in Italy

Also by Mary L. Volcansek

JUDICIAL IMPEACHMENT: None Called for Justice

JUDICIAL MISCONDUCT (*with Elisabetta de Franciscis and Jacquelyn Lucienne Lafon*)

JUDICIAL POLITICS IN EUROPE

JUDICIAL POLITICS AND POLICY-MAKING IN WESTERN EUROPE (*editor*)

JUDICIAL SELECTION (*with Jacquelyn Lucienne Lafon*)

LAW ABOVE NATIONS (*editor*)

WOMEN IN LAW (*co-editor with Rebecca Mae Salokar*)

Constitutional Politics in Italy

The Constitutional Court

Mary L. Volcansek
Professor of Political Science
Florida International University
Miami

First published in Great Britain 2000 by
MACMILLAN PRESS LTD
Houndmills, Basingstoke, Hampshire RG21 6XS and London
Companies and representatives throughout the world

A catalogue record for this book is available from the British Library.

ISBN 0–333–75442–5

 First published in the United States of America 2000 by
ST. MARTIN'S PRESS, INC.,
Scholarly and Reference Division,
175 Fifth Avenue, New York, N.Y. 10010

ISBN 0–312–22608–X

Library of Congress Cataloging-in-Publication Data
Volcansek, Mary L., 1948–
Constitutional politics in Italy : the constitutional court / Mary
L. Volcansek.
   p.   cm.
Includes bibliographical references and index.
ISBN 0–312–22608–X (cloth)
1. Italy. Corte costituzionale.   2. Constitutional courts—Italy.
3. Political questions and judicial power—Italy.   4. Law and
politics.   I. Title.
KKH2620.V65   1999
342.45'00269—dc21   99–37889
                                                              CIP

This book is printed on paper suitable for recycling and made from fully managed and sustained
forest sources.

10   9   8   7   6   5   4   3   2   1
09   08   07   06   05   04   03   02   01   00

Printed and bound in Great Britain by
Antony Rowe Ltd, Chippenham, Wiltshire

For 'H' and the 'Kits'

Contents

List of Tables and Figure

Acknowledgements

The research for this book would not have been possible without the benefit of a Jean Monnet Fellowship in the Law Faculty of the European University Institute and a sabbatical leave from Florida International University. The faculty and fellows at the European University Institute provided a stimulating environment for discussion and exchange that affected my approach to the project. The earliest stages were assisted by Carlo Mongardini who invited me to serve as a visiting professor in Political Science at Università di Roma, La Sapienza. Many people were instrumental in helping me locate materials. Chief among them are Philip Cannistraro, Giovanni Cattarino, Elisabetta de Franciscis, Carlo Guarnieri, Silvano Labriolo and Giovanni Salvo. David O'Brien was the first to suggest this enterprise, and he was very helpful in reading early drafts. I was saved from making a number of blunders by the suggestions offered by Luisa Chiarelli, Raffaele Chiarelli and Robert Evans. Alec Stone Sweet made some invaluable suggestions on the theoretical level. A very special note of appreciation is due to Alessandro Pizzorusso, who likely disagrees with my premises and therefore my conclusions, but who painstakingly read earlier drafts for accuracy and offered many insights that have improved the final product. I wish to thank Aracelys Montoya and Phil Stroud for helping me with computer glitches, and Nicol Rae, John Stack and Lisa Stroud for their unfailing support and encouragement. My very special thanks are due my husband, Harry Antrim, who has read, discussed, questioned and edited every draft. If errors remain despite the selfless efforts of all of these people, they must be laid at my door.

1
Courts as Political Institutions

On Monte Cavallo rising from the center of Rome sit two eighteenth-century buildings that, like so much of the city, now house political institutions. The Italian Constitutional Court sits in Palazzo della Consulta, facing the seat of the President of the Republic in Palazzo Quirinale. Whether by design or not, the two are symbolically separated from the centers of political power, as the houses of Parliament, government ministries and party headquarters are clustered below, nearer the Tiber. That arrangement underscores the supposedly apolitical nature of the two postwar institutions that were intended to guarantee the republic, as well as to differentiate the new era from those past.

The Italian Constitutional Court, implemented in 1956, has been praised by many as having played 'a progressive role in Italian politics',[1] 'earned a position of solid prestige'[2] and recognized as 'one of the chief institutional successes of the republican order'.[3] Its position as a body presumed to be above politics has led, however, to its being largely ignored by students of Italian politics,[4] but the Italian political class knows that the Court can wield considerable political clout.[5]

This book is a study of the Italian Constitutional Court as a political institution through its first 40 years. Analysis of individual behavior has been the preferred approach of political scientists for some time, but the so-called 'new institutionalism' offers directions for analysis of political institutions as political actors. Legal institutions are clearly, at least in western societies, among those that have become visibly important for collective life.[6] And courts, particularly ones with the power of judicial review, present the clearest juncture between law and politics. Constitutional courts possessing that power have proliferated in Europe, first after the Second World War, then with the democratic regimes in Spain and Portugal, and again with the third wave of

1

democratization in Eastern Europe and the former Soviet Union. Constitutional courts in Western Europe clearly have political influence,[7] but they are hybrid institutions sitting astride the legal–political divide. Because these courts are semi-judicial and semi-political, they stand at the 'frontier of law and politics'.[8] The links between the Constitutional Court, other political institutions and Italian society are interactive, and constitutional claims affecting individuals, organizations and other political actors are regularly – and often, repeatedly – adjudicated before the Court.

What follows is a case study that will add to the growing field of comparative judicial politics. As more and more nations' judicial institutions are studied, presumably we will be able to construct broad and overarching theories to explain legal and judicial institutions and their reciprocal influences on and from the larger political world. My intention is to contribute another building block to that effort.

Courts as political institutions

The political bent of a court is a function of the actions of the judges, individually and collectively. Decisions of judges are, like those of other government officials, 'a function of what they prefer to do, tempered by what they think they ought to do, but constrained by what they perceive as feasible to do'.[9] Students of courts in the United States have generally focused on the first part of that formulation and attempted to explain judicial behavior as determined by the individual's ideology or values. That has been especially true for studies of the US Supreme Court. The latter two aspects, role orientations and institutional constraints, have been largely on the margins because, according to Segal and Spaeth, attempts to test their influence empirically have not cleared the hurdle of 'predictive validity'.[10]

The new institutionalism offers, however, alternative theoretical perspectives for considering the interface of law and politics. Approaches subsumed under that rubric open particularly fruitful avenues for consideration of courts elsewhere. In Europe generally and in Italy particularly, the actions of individual judges on collegial courts are masked by the use of a single opinion 'of the court'. The logic behind the single opinion is the same as that voiced by Chief Justice John Marshall in 1801: to enhance prestige and legitimacy.[11] The appellate courts of England and Wales, the German Constitutional Court and the Portuguese Constitutional Tribunal might be susceptible to analysis via the votes of individual judges, but the Italian Constitutional Court and a number of others are not. As a result, the unit of analysis must be ratcheted up a notch, and the focus shifted to the institution with its collective decisional apparatus.

The term 'institution' relates to more than formal placement on an organizational chart and extends to practices, both formal and informal, and includes ideas and symbols.[12] The essence of an institutional level analysis of courts is 'that legal doctrine and legal institutions, law and office, are comprised of social practice, the same aspects of social life from which conflict stems and to which it must appeal'.[13] The judges on the Italian Constitutional Court, like people on other courts and organizations, 'engage in continuous exchanges between themselves and their environment, and they struggle to manage the environment so they may govern their own destiny'.[14]

Can individuals be considered separately from the institutions in which they operate? Some analyses of judicial behavior found that institutional factors provide the backdrop,[15] while others confirmed that institutional features exerted an independent influence on judges and that judicial behavior was contingent on institutional factors.[16] Thus the judicial organization in which decisions are made shapes values and beliefs.[17] Indeed, 'the activity of politics cannot take place without the existence of sets of structures; these are the means – and the necessary means – by which and through which decisions can be made'.[18]

Individual political actions can be seen, in other words, as defined, channeled and constrained by institutional structures. That perspective is particularly inviting in the context of legal institutions, where tradition, custom, rules, ritual, symbolism and a learned tradition of the law combine to limit both the playing field and the options available to judges, lawyers and litigants. It also lends itself comfortably to comparative analysis and to cross-national considerations of similar institutional structures.[19] Laver and Schofield were able, for example, to explain variations in coalition behavior in Western Europe by including 'the role of some institutional and procedural features of the bargaining system under consideration'.[20] Structural constraints clearly exerted different influences from one system to another.[21] Similarly, Richard Rose found that variations among institutional arrangements were more important than personality or circumstances in explaining the office of prime minister.[22]

In the field of comparative politics, a concept that allows systematic consideration of courts and judges is particularly welcome. The language of law and the myriad technical variations from nation to nation have long been barriers to meaningful comparisons; the absence of explicitly defined independent and dependent variables has likewise inhibited the process. The new institutionalism offers a vehicle that explicitly recognizes the position that institutions as actors have in a political system. Simultaneously, it permits and even invites inclusion of the important elements of individual choice, albeit constrained by the institutional framework that includes political context. It leads to a model elegant in its simplicity: individual-level decisions (antecedent variables) are molded and funneled by institutional factors, both orientation and structure (independent variables), and then result in judicial policies (dependent variable). Because each new policy subsequently influences both individual actors' choices and the environment in which the decision is received, the model is a dynamic one. That simple, linear abstraction can be expanded and completed to fit a wide variety of judicial structures and to facilitate comparative analysis.

Judicial policy: dependent variable

Judicial policies are the products of courts that are politically relevant and, in this study, are the dependent variable to be explained. Courts make policies through the process of rule adjudication, a mode of decision-making that differentiates their approach from those of legislatures or executives. It essentially takes the form of 'rule-application, as the aim is to discover what rule should be implemented in a particular context'.[23] Courts have a distinctive style of political action that is passive, where issues are decided only after the fact and in which deciding requires a tediously detailed attempt to ascertain the factual situation and then what rule should be applied. This passive quality, together with the inability to enforce decisions, renders courts weak in contrast to other institutional players.[24]

Judicial policies are distinct from legislative and executive ones, particularly in their origins, but nonetheless 'they are also public policies'.[25] Judges directly make law when choosing among a number of potential rules or interpretations and eliminating rival ones. Even when courts are deciding a narrow dispute between individuals, they directly make law when the rule settling the issue is applied to future cases. The broader the statement of the rule, the more akin to law-making the judgment becomes. Courts can also be part of the causal chain of government policy-making by signaling problems to be addressed or by providing incentives or inspiration to other government actors. Courts have, moreover, the prerogative of lending legitimacy – or not – to political choices of other institutions, because of their presumed authority to say what the law is.[26] Rule adjudication results, then, in public policy, be it direct or indirect. The political importance of what courts do can, moreover, be recognized in any area of rule adjudication by the answer to a simple query: would the policy look the same had the court not been involved?

Policies made by courts can, at least from an analytical perspective, be categorized according to the motives that underlie them. Because such classifications imply knowledge of what was in the judges' minds, we 'travel a rather circuitous, inferential pathway' in our attributions.[27] Evidence from American courts has, even so, 'produced a series of strong hunches about how decisions get made'.[28] The two leading theories are the legal model and the extra-legal model, with the first focusing on the primacy of legal motivations and processes. The extra-legal model suggests, on the other hand, that factors other than strictly legal ones, such as values, preferences, institutional position and political or social environment, enter into the equation when judicial decisions are reached. Judges are motivated primarily either to achieve good law or to make good policy. The apparent simplicity of the distinction has an iceberg like quality, where much more is concealed beneath the surface. More to the point, the two are not discrete categories, and both motivations are likely intertwined in any given decision; one may, however, predominate. For analytic purposes, the dependent variable of judicial policy in this study will be dichotomous, inclining either toward the legal/jurisprudential or toward the policy/outcome.

The legal model is predicated on the view that all judges seek legal goals, but it implies something far more complex than Montesquieu's notion that judges are no more than '*la bouche ... de la loi*'.[29] It recognizes that judges have discretion, but suggests that they use their discretion to achieve good law rather than good policy, that legal clarity and legal accuracy are the foremost objectives. Legal clarity means, in this sense, that the law is both clear and consistent, and legal accuracy refers to a quest for the correct legal interpretation. A policy-oriented judge would not deny either of these two goals, but, as Lawrence Baum explains the distinction, 'law-oriented judges eschew opportunities to make what they see as good policy in order to make good law'.[30] There remains ample room for judicial discretion and even for disagreement as to legal answers among judges who are law-oriented.[31] The critical distinction between law and policy orientations depends on how discretion is channeled.

That judges are policy-oriented has been acknowledged in the US at least since the 1948 publication of C. Herman Pritchett's *The Roosevelt*

Court, which bore the subtitle, 'judicial values and votes'.[32] The major paradigm that has dominated the political science sub-field of public law in the US thereafter has been the so-called attitudinal model, which emphasizes the values and ideological preferences of judges.[33] The extra-legal model includes that dimension, but expands beyond it to reach an array of 'factors not only internal but also external to the Court'.[34] The judge who is policy-oriented is aware of and affected by all of those influences and aims to make good policy through judicial decisions.

The two types of judicial goals are difficult to discern and separate, in part because they are so similar and both are couched in the language of the legal model. Judges are, rather obviously, trained in the law and believe they '*should* base their decisions on legal considerations'; that predisposition 'biases the ways that they describe the sources of their behavior'.[35] Very likely every judge and every court approaches questions presented in both ways, some with greater concern for legal goals and others with more interest in the policy outcome. This is akin to what Perry found in his study of decisions to grant *certiorari* by the US Supreme Court; 'what triggers one mode or the other is simply the degree of concern about the outcome on the merits'.[36] Analysis of a single decision to attribute a motive is difficult, and the obstacles are compounded for collegial courts issuing only a single opinion. To place a decisional goal label on any one decision must be largely conjectural. However, examination of a line of decisions on an issue area over time permits deciphering the institutional inclination toward either legal goals or policy goals. Notably, in a comparison of capital punishment cases before the US Supreme Court, both the legal and extra-legal models have been found useful for predicting decisions, but a merged model that combined the two was the most successful in explaining the evolution of the judicial policy.[37] There is, consequently, no expectation even at the institutional level that a court will approach all subjects strictly from one or the other perspective. The design of my study is, therefore, an analysis of five lines of decisions to determine any tendency toward legal or policy goals in each. Finally, relying on the independent variables proposed, variations among issue areas will be explained.

Explanatory variables

The statement that judges' actions 'are a function of what they prefer to do, tempered by what they think they ought to do, but constrained by what they perceive as feasible to do',[38] provides an outline of the independent or explanatory variables for judicial policies. Attitudes, values and ideology constitute what judges would prefer to do. These individual-level attributes are antecedent variables, since they are voiced on the Italian Constitutional Court only in the privacy of the Court's chambers and are not reflected in distinct votes on any case. I focus on the institutional level of analysis for which the inclinations of individual jurists are assumed to be channeled by the institution.

What judges think they ought to do is their role orientation, which tempers their personal inclinations. Role theory has not been a particularly productive avenue for research, since the typical means of determining the role to which a judge subscribes has been to ask the judge. These self-described conceptions are likely influenced by the milieu of attitudes that a judge carries with him or her. Despite that obstacle, there is evidence that roles are a mediating factor between preferences and decisions.[39] Some early anthropological work on role theory offers a means of conceiving and isolating judicial roles at the institutional level. S. F. Nadel argued that there are three dimensions to any ascribed role: the peripheral, relevant and pivotal aspects. The peripheral allows considerable individual discretion, whereas the relevant recognizes some structural control but still permits variation. It is the pivotal dimension that is determined by the institution, and the absence of qualities on that dimension alters the whole identity of the role.[40] For a constitutional court, these pivotal elements are independence, authority and accountability, and the three are intimately interconnected.

Independence is a critical quality for courts, since the ability to declare authoritatively what the law is hinges on the perception, both of elites and the pubic, that judges decide impartially. Some argue that virtually no court is truly independent,[41] and others see courts as possessing degrees of independence.[42] Judicial independence is perhaps best defined as a court's having 'some degree of freedom from one or more competing branches of government or from centers of private power such as corporations, unions or religious organizations'.[43] Institutional independence is always tied to the qualifier, 'some degree', and that degree varies over time and subject.

The degree of independence of a court can be gauged by the manner of recruitment and security of tenure and compensation and is protected by the secrecy of deliberations and votes. The recruitment of judges is rather obviously political, and knowing who is responsible for naming the judges tells us something about the degree of independence a court may exercise. When, as is the usual pattern for constitutional courts, the appointing authority is another political institution, there is an apparent bias toward naming individuals who are presumed to share or support the political values of those responsible for the appointment. This tendency has been demonstrated on both sides of the Atlantic, but any given nominee's selection has failed to guarantee that, once wearing the robes, the appointee will behave in the manner the appointer anticipated or desired. Even accepting that caveat, those named by the sitting political elite likely share the prevailing values of that elite or are, at least, not out of line with them for very long.[44]

Fixed tenure and compensation are intended to enhance the independence of those serving on courts, but judges, like most people, often have other goals that may inhibit complete autonomy. Career and standard of living are assumed to exert no influence on Supreme Court justices in the United States, for whom a lifetime appointment and a capstone legal position are seen as sufficient. Judges who do not serve, however, for life may find ambitions and financial security relevant and, therefore, impediments to complete independence.[45] The cloak of anonymity in decisions and votes may serve as a counterbalance to external influences where future career and security may be implicated.

The *authority* or discretion of a court is linked in some measure to its independence. The hierarchy of laws and type or level of court often define the reach of a court's institutional authority. For that reason, Carlo Guarnieri's conceptual scheme that merges independence and discretion seems useful. He proposes a two-dimensional continuum that combines a court's autonomy with its legal competence or discretion. At the extremes are the executor judge, with low discretion and low autonomy and the politico judge, with both high autonomy and high legal discretion or room for creativity. Between those two extremes are the delegate and guardian judges.[46] When courts may invalidate actions of other branches of government or exercise a 'veto point' by substituting their own will for that of another institutional actor, they have the greatest authority or legal competence.[47] However, that authority may not always be exercised, and a judicial institution may be located on different points on the axes, depending on context and issue area.

Accountability is a term not usually associated with courts on which the judges are appointed to a fixed term, but there are, nonetheless, audiences in which the judges' standing matters.[48] These may include other office-holders, interest groups, the media, the legal community

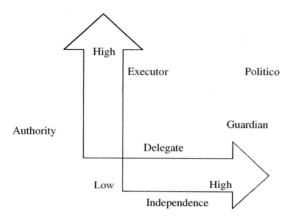

Figure 1.1 Judicial authority and independence. Adapted from Carlo Guarnieri, *Magistratura e Politica in Italia* (Bologna: Il Mulino, 1992), p. 27.

and the public at large.[49] Interest in the acceptance or 'approbation of certain audiences gives these audiences potential influence over the judges', though there is 'great difficulty of ascertaining influence and its sources'.[50] This form of tangential accountability may serve to reinforce an institutional role conception or incline a court toward a legal or policy preference on any given subject.

In addition to the institutional role, there is also the factor of what judges believe it is feasible to do. This is a second facet to institutional constraints that can influence judicial policies. These qualities may have been best captured by Yves Mény, when he asked should the emphasis in the term 'constitutional court' be 'on the noun or the adjective'?[51] Accenting the 'constitutional' underscores the political character, while 'court' highlights the judicial quality. Mény notes that certain institutional characteristics can lean more in one direction than another. Those that he points out as relevant are the mode of access to the court, the presence or absence of public debate, and abstract versus concrete review. In addition, the institution is also structurally affected by its place in the political scheme and its standing with the public. The context or environment in which a decision is made imposes a related structural determinant.

Access or the mode of application to a constitutional court limits who can bring a case. Unlike access to ordinary courts in Europe and virtually all courts in the United States, avenues to European constitutional courts tend to be strictly limited. May only other political institutions question the constitutional validity of a law, as is the case with the French Constitutional Council, or may an individual bring a constitutional complaint, as is possible in the Spanish and German courts? Access restricts, in turn, the range and scope of the questions that a court will be able to decide.

Likewise, the possibility for *public debate* can implicate a more judicial or more political quality for a constitutional court. Is there a public, adversarial discussion of the issues involved in a case, in which the interested or affected parties may present their positions? Rather obviously, public audiences where media coverage is possible and where airing of disputes is permitted push courts toward the goal of making good law, unless of course the issue is one that is politically divisive. Thus, despite the limited public awareness of court decisions, open forums for debate can facilitate judges' attentiveness to how the populace might respond and how other audiences will evaluate their decisions.

Abstract versus concrete review of laws and other official acts set some structural limitations on what and how a court may decide. Abstract review is akin to what Americans would call advisory opinions since there is no litigation involving a case. Concrete review refers to deciding constitutional legitimacy in the context of a real controversy with specific facts and live, disputing parties. The French Constitutional Council has only the power of abstract review before a law has been enacted, whereas the German, Italian, Spanish and Portuguese constitutional courts exercise *a posteriori* abstract and concrete review and both the Spanish and German ones receive constitutional complaints directly from citizens.[52] There are potential political implications, as well as strictly judicial ones, for either type of review. The ability to act on concrete cases gives a court a broader field of action and a greater potential to adjudicate rules involving old as well as new laws and to interpret the rules in specific factual contexts. The abstract variety is, however, more likely to place the court in the center of controversies between competing branches or levels of government.

A court's *political placement* in the scheme of government offers explanations for the types of policies it makes. For example, much of the effectiveness of the French Constitutional Council can be attributed to its position as a third legislative chamber, operating within the legislative space and on the legislative process.[53] Courts may also be within the judiciary itself, as is the situation of the US Supreme Court, or they can be separated from the judiciary and even rule on allegations of wrong-doing by the judges on other courts. Placement in the political scheme need not be limited to an organizational chart; institutional context includes the court's relationship with other political institutions. Courts are passive institutions, and their policies must be respected and enforced by other institutions; trust in and approval of court policies becomes especially important.[54] The rules that govern interactions with the other institutional actors are significant if judicial policy is to have any efficacy,[55] and the extent to which a court 'prevails in opposition to other political institutions is a strong test of how much impact it has in determining public policy'.[56]

Yet another structural dimension of political placement is a court's standing with the public, which is linked to legitimacy and prestige. Institutional legitimacy for national high courts in Europe has been related to the age and saliency of a court's decisions.[57] Evidence of the public's reactions to decisions of the US Supreme Court is mixed,[58] but in certain circumstances 'public knowledge of a decision can be quite high'. That finding may similarly shed light on public responses to high courts elsewhere. Clearly, legitimacy and prestige form the amorphous sources of authority on which courts are particularly reliant, even though much of the stable evaluation accorded, for example, to the US Supreme Court may be attributed to a general lack of public awareness.[59] Consequently, it is likely that a court's perception of its standing in the popular eye or public reaction to a decision may affect some of its decisions.

Context is the final institutional variable. This is a rather broad term with a temporal quality, referring to the social and political environment in which decisions are made and in which they will have an effect. Most environmental theories have been presented to explain how decisions are received and followed,[60] but environment also refers to 'the political context in which the controversy took shape'.[61] The external environment in which a dispute is formed and into which the decision must be received changes, yet remains a structural determinant of court policies. It also allows for a dynamic quality to judicial decision-making, since policies may be reconsidered once their reception in the larger political environment is gauged.

The possible range of cases decided by a constitutional court is vast, and many – indeed, possibly most – do not touch an exposed nerve that would trigger a policy response. Variations in judicial products between good law and good policy are likely to be located in those issue areas for which constitutional courts have a particular competence. The constitutional courts of Western Europe do not function as courts of first instance or as appellate courts following the British or

American models. Instead, their functions tend to be limited to three specific arenas. The first is guaranteeing the constitutional equilibrium both territorially and functionally. The territorial dimension refers to vertical arbitration between the powers of the central authorities and those on the periphery, whether local, regional or state. Functional equilibrium is the maintenance of balance horizontally, among the various central constitutional powers to preserve their respective spheres of authority.[62] The second jurisdictional realm is protection of rights and liberties.[63] Part of the rationale for a written constitution and for judges with the power to examine legislation for consistency with that constitution is that rights may be protected from the tyranny of the majority, as reflected in the legislature. Usually there is also a third, residual category that includes some kind of monitoring role in the political scene or organization of national elections, and it varies widely from country to country.[64]

These are the issue arenas on which I focus to examine the goals behind decisions of the Italian Constitutional Court. Maintaining constitutional equilibrium at the national level will be explored by looking at the Court's treatment of executive decree laws vis-à-vis the legislative branch. Territorial equilibrium will be considered through the Court's policies defining central versus regional authority. The Court's jurisprudence on radio-television pluralism represents its activity in application of Constitution Article 21, protections for freedom of expression, and is an example of the Court's treatment of rights and liberties.

The Italian Constitutional Court was given, like other such courts on the continent, responsibility for monitoring functions that are not normally in the orbit of courts. The first was to judge accusations against the President of the Republic and ministers. That has occurred only once, in the Lockheed case in the late 1970s, and the Constitution has subsequently been amended to involve the Court only in accusations against the Head of State. Also, the Court has been assigned a role in determining which referendum proposals will reach the electorate. Both of these more overtly political areas of the Court's policy-making will be considered. My intention is not merely to describe the Italian Constitutional Court, but to demonstrate that this court, like other institutions, is 'neither a neutral reflection of exogenous environmental forces nor a neutral arena for the performance of individuals driven by exogenous preferences and expectations'.[65] The Italian Constitutional Court is, in other words, a political actor.

Origins of the Constitutional Court

Studies of political institutions should include 'some indication of the origins of the structures or institutions' and, in particular, 'how those structures may have arisen from past, controversial political choices'.[66] The Italian Constitutional Court's early struggle to locate a place within the Italian political scene molded how it would act subsequently, and defined its role, both institutionally and structurally. Though the Constitutional Court (*Corte Costituzionale*) was a product of the work of those writing the first republican constitution for Italy in the aftermath of the Second World War, its antecedents can be found in earlier Italian constitutional history.

Monarchy and fascism

Four major phases in Italian constitutional history that preceded the republican one can be identified: the 'pre-Italian', the liberal state under *Statuto Albertino*, the Fascist regime, and the 'pre-constituent' phase.[67] The Italian peninsula was, after the Napoleonic occupation in the early nineteenth century, a mosaic of kingdoms and duchies with the Papal States bisecting it. The pre-Italian era served as a constitutional prelude to unification of the Italian state. There was, for example, a brief experiment with parliamentary government in Sardinia in 1793, but the monarchy withstood that challenge. On the Italian mainland the French example of republicanism was also challenging monarchical absolutism, and pressures for a democratically inspired constitutional monarchy were manifested all over the penninsula.[68]

At the end of the Napoleonic occupation in 1814, the House of Savoy was returned to power in Piedmont, setting the stage for the ultimate unification of Italy. Of particular relevance to later developments were the revolutions of 1820–1 in Naples and Turin, inspired by policies from liberal Spain that championed placing legislative power in an elected assembly. That inclination was later reflected in the constitutions of the Kingdom of the Two Sicilies, the Grand Duchy of Tuscany, the Kingdom of Sardinia, the Papal States, the Duchy of Parma and the 1848 *Statuto Albertino* of Piedmont, which eventually was extended to the whole of a united Italy as the first national constitution. *Statuto Albertino* borrowed from the 1814 French Constitution, the 1812 Spanish one, and the 1831 Belgian document, and the British model overlaid much of the whole. The guiding principle was that of constitutional monarchy.[69]

The Piedmont/Italian King retained considerable power – the whole of the executive and a share in the legislative. Parliament was composed of a Senate appointed by the monarch and a Chamber of Deputies elected by a very limited electorate. The *Statuto* also enumerated a number of liberal guarantees, including equality before the law, sanctity of domicile, freedom of press, protection for private property and the guarantee of individual liberty. The Constitution was, perhaps most importantly, a flexible one, and interpretation of the law was exclusively the prerogative of the legislative power.[70]

The elastic nature of the *Statuto* allowed it to be transformed in 1891, 1922, 1925, 1943, and again in 1946.[71] The expansion of the franchise in 1891 under Francesco Crispi was followed by a reactionary contraction under Giovanni Giolitti. But the most dramatic changes were those of 1922 and 1925 that heralded 'the great parentheses', or the 20 years of Fascist rule. In October 1922, in anticipation of Benito Mussolini's March on Rome, King Vittorio Emmanuele III acted without consultation and invited Mussolini to form a new government, an act that was subsequently ratified by the Chamber of Deputies.[72] The following year a militia was created and, in 1925, opposition parties were expelled from Parliament. The formation of the militia was described by Mussolini as condemning 'to death ... the old liberal democratic state' and expulsion of the opposition he likened to its funeral, that 'took place with full honors on 3rd January 1925'.[73] The pliable *Statuto* could also accommodate, as it did on 25 July 1943, the ouster of Mussolini and the King's appointment, without consultation with the Grand Fascist Council, of a new prime minister, Pietro Badoglio, and eventually the repudiation of the Fascist regime.[74]

An armistice was signed between the Italian state and the British and Americans in September 1943, and by June of the next year, a coalition of all major parties in Italy had joined in a Committee of National Liberation.[75] King Vittorio Emmanuele III abdicated in favor of his son Umberto II, and a decree provided that a Chamber of Deputies would be elected when the state of war had passed.[76] At the war's end, a new era of Italian political life began with the election of a Constituent Assembly in June 1946 that was charged with writing a new constitution. Simultaneously, through a national referendum, a republic was chosen over a monarchy by 54 per cent of Italian voters. Those two polls were the first in which universal suffrage had been practiced. The steady expansion of the franchise from a mere 1.9 per cent in 1861 to even allow women to cast their ballots in 1946 had been possible under the elastic *Statuto*.

Republican constitution

The Constituent Assembly reflected the cultural and ideological divisions within the Italian state. The Socialists held 115 seats, and the Communists 104, giving the left just over one-third of the 556 positions. The far right and monarchists won 46 seats, while the Christian Democrats had 207; the Liberals 41; and the Republicans 23.[77] This diverse body was not especially innovative, and its major additions to the old scheme were a rigid constitution, a constitutional court and regionalism.

Some kind of check on the constitutional validity of laws had been discussed as early as 1925, but had lain dormant until the fall of Fascism.[78] In 1946 the only models of such an institution were the United States Supreme Court and the brief pre-Nazi Austrian experiment (1920–34) that had been the handiwork of Hans Kelsen. Kelsen's notions, not those of the US, were the inspiration for the Italian Constitutional Court. Kelsen recognized a hierarchy of laws, with the constitution on the highest rung.[79] He argued, more importantly, that the position of a constitution could only be guaranteed 'if some organ other than the legislative body is entrusted with the task of testing whether a law is constitutional and annulling it if…it is "unconstitutional"'.[80] He rejected the US style of decentralized judicial review and advocated instead a special institution that alone held the power of constitutional review.[81]

The Constituent Assembly delegated initial drafting to a commission of 75 of its members, which was proportionally representative of partisan strength in the larger group. The commission's draft that was presented to the parent body on 31 January 1947 formed the basis for discussions and is remarkably close to the final version and included a Kelsen-style constitutional court. The most contentious debates and most vital compromises in the Assembly did not involve the Constitutional Court, but it was nonetheless subjected to criticism.

Early in the deliberations of the Assembly, Socialist Pietro Nenni challenged several elements of the initial draft, including the proposed constitutional court, as undemocratic. 'The secret flaw of this constitution is', he contended, 'the same found in our history from the *Risorgimento* and now: distrust of the people, fear of the people and sometimes terror of the people.'[82] The Constitutional Court was undemocratic, he argued, since 'the constitutionality of law that is not debated in the National Assembly, in Parliament, is not susceptible to control by the people'.[83] The fear that the Court would infringe on popular sovereignty was echoed by Nenni's Communist colleague,

Palmiro Togliatti, who asserted that a constitution must recognize that 'all power emanates from the people',[84] and, from that perspective, a constitutional court that would place judges above the parliamentary system was 'bizarre'.[85]

Others in the Assembly proposed instead to assign the power of constitutional review to the existing highest ordinary court, the *Corte di Cassazione*. Part of their reasoning was that the proposed new court would emanate either directly or indirectly from Parliament, 'reflecting the vices, the virtues, the contrasts and the defects of that body'.[86] The ordinary courts were viewed, conversely, as apolitical and able to resolve questions of constitutionality free from politics. The counterargument was that the ordinary courts had not behaved very independently during the Fascist era and could not be expected to do so in the future.[87] That point was particularly salient in 1947, since the judges sitting on the highest ordinary court then 'must have had some connection with the ideology of the past regime'.[88]

Codacci Pisanelli argued that legislatures on the Italian peninsula since the Middle Ages had abused every power, which suggested the need for an organ to protect the constitution from legislative usurpation. He expressed skepticism, however, that the proposed court, as a creature of Parliament, would effectively block an abusive legislature,[89] and his cynicism was shared by others.[90] The proposed constitution included a lengthy list of rights and responsibilities, subjective individual and community rights. The argument that a constitutional court was essential if any or all were to be protected from legislative encroachment persuaded many in the Constituent Assembly of its necessity;[91] it would act as 'the guardian and custodian ... of the spirit and the letter of the Constitution'.[92]

The 139 article long Constitution and 18 transitory provisions were approved in final form on 22 December 1947 in a secret ballot with 62 votes against and 453 votes in favor.[93] It was signed by the President of the Republic five days later and took effect on the first day of 1948. The articles describing the Constitutional Court are grouped at the end of the document, under the title, 'Constitutional Guarantees'. Article 134 authorizes the Court to resolve disputes on the constitutional legitimacy of laws and actions having force of law, settle conflicts of power and judge accusations against the President of the Republic and any ministers. Article 135 describes the Court's composition and method of appointment, while Article 136 addresses the publication of decisions and the immediate effects of a law that is declared constitutionally illegitimate. Article 137 requires a constitutional law to specify the forms of judgments and preservation of independence for the judges.

Birth of the Court

The Italian Constitutional Court was stillborn in 1948 and was not to hear its first case until 1956. Though the Court had been one of the less contentious provisions of the new Constitution, forces in the political world transformed it into a controversy during the first decade of the Republic. The Court's defenders in the Assembly had been from the centrist parties, and the left had openly opposed it. The motives of each, despite their rhetoric in the Assembly, had been relatively transparent. The left had been confident of its ability to win at the polls and had opposed measures, such as the Court, that could dilute its power. The Christian Democrats (DCs) and their more moderate allies had favored institutions that could check a left-dominated Parliament and, hence, had staunchly supported the Constitutional Court.

The major parties had united in a coalition, the Committee for National Liberation, in 1944 and jointly governed Italy until April 1947, when Prime Minister Alcide De Gasperi ousted the Communists and Socialists from the government. His action set the stage for constitutional implementation over the next two decades and for the shape of Italian politics until 1994. Two vast opposing fronts emerged, on both the national and the international levels: 'the one having its focal point in the employing classes, the Christian Democrats and the United States; the other centered on the working-class movement, the Communists and Russia'.[94] The first parliamentary elections in April 1948 shifted the political landscape and disproved the fears and ambitions of the two sides during the Constituent Assembly: the Christian Democrats won 305 of the 574 seats in the Chamber of Deputies. This was an absolute majority, even though the actual vote gave them just short of that mandate (48.5 per cent); the joint Socialist (PSI) and Communist (PCI) list won only 31 per cent of the vote and 183 seats.[95]

The partisan postures assumed at the Constituent Assembly quickly shifted as more basic issues of power arose. The DCs and their allies were bent on consolidating their hold, and the parties of the left found themselves seeking a means to gain a foothold. Since the Constitutional Court was potentially a rival power center, its implementation was not a priority on the agenda of the governing party. Still, Article 137 of the new Constitution required parliamentary action to determine 'all other provisions necessary for the constitution and functions of the Court'.

Legislative debates began in the Senate on 25 January 1949 and focused exclusively on the issue of the Constitutional Court's potential to control Parliament through its power of constitutional review and its potential to obstruct the majority. A text passed the Senate in March of that year and was forwarded to the Chamber of Deputies, that did not take it up until November 1950. The version that ultimately passed the Chamber in March 1951 included a variety of changes and significant amendments. It was returned to the Senate, where it was amended again before passing back to the Chamber. Law No. 87, 1953, was finally passed on 7 March 1953, more than four years after the debates had begun.[96] It was followed four days later with Constitutional Law No. 1 – norms integrating constitutional concerns relating to the Constitutional Court – that set terms and salaries for judges and defined impeachment and referendum review processes.[97]

The Christian Democrats' five-year rule with an absolute majority of Parliament led them to take even bolder actions to block the so-called 'obstruction of the majority' by altering the electoral system so as to cement their dominant position. The 'fraud law', as the Communist Party dubbed it, essentially prescribed that if a party or coalition of parties won an absolute majority of the popular vote, it would gain two-thirds of the seats in the Chamber of Deputies. The centrist party allies of the DCs – the Liberals, Social Democrats and Republicans – lent their support to the proposal, if only to prevent the Christian Democrats from shifting their allegiance to the parties of the far right. The law was passed just days after those implementing the Constitutional Court.[98] That law and the question of land reform were the central issues in the June 1953 elections, in which the parliamentary balance tilted. After the election, though Christian Democrats retained their dominant position, they no longer held an absolute majority. Their share of the vote fell to 40.1 per cent, while the PCI won 22.6 per cent and the Socialist Party 12.7 per cent.[99]

Results of the 1953 elections might have been expected to move implementation of the Constitutional Court on to the fast-track, but, in fact, the increased presence of the left in Parliament may actually have impeded the process. Selection of the judges then became the stumbling block. This process will be discussed in detail in the next chapter, but briefly controversies over how to select the judges and who had the authority to make appointments delayed implementation for more than two additional years, with the first judges finally being sworn into office in December, 1955, and the first session of the Court occurring in April 1956. During this entire period, all of the civil and penal codes, along with security laws from the Fascist era remained in force, and many of them were clearly inconsistent with the new Constitution. Some alleged that the Christian Democrats consciously intended that these laws continue so as to perpetuate a partially authoritarian state.[100]

Attempts were made in the eight-year lag between the Constitution's promulgation and the implementation of the Constitutional Court to undermine the new institution. The argument was made in Parliament, the press and the scholarly community that the Court could not rule on the constitutional validity of laws that pre-dated the Constitution (1948) or even the Court itself (1956). This position contradicted both the rule on chronology of laws (*les posterior derogat legi priori*) and Kelsen's conception of a hierarchy of norms that was implicit in the concept of a constitutional court. It was an undisguised attempt to preserve the entire corpus of Fascist law, despite the lengthy enumeration of citizen rights in Articles 13–54 of the Constitution. The very first decision of the Constitutional Court addressed the controversy head on. At issue were a series of laws and sections of the criminal code dating from 1931 that required authorization from the public security office to distribute flyers or newspapers on a public street or to hold public demonstrations or meetings using amplifying equipment. Article 21 of the new Constitution guaranteed, on the other hand, freedom of expression, both written and spoken, and freedom of the press unrestricted 'by any authorization or censorship'. Notably, the same question had already been raised in ten ordinary courts.[101] The Court announced its conclusion straightforwardly and without reference to the political or academic debate: Article 134 of the Constitution 'speaks of the constitutional validity of laws without distinction … among them by logic of date or grade … both anterior ordinary laws and posterior constitutional ones'. That is, the judges declared, 'the intrinsic nature of a rigid constitution'.[102] The public security laws fell to the requirements of Article 21.

The Italian Constitutional Court did not take its first official action until almost a decade after the advent of the Italian Republic. Many of its institutional features were defined by political choices made in the political arena, first by the Constituent Assembly and then by Parliament. The Court's subsequent field of action was colored and constrained by decisions pre-dating the Court's existence. The boldness, caution or accessibility of the Court over the next four decades was somewhat predetermined before its full implementation in 1956. The form in which the institutional characteristics of the Court have evolved are considered in the next chapter, and how they have affected different lines of policy decisions is explored in the subsequent five chapters.

2
Institutional Properties

Though the Constitutional Court is a twentieth-century creation, its setting and rituals evoke an earlier era. Palazzo della Consulta, the seat of the Court, is an elegant eighteenth-century edifice built by Pope Clement XII and one of many clerical properties converted to use by the secular state after the conquest of the Papal States. It housed the Ministry of African Affairs until its post-Second World War designation for the Court, but the transformation did not erase its heritage. The building is adorned with images of Justice and Religion, as though the original architect had foreseen the multiple functions that the building would serve. It is ironic that the edifice even bears the coat of arms of Pope Clement XII, since the Court was prominent in dismantling many prerogatives of the Catholic Church.

Rome is cluttered with historic buildings, many of which are now used by government agencies, but the importance of the Consulta derives not from its architectural features, but rather from what occurs within its walls. Whatever values or predispositions a judge, lawyer or law professor might hold before joining the Court, their eventual reflection in judicial policies is constrained by the institution's rules and practices. What each individual jurist is able to do is both limited and enhanced by the institutional role and by structural determinants. The historical legacy of the Court and its relationship with other judges, Parliament, the executive and the public set parameters for acceptable judicial policies. Independence and discretion, access and authority, are funneled by traditions, rituals, symbols and procedures that have developed since the founding of the Italian Republic. Recitation and explanations of rules is often dry, but these norms define both the game and the playing field.

Recruitment and independence

Selection of judges for the Constitutional Court is where direct political influence on them is most apparent. Judges for the Italian Constitutional Court are assumed to be insulated thereafter, since their appointments are for a single, non-renewable term. Politics may govern selection, but conventional wisdom holds that secure tenure and compensation bar direct political influences on sitting judges. That expectation fails to account, however, for the aspirations and ambitions that judges may have for post-Court careers.

Article 135 of the Italian Constitution describes the selection mechanisms, qualifications for the office, length of tenure and limits on non-court activities. The Constituent Assembly consciously chose to divide authority for naming the Court's 15 judges: one-third are appointed by the President of the Republic, another one-third by the two houses of Parliament in a joint sitting and the final third by the judges of the ordinary and administrative courts. Those eligible to sit on the Court are judges on the ordinary or administrative courts, including retired ones, and full professors of law or lawyers with at least 20 years of experience.

Law No. 87, 11 March 1953, delineated procedures for appointing the five judges named by ordinary and administrative judges and the five selected by Parliament. The judges are divided into three colleges to elect from among their number the constitutional judges. Those of the *Corte di Cassazione* (the highest ordinary court) elect three, and the Council of State and the Court of Accounts, both administrative courts, each elect one.[1] Those procedures have been only slightly modified subsequently,[2] such as provision for second ballots in the event of no majority on the first.[3]

The five parliamentary appointees are elected in a joint sitting of the two chambers using a secret ballot. To win on the first ballot, a nominee must garner three-fifths of the total number of parliamentarians, but on succeeding ballots, the requirement drops to three-fifths of those voting.[4] The super-majority was explicitly designed, according to DC leader Luigi Sturzo, to prevent any judgeships from going to the Communists, who would be the 'eyes of Moscow'.[5] In spite of Sturzo's efforts, the Communists won a presence on the Court, when the June 1953 elections altered the partisan balance in both houses of Parliament and the DCs and their allies no longer controlled three-fifths; the Communists were able to negotiate for one judgeship.

Implementing legislation ignored the five judges to be named by the President of the Republic, and an amendment of clarification was once passed by the Chamber but not by the Senate.[6] Confusion resulted, because of an apparent conflict between Articles 89 and 135 of the Constitution. Article 89 states that actions by the President of the Republic are valid only if countersigned by the proposing ministers, whereas Article 135 mentions the President alone as the appointing authority for constitutional judges. Prime Minister De Gasperi claimed, under the former provision, that the choice of constitutional judges was the prerogative of the Council of Ministers and that presidential action was merely ceremonial. President Luigi Einaudi refused to accept this interpretation, pointing out that Article 135 did not mention the Council of Ministers and, moreover, that the appointment of judges was clearly separate from any provisions requiring a counter-signature by the Council. Einaudi outlasted Da Gasperi and two – almost three – of his successors, but he was never able to name a single judge to the Constitutional Court. That fell to his successor, Giovanni Gronchi, who acting alone named the first five presidential appointees, but in practice, presidential nominations have paralleled the partisan affiliations of the parliamentary appointments.[7]

The first 15 judges named set a pattern that persisted for the next four decades. The ones chosen by their fellow judges were elected rather expeditiously. The three named by the highest ordinary court included the presidents of two sections and an advocate general. Presidents of sections were also elected by the Council of State and the Court of Accounts. Elevation of section presidents has been the norm and that practice opens vacancies for other judges to advance within the judicial hierarchies. Parliament named one lawyer and four professors of constitutional law. Appointees of the President of the Republic were diverse and particularly distinctive. Gronchi appointed the first President of the Republic, Enrico de Nicola, who was a lawyer of requisite standing and a senator; Gaetano Azzariti, who had been an active participant in the Constituent Assembly and was honorary president of the *Corte di Cassazione*; Tomaso Perassi, who had also been an important member of the Constituent Assembly and a professor of international law; Giuseppe Capolgrassi, professor of philosophy of law; and Giuseppe Castelli Avolio, president of a section of the Council of State. The noted lawyer, professor and legal philosopher, Costantino Mortati, who had also been an instrumental player in the Constituent Assembly, was appointed to replace Perassi in 1960. Once President Gronchi independently made his appointments, the precedent was set that presidents named individuals to the Court without formal consultation, and President Giuseppe Saragat even appointed judges after a government had resigned.[8] The Council of Ministers co-signs the appointments, but that is now a mere formality.[9]

Nominations by Parliament are clearly driven by politics and not just by the desire to name a like-minded judge to the Court. These appointments are part of a larger patronage system, known as the *lottizzazione*, that dictates allocations of a bargained proportion of positions to each political party. The formula followed by Parliament from 1956 to 1994 and, in practice by the President, called for two for the Christian Democrats, one each for the Communists and Socialists, and the last for rotation among the lay parties (Republicans, Liberals and Social Democrats).[10] A candidate forwarded by a party was not, however, assured of the appointment, but rather some person nominated by the party must get the seat.[11]

The Italian political system was dramatically altered after 1994,[12] with the demise of the old parties; only the former Communists, now renamed the Democratic Party of the Left (PDS), of those previously part of the *lottizzazione* remained.[13] The major new alignments did not have an agreement on apportioning seats on the Constitutional Court, so when a vacancy occurred, nominations were simply subjected to a vote by the two houses in a joint sitting. Without any agreements, partisan bickering left the Court operating with a bare quorum of 12 for a goodly part of 1995. The vacancies, when finally filled in 1996, retained the flavor of the earlier distribution.[14]

From 1956 until 1997, 77 people served on the Constitutional Court. All 25 named by the judges were, not surprisingly, other judges. The ordinary judiciary typically has three to four factions representing them at any given time, factions that are linked with differing ideological positions, clearly left, center and right-center of the political spectrum,[15] but not associated with political parties or candidates for the Constitutional Court.[16] Presidents of the Republic have the greatest flexibility in selecting judges and, while adhering to the prescribed partisan distribution, have also made other symbolic statements through their appointees. In 1996, for example, President Oscar Luigi Scalfaro named the first woman, Fernanda Contri. Presidents have tended to favor law professors for the Court, with 80 per cent of those appointments going to academics, and only three judges and three practicing lawyers have been named by the head of state. Parliament has also favored law professors, but there have been seven practicing lawyers and two judges named by the legislature, along with 14 academics.

Ideological persuasions, party ties and personal allegiances color nomination and selection. Once judges are named, however, the goal of judicial independence was thought to be secured by the twin features of lengthy tenure and secure salaries. Tenure was originally for 12 years, according to the 1953 implementing legislation, but reduced to nine years in 1967. Judges have always had only a single, non-renewable term. Their salaries were made equivalent to those of the highest judges on the ordinary courts, and they were granted immunity for their votes and opinions expressed in the course of their duties.[17] Judges were also prohibited from practicing their professions or accepting any other position while on the highest court.[18]

The average age of the first 73 constitutional judges at the time of appointment was nearly 62. Some were appointed, though, at quite young ages: Francesco Bonifacio was only 40; Aldo Sandulli, 42; Livio Paladin, 44; Antonio Baldassarre, 46. At the other end of the age spectrum, Enrico de Nicola, the first president of the Court was 78 when he took office, and five others were 70 or older. The relative youth of many of the appointees and their non-renewable terms has led to a rather novel phenomenon implicating judicial independence. A number have gone on to other political positions at the conclusion of their time on the Court, and even those who began their terms at chronologically more mature ages have not been deterred from further political careers. Consequently, career choices *after* one's service is completed introduces a measure of self-interest, be it standard of living or career ambitions, that may impinge on judicial independence.[19] There are several notable examples of careers following a stint on the Court. President of the Court Leopoldo Elia was regarded in 1985 as a candidate for President of the Republic, but a Court decision on a proposed referendum that year may have ended his chances.[20] Presidents of the Court Giuseppe Branca, Francesco Bonifacio, Paolo Rossi, Leonetto Amadei, Leopoldo Elia and Antonio La Pergola were all subsequently candidates for either the Italian or the European Parliament,[21] and Giovanni Conso, Ettore Gallo and Vincenzo Caianiello later served as Ministers of Justice. Interestingly, Giuliano Vassalli reversed that career track, having been Minister of Justice before he went on to the Court.

Partisan or ideological voting by constitutional judges is concealed by the prohibition on separate opinions, either dissenting or concurring. The pluralistic composition of the Court resulting from the party formulas has likely moderated some individual inclinations, and shared interests in maintaining intra-court harmony and limiting workloads emerge as goals that can transcend ideological divisions.[22] The collegial nature of the Court and its pluralistic composition are intended to protect institutional independence.

Access

Avenues to a court limit policy questions in two ways – who can bring cases and what questions can be raised. The issues raised by political institutions differ from those presented in cases reaching courts through appeals or referrals. The very nature of the questions decided, those of constitutional validity, makes both forms of access politically relevant. A constitutional court not only allocates values, but also arbitrates among fundamental values for the polity. Article 134 of the Constitution defines the jurisdiction of the Court as deciding the constitutionality of laws and actions having the force of law, resolving conflicts among various parts of government and trying accusations against ministers and the President of the Republic. The last of these has been invoked only once, in the Lockheed scandal of 1979, and the Constitution was modified in 1989 to limit the Court's role to trying accusations only against the President of the Republic.[23]

One route to the Court is by indirect access, a procedure akin to, but not the same as, an appeal. It occurs when, in the course of litigation involving a concrete case, an issue of constitutionality is raised. The judge trying the case, the judge *a quo*, halts the litigation and refers the constitutional question to the Constitutional Court, which decides only the constitutional issue. Then, the judge *a quo* applies it to the merits of the case. This form of preventive review separates the two categories of judges, placing the issues of constitutionality in the hands of the judges of the Consulta and the decision in the specific case in those of the ordinary judge.[24] The judge *a quo* retains the prerogative at the outset to decide if the constitutional claim is relevant to the merits of the case and, at the end of the process, to apply it directly in the case. This is called constitutional control *in via incidentale* (or as incidental to the case), and 90 per cent of the Court's caseload involves this type of access.[25] The system maintains a balance, then, whereby the judge *a quo* possesses total discretion in deciding if the outcome of the case hinges on a viable constitutional challenge to a law and can deflect questions away from the Court. In a parallel manner, the Court may sidestep a question by declaring it inadmissible or unfounded.

Only organs of the state can use direct access whereby a complaint is lodged directly with the Court: a region or regions may challenge the national government and visa versa or regions may sue one another. Similarly, the Constitution charges the Court with arbitrating 'conflicts of attribution' or controversies among the branches of the national government. Both types of case begin directly with the Court, acting as the court of first instance. These are cases *in via principale* (principal issues of the case),[26] and when cases are brought in this fashion, the review is abstract. Obviously, when review is limited to the abstract kind and coupled, as in Italy, with direct access from political institutions, the questions posed are limited but touch major political controversies. Preventive review involving referrals allows, however, consideration of a much wider field of questions, ones that other political actors might prefer to leave unanswered.

A distinctive competence of the Constitutional Court lies in the referendum process, whereby a law passed by Parliament may be revoked through a popular vote. The Constitution restricts the laws that are susceptible to this form of repeal and sets certain subjects beyond the reach of popular referendums. The 1953 constitutional law charged the Court with determining the constitutional admissibility of proposed referendums.[27] The Court's management of referendum questions will be considered in Chapter 6.

Public or secret

Public debate and use of a single opinion are intended to preserve prestige and emphasize that decisions represent legal policies. Public audiences are the norm for the Italian Constitutional Court, except for decisions on admissibility of referendum cases. Audiences are held on an upper floor of Palazzo Consulta and conducted with elaborate staging. The 15 judges in their black robes and hats occupy a semi-circular table, and advocates presenting cases also don robes for the recitation of their arguments. A dozen or more cases may be heard in a single morning, and the audiences are rather routine. The judge assigned as the reporter for each case explains its essential elements, and then the advocate or advocates for each side present brief arguments. There are no questions, no interchanges, no theatrics and little moving rhetoric. At the conclusion of the morning's audiences, the judges retire to the adjoining council chamber for deliberation and decision.

Decisions are made by majority vote, and in the case of a tie, the president's vote carries the decision. Votes are secret, and porters at the Court delight in pointing to the fireplace in which the ballots are burned. Whether that is mere apocryphal lore or the actual practice, the Court has conscientiously preserved the secrecy of its deliberations. The judge who served as the reporter for the case votes first, and is followed by others according to age, beginning with the youngest and ending with the president, who votes after the oldest judge. The reporter judge then drafts the decision of the Court, which will be approved at a later meeting.[28] The prescribed form of the decision is unitary, with neither dissents nor concurrences. Despite the prohibition on individual opinions, judges have on at least two occasions voted against the Court's ruling and made their positions public, once in 1980[29] and again in 1994.[30] The question of separate or dissenting opinions is usually answered by the Constitutional Court quite simply: a single opinion protects the independence of the Court and insulates judges from political or other pressures. The Court in fact declared in a 1989 case: 'half of the security of independence comes from the impersonal nature of decisions'.[31]

Aspects of form and style of decisions were lifted from the practices of the ordinary courts. Decisions can be either judgments (*sentenze*) or decrees (*ordinanze*), with the former constituting a final order that concludes the case, while the latter decides only a procedure or question, but does not settle the case. For both, the Court follows a format in which the facts and legal issues are recited and then a decision declared. The Court has no formal mechanism for refusing cases, but has devised a means of calendar management that both limits the number of cases and avoids some issues. The Court simply rejects cases as inadmissible, when the question referred is seen as irrelevant to a decision in the case, or as unfounded, which implicates the merits of the case.

Judicial outcomes

This study focuses on policy-making by the Italian Constitutional Court, both public policy and legal policy. Specific lines of decisions will be discussed in the chapters that follow, but the Court's overall workload in aggregate numbers frames those cases (see Table 2.1). A complete portrait of the Court's work is impossible, since some information, specifically the number of laws that have been declared unconstitutional, is not available. No records are maintained on that subject because of the disorganization of the statute books.

A sense of the Court's use of constitutional review can be gleaned from published sources. Each year, for example, a leading reporter of Constitutional Court decisions, *Giurisprudenza Costituzionale*, published, until 1966, a compendium of all cases in which a law had been declared unconstitutional. For that ten-year period, 108 national laws and 13 regional laws had been invalidated in whole or in part, along with eight sections of the Civil Code, one of the Code of Civil

Procedure, five of the Navigation Code, 16 of the Criminal Code, and one of the Military Code.[32] That pace did not slow. In 1967 another 41 national laws and nine sections of the codes were found to run afoul of the Constitution,[33] and, more recently, in the first four months of

Table 2.1 Caseload of the Constitutional Court

Year	Cases received	Judgments	Ordinances	Indirect access	Direct access	Conflict of power	Other
1956	414	22	12	349	50	15	
1957	132	102	27	105	19	8	
1958	80	49	34	52	15	13	
1959	152	47	22	130	16	6	
1960	119	49	26	95	13	11	
1961	241	60	19	224	2	15	
1962	226	68	59	210	9	7	
1963	270	109	65	213	55	2	
1964	211	82	38	193	9	9	
1965	266	72	29	234	19	13	
1966	272	93	37	245	21	6	
1967	315	119	37	279	17	19	
1968	310	111	32	288	8	14	
1969	489	124	42	473	8	8	
1970	420	137	68	395	14	11	
1971	525	139	71	490	11	23	1
1972	507	170	54	421	61	25	
1973	490	144	45	454	20	16	
1974	587	215	86	550	18	18	1
1975	697	197	54	635	24	37	1
1976	840	192	83	764	38	38	
1977	672	nr	nr	nr	nr	nr	1
1978	771	31	56	nr	nr	nr	
1979	1085	88	59	nr	nr	nr	
1980	989	116	82	nr	nr	nr	
1981	964	115	90	nr	nr	nr	
1982	1025	154	112	952	51	21	
1983	1173	134	243	1101	41	31	
1984	1493	121	188	1448	47	58	
1985	1271	179	207	1116	54	1	1
1986	1247	162	157	1160	49	27	
1987	916	239	402	864	25	25	
1988	1298	876	422	1083	102	113	
1989	833	370	226	698	107	24	4
1990	884	241	354	760	81	40	3
1991	863	259	262	753	54	55	1
1992	939	267	230	807	72	46	14

Table 2.1 (Continued)

Year	Cases received	Judgments	Ordinances	Indirect access	Direct access	Conflict of power	Other
1993	942	294	219	809	83	43	7
1994	955	286	207	803	90	46	16
1995	972	308	233	827	84	46	16
1996	1122	234	203	1062	32	6	
1997	1073	242	229	918	78	18	30

Note: nr – not reported.
Data for this table are taken for years 1956–76 from Nicola Occhiocupo (ed.), *La Corte Costituzionale tra Norma Giuridica e Realtà Sociale* (Padua: CEDAM, 1984), 518–20. Subsequent years were gleaned from Alessandro Pizzorusso, 'Attività della Corte Costituzionale nella Sessioni, 1987–88', *Il Foro* (1988), IV 389–410; and 'La Giustizia Costituzionale 1956–1989, 1990, 1991, 1992, 1993, 1994, 1995, 1996, and 1997: Discorsi e Conferenze Stampa dei Presidenti della Corte Costituzionale' (Rome: Unpublished Documents of the Constitutional Court).

1995, 18 laws and two code sections were wholly or partially invalidated by the Court.[34]

By way of contrast, the French Constitutional Council examined only 44 laws between 1958 and 1980 and, although much more active later, had considered a total of only 135 during the almost 30 years from 1958 to 1987.[35] The German Constitutional Court invalidated only 190 national laws between 1951 and 1990,[36] and the US Supreme Court has declared 152 national laws unconstitutional from 1803 until 1997.[37] The raw numbers have a clear meaning in France, Germany and the United States, but they can be misleading in Italy for two reasons. The first is the sheer number of laws that exist in Italy. Rudolfo Pagano estimated the number of laws by counting the volumes of *Raccolta Ufficiale*, which publishes all laws and decree laws; from the beginning of the Italian state in 1861 until June 1993, there were 1065 volumes.[38] An additional 42 volumes were published between the end of June 1993 and December 1995. Another study of the number of laws active in Italy in 1993 concluded that no one knows how many laws exist and estimated somewhere between 100 000 and 150 000. That can be compared to France, with 7325 statutes, and Germany, with 5586 federal laws.[39] Pagano verified that 13 316 national laws and 27 592 regional ones had been enacted between the founding of the Republic in 1948 and mid-1993.[40]

The matter is even more complicated since active laws in Italy include those dating from the monarchy and the Fascist regime. Indeed, much of the prestige the Court enjoys results from its role in dismantling portions of Fascist-era legislation.[41] The number of laws is further skewed toward the high side because many are what are called *leggine* or 'little laws'. Though there is no formal legal designation for 'little laws', the label derogatorily refers to incremental legislation that affects marginal sectors of society.[42] These 'little laws' inflate the number of laws on the books[43] and distort perceptions of the performance of both Parliament and the Constitutional Court.

The Court refrains, moreover, from striking down all laws that it deems unconstitutional and, instead, 'reinterprets' some offending acts so as to render them constitutionally acceptable. The result is a body of 'judgment laws' (*sentenze-legge*).[44] The German Constitutional Court also uses these 'weapons of limited warfare and, in doing so, limits the room available for parliamentary maneuver'.[45] The Italian Court uses similar weapons and, particularly in the early years, would validate the constitutionally acceptable portions of a law and eliminate the offending sections with declarations of 'constitutionally illegitimate *in the part that…*'.[46] It also uses 'substitutive' decisions that conclude with a declaration using the connective language of 'rather than' (*'anziche'*), whereby the Court does not leave a fragment of a law but removes unconstitutional elements substitutes an acceptable interpretation.[47] 'Additive' decisions are, on the other hand, ones in which Court-imposed language completes laws that would otherwise be unconstitutional because of omissions.[48] The Court's repertoire also includes so-called 'warning' decisions or *'moniti'*[49] and 'mechanical' decisions,[50] but additive and substitutive ones are the most prevalent.[51] The Court uses these creative interpretations when it believes only a single interpretation will achieve a constitutional result; when it sees several possibilities, the Court invalidates the law and leaves the choice to Parliament to do what it wishes.[52]

Good law or good policy

Stefano Rodotà recalls that at a conference on the Constitutional Court in 1981 the political role of the Court was off-handedly mentioned by all of the participants, whereas ten years earlier, such characterization would have been disputed vigorously.[53] More recently, the politicization of all Italian judges on high courts, including those on the Constitutional Court, has been studied.[54] Recognition that the Constitutional Court at times behaves politically, though, does not necessarily further an understanding of the legal versus policy goals of judicial institutions cross-culturally. Political consequences may follow decisions motivated by achieving only legal accuracy and legal clarity. The goal of making good policy implies, however, political incentives.

The model from Chapter 1 as applied to the Italian Constitutional Court assumes that whatever biases or ideological predispositions a judge carries to the Court will be channeled by the institutional setting. The attributes of the institution, both in role orientation and structure, vary cross-nationally and over different subjects. Pivotal aspects of the Court's role are shaped by the mix of independence and authority of the judges. Whereas judges' independence is preserved by appointment to a single, non-renewable term, appointments by Parliament and the President are quite openly along party lines. Even though the formula that governed the distribution of positions among the parties was rendered obsolete after the 1994 elections, an equilibrium of right and left has been respected in subsequent appointments.

Judicial independence, whether absolute or in a reduced measure, is relevant primarily as it exists in tandem with the authority that the judges wield. Judges may, to use Guarnieri's terminology, be delegates with high discretion and low autonomy, executors with low autonomy and low authority, guardians with high degrees of independence but minimal room for creativity, or politicos, with both high insulation and high authority.[55] The categories are not discrete ones, and both independence and authority connote relative degrees on a continuum. More importantly for the Italian case, the judges may assume different points on those two axes depending on the subject before them and the specific time period.

Though independence is protected by secure tenure and compensation, the Italian Court has chosen to reinforce the autonomy of individual judges through the use of a single opinion of the court. The use of a single decision is self-consciously intended to enhance the Court's prestige and to create the impression that the judges' conclusions are driven only by the goal of good law. Individual judges also benefit from the mantle of anonymity that the single decision offers, masking self-interest or other motivations. Judges everywhere have audiences to whom their work is addressed – political branches of government, the media, the legal community, the scholarly world and the public. A desire for the approbation of these extra-court groups can influence certain decisions. The Italian experience presents a peculiar situation that makes the thesis of other audiences' impinging on judicial decisions quite plausible. Aspirations of judges for post-judicial careers would naturally depend on reception of their work by other audiences. Though such goals are rarely a consideration for justices on the US

Supreme Court who have life tenure, it is a realistic one for judges situated otherwise. That potential influence must be calculated in the independence–authority equation.

Structural features of the Italian Constitutional Court must also be counted among the attributes that may temper the goals that judges pursue in their decisions. Access to a court may extend or restrict the content of judicial policy. In the Italian case, more blatantly political issues may reach the Constitutional Court through direct access from the other branches of the national government and from the regional governments. Most direct access questions leave little room for judicial creativity, but they constitute a mere fraction of the Court's work. Most cases come through indirect access and permit the Court a wider range of questions for preventive review. The Court is dependent in direct access, however, on referrals from judges on other courts. The route to the Court does not necessarily implicate a result that is more likely good policy than good law.

The same can be said of abstract versus concrete constitutional review. Neither automatically provokes a jurisprudential or policy mode for the Court. The number of abstract constitutional review cases is small and restricted to determining the validity of regional legislation; its relevance is minimal. The bulk of the Court's work involves concrete review. Likewise, public debate and open hearings need not denote more policy versus legal goals for the Court. Rather, the open airing of the issues preserves the legitimacy of the Court and lends an aura of legalism for public consumption. At the same time, crucial decisions on admissibility of cases are made in council without benefit of a public airing, as are decisions on referendum questions.

A final structural component of the institutional role is the place of the Court in the larger political scheme. The Republican Constitution of Italy provided an outline in which the Court was assumed to serve, like the President of the Republic, as a guarantor of rights and institutional equilibrium. Since courts generally depend on perceptions of their legitimacy as a source of authority, they cultivate a bond with the public for their standing vis-à-vis other governing bodies. Timing is essential in attaining that place. The Court's standing in the Italian political scheme has evolved, and evaluation of its policies must always look to the political environment in which decisions were made. Institutional place is movable, and in trying to identify it one must always consider the political context. Judges, like other political actors, 'consider the environment under which they are operating',[56] and links between the Court and the other institutions of government and between the Court and the public determine what is feasible in any given situation.

Good law and good policy are both achieved by affecting the substantive content of the law. That is accomplished sometimes by upholding actions of other political actors, as well as by invalidating them. The Italian Constitutional Court has not limited itself to a dichotomous set of options, but has introduced an intermediate level of interpretation, either additive or substitutive decisions that stop short of overriding an act. An analysis of how the Court has used the weapons in its arsenal of constitutional review in five lines of cases will permit inferences about the goals of good policy versus good law, of jurisprudential versus outcome motivations of the Italian Constitutional Court.

3

Executive–Legislative Relations: Decree Laws

A major role of constitutional courts is ensuring constitutional equilibrium by balancing and arbitrating among competing powers within the central government and between the national and regional or local levels. The US Supreme Court is called upon to referee between Congress and the president only when issues of constitutionality are involved, and even then it will seek refuge in the political question doctrine or some other jurisprudential dodge to avoid being drawn into inter-branch disputes.[1] The US Court considers the preferences of Congress and the president in the regular course of its decisions, even when it is not necessary to do so.[2] European constitutional courts are not, however, equally able to skirt power disputes because most are directly charged with resolving conflicts between warring branches or levels of government. This function is a particularly delicate one, for the courts are in treacherous territory when they demarcate the boundaries of other powers. Moreover, because of the nature of their recruitment, most constitutional judges are also ruling in such cases on the prerogatives of those who placed them in office.[3]

The Italian Constitutional Court is, like its counterparts elsewhere in Europe, the umpire in disputes over power. Most such conflicts reach the Court not as Parliament versus government or region against central government, but rather when a private party alleges injury as a consequence of *ultra vires* exercise of power by one or another branch. That is how the Court was drawn into one of the longest tugs-of-war between the legislative and executive branches – the dispute over executive use of decree laws. The Court's handling of that conflict illustrates how it has maintained the constitutional balance at the national level.

The Italian executive is authorized by Article 77 to issue decree laws, or more simply decrees, in 'extraordinary cases of necessity and urgency'. These are 'provisional measures having the force of law' that are invalid retroactively if 'not converted into law within sixty days of their publication'. Parliament can, even so, regulate the extent of the retroactive effects of decrees that were not converted. The executive came progressively to rely on decrees to govern, thus skewing the relationship between legislative and executive bodies. With increasing frequency, the Constitutional Court was called upon to intervene. The Court trod cautiously around the controversy, even though governments pushed the outer limits of their authority and Parliament periodically rebelled. More than 2000 decree laws were issued, and half of those were then reissued, a controversial practice with no constitutional foundation. Of those, only one decree, a reissued one, was annulled by the Court, until the judges finally drew a line in 1996 and declared the executive practice of reissuing unconverted decrees unconstitutional.

Earlier political choices

Decree laws had been a regular feature of Italian politics under the monarchy, as *Statuto Albertino* had, in Article 3, enabled Parliament and the King 'to exercise collectively' the legislative power,[4] and executive decree laws evolved as one means of legislating. Pre-republican practices set the tone for how executive decrees might be employed. The number of decree laws was not large initially, numbering only about 70 until after the First World War.[5] There were from time to time isolated attempts by the ordinary judiciary to limit their use, but these were notably unsuccessful. Later, the number of decree laws grew exponentially in an attempt to confront the economic and social problems that the First World War had produced,[6] and 1043 decrees were issued in 1919 alone.[7] Under the Fascist regime decree laws were supposedly regulated by statutes passed in 1926 and again in 1939,[8] but the executive nonetheless frequently bypassed the legislature through the decree device.[9]

The practice was carried over into the republic, and Article 77 of the postwar constitution governed its use. The major difference was the new system's emphasis on the temporary nature of decree laws, calling them 'provisional measures' and stipulating that they 'lose effect from their inception if they are not converted into law'. What occurred over the next half century has been described as 'somewhere between a solemn institutional clash and an opera buffa'.[10] The executive exercised legislative power by passing decrees that become priorities on the parliamentary agenda, since they must be enacted or rejected within 60 days from the date on which they are published. The chambers of the legislature have options beyond simply accepting or rejecting the decree; they may change it through amendments. When Parliament did not act within the specified 60 days, the government began in 1964 to 'reiterate' or reissue the decrees for another 60 days. Then, one was reissued a second time and eventually the extensions were nearing three years.

Judges' initial responses

The use of decree laws raised a number of constitutional questions, ranging from their legal character to their validity if not converted. There were also issues relating to the retroactive effects of amended decrees and rejected ones. How was the situation of 'extraordinary necessity and urgency' to be assessed, and, of course most central, how much could the executive manipulate or control the legislative process through decrees?

The Constitutional Court's handling of these and other queries is best understood in the larger context of legislative–executive relations. Throughout the Republican era, political parties rather than institutions have been the central actors on the political stage and were the conduits to the institutions of the state. Hence the Italian government has been labeled a *partitocrazia* or government by the parties.[11] Policies were formulated and negotiated through the parties, with parliamentary composition as the measure of relative party strength. From the early postwar years until roughly 1965, Parliament was the central institution of government.[12] The Constitutional Court came into being only toward the end of that period and, as a consequence, was peripheral to early inter-institutional conflicts.

In 1957, the Court considered the time limits for parliamentary conversion of a decree law. Its decision demonstrated that early inclinations of the Court were to allow the executive–legislative process to find its own equilibrium. The case involved decree law No. 1227, issued on 17 December 1955, governing conversion of real estate into hotels or pensions. The decree was not converted into law until 30 April 1956, well beyond the constitutionally prescribed time. The Court dismissed as a mere technicality that more than 60 days had lapsed between the decree and its conversion. What was important was that the decree had, in fact, been converted.

The Court's strategy in its second decade was simply to avoid the issue of executive use of decree laws when possible. In 1967 it declared the policy that would dominate its jurisprudence thereafter: decree laws have only limited effects without legislative conversion; therefore, only the constitutionality of the converted decree law merits judicial scrutiny.[13] Notably, the Court showed absolutely no restraint about reviewing converted decree laws and no hesitation about invalidating offensive ones.[14]

Some decrees were actually motivated by the Court. In 1970, for example, the Court invalidated one element of a law governing preventive detention, and the government responded with a corrective decree law. Another was prompted in 1974 to adjust the law on radio-television pluralism to conform with a pair of decisions by the Court. Other decrees were reactions to international necessities, as when an adjustment was necessary in the Italian laws involving export of objects of art and antiquities to achieve compliance with the Treaty of Rome as interpreted by the European Court of Justice.[15]

The Italian Parliament had moved from a position of centrality to one of marginality, becoming an 'empty legislature'. The Court was an accomplice in this shift since its acceptance of government decree laws as constitutional further diminished parliamentary prerogatives.[16] Parliament reacted in 1971 by rewriting its rules to expedite its processes.[17] That coincided with a progressive weakening of executive influence, such that in Parliament VI (1972–6) less than 70 per cent of government sponsored legislation was passed. Governmental stability simultaneously became elusive,[18] but the number of decree laws escalated. In the 16 years and five legislatures that had preceded Parliament VI, a total of 282 decree laws had been issued, of which only six had been allowed to lapse and four had been rejected. However, in the span between 1972 and 1976, 124 decree laws were issued by the executive and accounted for more than 10 per cent of all laws passed. That trend persisted and even accelerated.[19] Parliament became resistant, and the Court was approached more and more often with charges that the government was pre-empting Parliament's law-making power.

Non-intervention: the Court on the sidelines

Neither Parliament nor the Court reacted boldly to the increasing use of executive decrees, but by 1976 major changes were occurring in Italian politics. Parliamentary elections that June saw the Communist Party garner close to 13 million votes, trailing the Christian Democrats by a mere 4 per cent.[20] More importantly, the distinctions between government and opposition became blurred when all parties supported the government under a non-no confidence agreement.[21] Parliament VII's (1976–9) legislative record was largely a consequence of that agreement which collapsed in 1979 and brought early parliamentary elections. The Court stood on the sidelines as executive decrees became more numerous, accounting for one-fifth of all laws passed.[22]

In March of 1977 the Court again refused to hear a challenge to a decree law, when an ordinary court judge questioned a 1974 decree that made failure to have insurance coverage for automobiles a criminal act. The referring judge specifically questioned the constitutionality of decree law No. 99 of 1974 on the grounds of the absence of urgency or emergency to justify executive action. The Court responded consistently with its earlier pronouncements: the question was irrelevant, since the decree had ultimately been converted.[23]

The government's use of decree laws and the consequences of that practice grew. Subjects of decree laws shifted away from minor, microsectional or local topics to ones of general interest.[24] Parliament emerged, however, as a more equal partner, since minority governments could not presume support for any program without considerable consultation. During Parliament VII (1976–9), 167 decree laws came from the executive, and 136 were passed by Parliament, but 99 of those were amended in the process.[25] When the so-called grand coalition collapsed in 1979, parliamentary subordination resumed.[26]

The 1980s have been described as the era of *decisionismo*, or toughness, as more decisive executive action became the norm.[27] That stylistic change was reflected in parliamentary activity, and Parliament VIII (1979–83) witnessed the introduction of 275 decree laws, of which 169 or 61 per cent were converted, even though more than three-quarters of them were altered through amendments.[28] The government and the legislature adjusted to a new mode of operations, while the Court refused to hear cases involving decrees that had not been converted by Parliament. The Court's explanation was predictable: decree laws that were not converted were not laws and questions of their constitutional validity were not admissible.[29]

Increasingly the executive seemed to have no way of governing without resorting to decrees. The two Cossiga governments during 1980 (Cossiga I – January to March 1980 and Cossiga II – March to September 1980) issued 63 decrees laws,[30] and Cossiga II met its demise in Parliament as a result. In fact, three decrees presented by the Cossiga government were rejected by Parliament specifically on the grounds that they interfered with the legislative will.[31] The rate of conversion of decree laws then became inverse to the number of decrees issued by the government.[32]

General consensus blamed the problem on Parliament and its ponderously slow and cumbersome procedures. Governments had no alternative but to rely on decrees to have their programs considered,[33] with the result that Italy experienced a period of 'government by decree'.[34] The conflict between the legislative and executive branches sharpened, and the number of decrees either not converted or amended in the process increased along with the rhetoric.[35] Yet, there was another side to the decree law questions. The opposition and, more particularly, parties of the executive coalition were able to control the government through threats not to convert decrees, which enabled them to negotiate changes or modifications in reissued versions. Indeed, the theory on which parliamentary systems rests assumes that Parliament and the government are closely connected and are not designed to check one another. 'Political power is unitary and divided only by formal competencies and procedures' and power is stabilized by merging political–legislative–government into a single continuum.[36]

The assumption that, in parliamentary democracies, the government of the day is consistent with the legislative majority did not hold in the years when executive use of decrees became abusive. In the slightly over five years from March 1978 until August 1983, there were eight different governments: Andreotti IV (March 1978–January 1979, 9 months), Andreotti V (January–August 1979, 8 months), Cossiga I (August 1979–March 1980, 8 months), Cossiga II (March–September 1980, 7 months), Forlani (September 1980–July 1981, 10 months), Spadolini I (July 1981–August 1982, 13 months), Spadolini II (August–December 1982, 5 months) and Fanfani V (December 1982–August 1983, 9 months).[37] Not only were each of these governments short-lived, but also only one time, Spadolini I and II, reconstructed the same parliamentary coalition following the fall of one government and the investiture of the next. Connections of a parliamentary majority to the government were merely tangential. The distortions existing in legislative and executive relations raised myriad constitutional questions, but the Court declined to hear cases raising the issue.

The turbulent 1980s

Both the Chamber of Deputies[38] and the Senate[39] revamped their procedures to receive and dispose of decree laws more expeditiously, but

Italian politics changed in the 1980s, particularly after Socialist Bettino Craxi became Prime Minister in August 1983. Craxi personified *decisionismo*, and his combative style enabled him to remain in that position longer than anyone had previously. For three years a stable coalition of five parties governed.

Finally, after having absented itself from the decree law controversy for more than a decade, the Court was presented in 1983 with a voluminous challenge to multiple decree laws regulating the finances of regional governments. The governments of the regions of Lombardy, Liguria and Emilia Romana jointly raised 21 questions about regulations, most of which had their origins in four decree laws that had eventually been converted by Parliament. The general questions raised focused on constitutional encroachments on the financial autonomy of the regions, but some others were challenges brought under Article 77 of the Constitution. Two of the challenged laws were decrees that had been converted by Parliament, but in an amended fashion, and one that had been allowed to lapse without passage, but was then reissued and finally converted. The Court responded consistently with all of its previous decisions and rejected the challenges as unfounded since the decrees had, in fact, been converted; had the decrees not been converted, their effects would have been obliterated. Applying that rationale, even though one of the contested elements was a provision in a decree law that was not carried over into the converted law, the Court found that portion of the decree was irrelevant. The Court's sympathies were clearly with the executive, since the opinion characterized decree laws as a 'necessary and automatic consequence of the inertia of Parliament'.[40]

The battle over executive decree laws escalated during Parliament XI (1983–7). The government issued a record number of 302, but the legislature converted less than half (136), and most of those (129) were passed in an amended form. More remarkably, Craxi's government reissued 134 of the decrees that had not been passed.[41] Various explanations were offered for the staggering increases. The fragmentation of Parliament, persistent legislative paralysis and growing social problems that required specific and immediate action were all cited as causes of the decree phenomenon.[42] Alternatively, decree laws were depicted as a consequence of a weak government, incapable of presenting coherent programs and without a parliamentary consensus that could ensure passage of any government initiative.[43] Clearly there were some peculiar conditions that required immediate government responses, such as staving off speculators by quickly altering prices or tariffs.[44] That might explain some decrees, but not the total lack of connection between the two political powers.

Parliament became more resistant to passing government decree laws, and the executive began to make conversion of the decrees a matter of confidence, thus preventing the chambers from amending the laws and shortening the time between issuance and passage. Even that technique could be and often was undermined by the secret ballot. For confidence votes, an open roll call is used, but that vote may be followed by another one on the identical legislative text, but with a secret ballot. The government may win the former, but the decree can be defeated in the second vote. That fate befell Francesco Cossiga when he was Prime Minister in 1980, and one of his successors, Giovanni Spadolini, just two years later. In both cases, the governments resigned. In 1986, Craxi I also fell, after winning a vote of confidence by a margin of 100 and then losing a vote in a secret ballot on the decree law that had been the matter of confidence.[45]

The legislative and executive branches appeared to be in stalemate, when a third institutional party, the President of the Republic, intervened. President Sandro Pertini refused in 1980 to sign a government decree that would alter the method of verifying signatures on petitions requesting a referendum, and, in 1985, Cossiga, then President of the Republic, used his power of persuasion to prevent the government from issuing a decree to change radio-television industry regulations and again in 1987 to block a budget regulation.[46] Presidents are expected to be aloof from politics, but Pertini and Cossiga said that their actions were part of their obligation to guarantee the equilibrium between the powers of government and between the majority and the opposition.[47]

Judicial intervention

The Constitutional Court re-entered the dispute in 1985, when it considered a decree law that had not been converted in full. The decree lessened the penalties for erecting certain kinds of buildings without the required licenses. When it was converted, the portion on penalties for lack of the necessary permits was not included. The omitted portion was, in the view of the Court, an unconverted decree law. That created a peculiar difficulty, since the decree had intended to change part of the criminal code and not recognizing its effects amounted to allowing *ex post facto* penalties. The Court's jurisprudence had always granted priority to any law that was 'more favorable to the accused' to avoid retroactive criminality or increased punishment. Moreover, as the Court itself noted, the prohibition on *ex post facto* laws was an exalted principle, found in the 1789 French Declaration of the Rights of Man and Citizen, in the 1948 United Nations Universal Declaration of Human Rights, in the 1950 European Convention on Human Rights and Fundamental Liberties and, closest to home, in Article 25 of the Italian Constitution. Not recognizing the unconverted portion of the challenged decree law would run counter to that principle. Nevertheless, the Court chose to defer to other constitutional values; the unconverted portion of the decree law had no effect, application of it was unconstitutional, and criminal punishments could be imposed.[48] Decree laws are by definition provisional, and any citizen choosing to act on them in advance of parliamentary action places himself in a 'risky and dangerous position'. Indeed, had the Court decided differently, a government could arbitrarily issue decree laws favoring its patrons by decriminalizing certain acts or lowering penalties for some crimes. Only the scrutiny of Parliament was a check on that possibility.[49]

In 1988, the Court made a more dramatic statement on the use of decree laws. Governments had become progressively more blatant in their abuse of the decree device and, in particular, in their willingness to reissue unconverted decrees repeatedly. Only four decrees had been reissued in Parliament V (1968–72) and Parliament VI (1972–6), and during Parliament VII (1976–9), nine were reissued. Then a torrent followed: 71 were reissued in Parliament VIII (1979–83), 134 in Parliament IX (1983–7).[50] In 1983, the practice expanded in yet another form as decree laws were reissued not once or even twice, but up to six times.[51]

In March 1988, the Constitutional Court added its voice to the chorus already condemning the government's use of decree laws and particularly its reissuing them. The Court's decision was not a condemnation of the system of reproducing unconverted decree laws per se, but its intent as an admonition was clear. The dispute reached the Court *in via principale* from the Region of Tuscany, that complained that a decree affecting its authority was initially issued in 1986 and was reissued eight times, before being converted in a modified form by Parliament in 1988. That constituted, according to the regional government, an unconstitutional infringement on the powers of the regional governments. The law in question concerned regulations controlling sanctions, recovery and rectification in cases of abuses in urban construction.

A litany of constitutional improprieties were asserted by the region, but the Court side-stepped ones it deemed merely symbolic and those challenging the absence of extraordinary urgency or emergency. Instead, the Court pinpointed the fact of multiple reiterations. Repeatedly reissuing decrees laws raised, according to the Court, 'grave doubts relative to constitutional equilibrium and constitutional principles', since such decrees are 'practically irreversible (as, for example, when they infringe on the personal liberties of citizens) or when the same effects are accomplished, despite the fact that the decree was not converted'. The Court noted that not all reissued decree laws were unconstitutional, but, in this specific case, the challenged decree had 'created undoubted interference in the regional administration', by shifting conditions and starting points for the law. Reissuance of the decree had, consequently, 'rendered the regional powers enumerated in Articles 117 and 118 of the Constitution empty'.[52]

The Court's reliance on Articles 117 and 118 that govern regional authority, in lieu of Article 77, governing decree laws, muted the impact of the decision. Ambiguity also resulted from the invalidation of only one reissued decree, but not all of them. Could decrees be reissued two or three times, or more, but less than eight? Though the decision offered no standard and no criteria,[53] the political arena read it as a call for reform and, indeed, the Court itself later cited its 1988 decision as the stimulus for the far-reaching parliamentary reforms that followed.[54] In October 1988, a reform law passed, entitled 'Discipline of the Activity of Government', that intended to usher in a new era of legislative–executive relations.[55] It addressed a long list of sticking points in relations between the two national powers and was a compromise document that gave something to both the executive and the legislature. Since secret ballots had so long been a source of executive complaint, their use was curtailed and was to be permitted only for constitutional and electoral questions or for votes involving personal morality and family. Secret ballots had defeated much of the two Craxi governments' programs (1983–7) and that of the Goria government (1987–8).[56] That part of the reform law was welcomed by the government.

Article 15 of the reform law attempted to rationalize decree laws and required that they carry in their preambles an explanation of the extraordinary circumstances of necessity and urgency that justified their promulgation. It further provided that the government could not: (1) treat a decree law as though it were a delegation of authority from Parliament; (2) use decrees to address constitutional or electoral matters or ratification of international treaties or budgetary issues; (3) reintroduce via a decree a regulation that had previously been the subject of a defeated decree law or of a law that had been invalidated by the Constitutional Court. The reform legislation further required that decree laws must be 'specific, homogenous and correspond to their titles'.[57]

The 1988 reform law was greeted with skepticism, but Enzo Cheli defended it with a reminder that 'everyone says they want reforms but they are rarely translated into reality', and this is one 'that I wish well'.[58] Unfortunately, the law was found wanting as it applied to decree laws, and its first test, conversion of decree law No. 522 of 10 December 1988, illustrated the problems. First, the Chamber of Deputies did not pass the law and refer it to the Senate until 58 of the 60 days had lapsed. The Senate committee that reviewed the text of the decree concluded that it violated the required homogeneity, since it addressed a series of unrelated provisions ranging from the state radio-television system, artisans and universities to health, public works and civil protection. An amended version of the decree law was ultimately passed, long after the 60-day limit had expired.[59] Parliament's failure to meet its own mandates in a timely fashion reinforced the long-standing claim of governments that decree laws were essential 'safety valves' in times of parliamentary inaction and necessary to move programs through the cumbersome parliamentary maze.[60]

Despite the Court's one-time invalidation of a reissued decree law and the legislature's reform to regularize and limit government use of decree laws, nothing changed. In fact, the reverse happened: the government exercised its decree law prerogative with greater and greater frequency and, as can be seen in Table 3.1, reissued unconverted decrees more often and with seeming impunity. The number of decree laws steadily increased from 1987 through 1995. In the first two years of Parliament XII, 514 decree laws were issued and 348 of them, reissued; one was reissued 13 times and never converted.[61]

Parliament also resumed its habit of allowing decrees to lapse and of changing them through amendments. The only checks were Parliament's occasional (only 32 times from 1987–95) refusal to convert the decrees and sporadic attempts by the President of the Republic to block executive abuses. President Oscar Luigi Scalfaro had, in fact, refused to promulgate a decree law already reissued four times that would have set a mandatory retirement age of 70 for members of the judiciary. He refused to promulgate another on financing political parties that was already the subject of a referendum. Twice in 1994, Scalfaro returned conversion laws to Parliament for reconsideration in light of their questionable constitutionality.[62]

Table 3.1 Government decree laws by legislature (number of decree laws)

Legislature		Presented	Converted	Converted amended	Rejected	Lapsed	Reissued	Success of gov't bills (%)
I	1948–53	29	28	0	0	0	0	89.9
II	1953–8	60	60	35	0	0	0	85.0
III	1958–63	30	28	11	2	0	0	83.1
IV	1963–8	94	89	50	2	3	1	79.2
V	1968–72	69	66	44	0	3	4	71.8
VI	1972–6	124	108	68	0	16	4	68.2
VII	1976–9	167	136	99	16	15	9	56.7
VIII	1979–83	275	169	129	13	93	71	56.7
IX	1983–7	302	136	105	27	139	134	47.3
X	1987–92	466	187	148	15	264	224	50.3
XI	1992–4	490	119	84	8	363	328	*
XII	1994–**	514	97	75	9	408	348	*
XIII	1996–***	447	87	*	277	83	8****	*

*Not available; **Through November, 1995; ***Through 16 March 1998; ****Practice of reissuance declared unconstitutional 17 October 1996.

Note: Data for the first seven columns of this table are from Alfonso Celotto, 'Gli Atti Legislativi del Governo e i Rapporti fra i Poteri' (Parma: Paper presented at the Annual Meeting of Associazione Italiana dei Costituzionalisti, November, 1995), p. 3 and Servizi dei Camera dei Deputati (Rome: Unpublished document, 1998). The last column data are taken from Maurizio Cotta, 'The Rise and Fall of the "Centrality" of the Italian Parliament: Transformation of the Executive–Legislative Subsystem after the Second World War', in Gary W. Copeland and Samuel C. Patterson (eds), *Parliaments in the Modern World: Changing Institutions* (Ann Arbor: University of Michigan Press, 1994), p. 61.

Judicial retreat

The Constitutional Court was nowhere to be found during this renewed abuse of decree laws, and though many challenges to them reached it, the Court demurred on all. The Region of Sardinia objected to a decree law that presumed to regulate another unconverted decree involving both budget and accounting procedures. The Court declared the question inadmissible, while adding almost in the margin that it doubted 'the correctness of the government's work in light of provisions of Article 77'.[63] It again refused to hear a case in 1994 when approached by the Region of Sicily regarding a new regime of preventive control for the Court of Accounts. The Court acknowledged the implications of the decrees in question and their successive reissuances, but emphasized that the decrees were finally converted and therefore had the imprimatur of the legislature.[64] Similarly, when six questions regarding a 1993 decree law that altered the land registry for urban buildings were referred, the Court rejected all as either unfounded or inadmissible. The Court repeated that even though the decree had been reissued multiple times, the decree law was irrelevant: 'how many times must this Court affirm that, after conversion, the relevance of the decree law is gone and with it, the constitutionality of the government's power to issue decree laws!'[65] With that strong language, the Court made clear that it had no intention of acting on the legitimacy of executive decrees. That inclination was underscored by its refusal to hear a similar question about a decree regulating the Court Accounts that was raised by four other regions in 1995.[66]

A change of course came in October 1996, when the Constitutional Court finally invalidated a reissued decree law on the broad ground that *all* reissued decree laws were unconstitutional. That dramatic about face came with reference to a decree that governed recycling and imposed criminal sanctions on violators. The decree had been issued initially in January 1994 and was repeatedly reissued, without ever being converted by Parliament, until September 1996 – a total of 32 months. The Court argued that, first, the constitutional requirements of extraordinary urgency are lost when a measure is reiterated. Second, legal certainty is jeopardized when, as a consequence of repeated reissuance 'it becomes impossible to predict how long the decree law will be in effect [because] there is no fixed end point for conversion'. This uncertainty, the judges added, is even more serious when, as in this case, criminal sanctions are involved. And, lastly, the Court focused on distortions that decree laws introduced into the constitutionally prescribed distribution of powers. The opinion concluded with a strong warning that the Court would be more rigorous in requiring that decree laws meet the requirements of urgency and emergency and in expecting the government to respect the role of Parliament.[67]

Assessing the Court's reluctant intervention

A decree law had first been reiterated in 1964, and even though no part of the constitutional text sanctioned the practice, the Constitutional Court stood on the sidelines as the practice was transformed into a clear abuse of power. Multiple appeals to the Court challenged the validity of decree laws and particularly of reissued ones. Yet, in over three decades the Court invalidated only one on the very narrow and specific grounds that it had changed the terms of the original version.[68] The result was that, with the 'exception of one isolated episode', the Court had 'substantially abandoned the field [and] recognized its impotency in the sector'.[69]

Until 1996, the Court was wholly consistent in its treatment of all decree laws. It had fashioned a legal policy to justify its non-interference. First, decree laws are by their nature provisional. Therefore, whatever flaws may inhere in the decree law that are absorbed into the converted version can be judged when that law is challenged. Finally, Parliament is the judge of the conditions of urgency and emergency that give rise to a decree law and, if it converts the decree into law, it must have concurred in the assumptions of extraordinary circumstances. Notably, the reiteration of decrees is not directly addressed by any element of that jurisprudence, except by implication.

The Court's adoption of a legal policy to apply to decree laws does not necessarily mean that there was no political policy involved. Indeed, the Court's decisions can also be viewed as a series of strategic actions. The Court never enumerated a legal policy akin to that of 'political questions'. Similarly, it has no court-made standards for jurisdiction or justiciability that allow it to avoid issues on grounds of standing, mootness or concreteness. The Court had, nonetheless, clearly applied some rather stable notions about why it would not interpose itself between the legislature and the government on the issue of decree laws. For example, acting on a decree law could amount to deciding an irrelevant or moot question if the law were never converted. Perhaps more importantly, Article 77 of the Constitution granted Parliament the power to annul any decree law and, thereby, to obliterate its efficacy from the moment of its publication. For the Court to act in advance of a parliamentary decision would have infringed legislative prerogatives. The constitutional text had clearly ascribed the power to accept or reject provisional decrees to the legislature.

Was the Court seeking good policy by perhaps protecting its own institutional position or was good law its only goal? If legal accuracy and legal clarity were the sole motivations, why did the court change its policy so abruptly? Notably, the 1996 decision addressed *only* the practice of reissued decrees, not all decree laws. With that perspective in mind, the 1996 judgment can be seen as a logical extension of the 1988 decision in which reissued executive decrees were assailed for undercutting legal certainty when there is no fixed point for conversion. Similarly, the 1996 judgment had at its core that legal certainty is jeopardized when a decree law is reproduced, even in identical terms, over a three-year period without legislative conversion. The other points cited in the decision – loss of urgency and the executive–legislative imbalance – have at their base the principle of legal certainty.

All other elements of executive decree law practices remained intact, and the Court did not say that it would examine executive motives or rule on the validity of decree laws not converted. The Court directed its aim squarely at the most abusive aspect of the decree phenomenon, the practice of reissuance. The decision left, however, unanswered questions of the force of decree laws pending conversion[70] and responded solely to the often posed query of the status of repeatedly reissued ones.[71] Jurisprudential consistency argues, it would seem, in favor of a legal policy explanation.

The fact that Parliament had apparently been incapable of checking executive abuse in a global fashion, on the other hand, offers an alternative view. Parliament's inability to stem the tide of decree laws would argue that, from a strategic perspective, a judicial action might also be ineffective. Parliament attempted to block executive invocation of emergency and urgency when there were no objective justifications by passing Law No. 400 of 1988. That law had also intended to limit the scope of decree laws to a single, homogenous issue. It was thought to have corrected the practice, but quickly proved to be insubstantial and neither the reissuance of decree laws nor the limitations of real emergency situation were respected by the executive. Pizzorusso went so far as to say that 'many (and perhaps all) of the limitations introduced by Article 15 [of Law No. 400] have … not changed the nature of the decree law'.[72]

Parliament succeeded merely in rejecting specific decree laws, amending some and allowing others to lapse, only to be reintroduced again. Its single overarching effort to redesign the relationship between Parliament and the executive failed, due in large part to its own inability to enforce the restrictions. Interventions by the President of the Republic were successful in the most limited way, blocking a single decree Law here and there. The Court could have rightly calculated until 1996 that its best strategy was to avoid making what might well have been no more than a useless gesture.

Assuming that the Court, as an institution, was seeking a rational policy in its relations with other institutions, why might it expect to succeed where neither Parliament nor the President had? Additionally, what institutional price might the Court pay for intervening? The Court's decisions on decree laws from 1957 to 1988 can be explained two ways. The first and most obvious is the judges were pursuing legal accuracy and legal clarity. A coherent jurisprudence was created that emphasized the temporary nature of decree laws and deferred to parliamentary authority to judge the urgency behind a decree and, more importantly, to modify or reject it. The Court retained the authority to evaluate any converted decree law for constitutional validity. Thus, each of the three national powers retained a measure of autonomy within its own sphere.

That legal model explanation is not in opposition to a parallel strategic choice hypothesis that asserts the Court could also have calculated that confronting the executive on the issue of decree laws would likely be futile. Perhaps even more importantly, the Court would win nothing if it succeeded only in upsetting already strained and fragile institutional relationships. Siding with a weak legislature was not going to bolster the Court's standing nor was it likely to win an effective protector. The so-called 'ungovernability'[73] of Italy is legendary, and various proposals for institutional reform had not altered the political stalemates that frequently blocked coherent government programs and parliamentary majorities. The Court's only foray into the decree law thicket had been its very narrow decision in 1988 to abrogate a single reissued decree law. The identical line of reasoning, that of loss of legal certainty, was followed in the broader 1996 judgment that invalidated all reissued decree laws.

The more intriguing question is why the Court chose to alter its strategy and intervene so boldly in 1996. Extra-legal factors are the only viable means of explaining that dramatic shift in the Court's law and policy. Three things had changed: the Italian political environment and, directly related to that, the formula for naming judges to the Constitutional Court and the system that could reward judges at the conclusion of their terms. After the 'Clean Hands' investigations began in 1992, the six political parties that had controlled the allocation of government offices slowly self-destructed or reinvented themselves. The Communist Party split into the hardline Refounded Communists and a social democrat version, the Democratic Party of the Left. What had been the dominant Christian Democrats splintered into the Popular Party on the center-left and two incarnations on the center-right. The old Social Democrats and Socialists were obliterated, and neither the Liberal Party nor the Republican Party retained any meaning outside larger coalitions of the center-right or center-left. For judges on the Constitutional Court, this translated into a type of enhanced independence, for their appointers and their potential patrons for future political careers were largely irrelevant. The judicial independence–judicial authority combination was altered.

My supposition can be illustrated by the actual composition of the Court at the time of the 1996 decree law decision. President of the Court Mauro Ferri and Judge Enzo Cheli had been appointed by former President of the Republic Francesco Cossiga and were identified with the broad area of socialists. Luigi Mengoni, also a Cossiga appointee, was associated with the Catholic political area. All three were at the end of their nine-year terms on the Court at the time of the October 1996 decision. Cheli has, notably, been cited frequently in this chapter, for as a constitutional law scholar he was a critic of the government's use of decree laws. Five others (Renato Granata, Fernando Santosuosso, Massimo Vari, Riccardo Chieppa and Cesare Ruperto) had obtained their positions through election by their fellow judges where partisan politics are irrelevant. The five parliamentary appointees could no longer be linked to a specific party. Rather, they were loosely tied to ideological clusters – Giuliano Vassalli and Francesco Guizzi are regarded as of the socialist area; Carlo Mezzanotte, to the center-right Il Polo; Cesare Mirabelli, with the Catholics; and Valerio Onida, to the center-left coalition, the Progressives.[74] Political ties and patronage expectations were lessened, and judicial independence enhanced.

Another element that cannot be ignored is the policy goal of institutional self-preservation, for the Court's standing and prestige in the political scheme. Since the Constitutional Court's inception in 1956, it has struggled with the ordinary and administrative courts for power. In the early years the ordinary and administrative judiciaries were hesitant to relinquish prerogatives to the new body. While the Court refused to act and where parliamentary and presidential attempts proved futile, another actor had mounted the stage. Judges on the ordinary courts dealing with criminal matters began tackling aspects of decree laws that had not been converted and those that were repeatedly reissued. Specifically, the criminal section of the highest ordinary court, *Corte di Cassazione*, concluded that a reissued decree law that affected criminal sanctions loses effect from the moment when first issued, if reissued successively. Otherwise, it would be retroactive and thereby violate Article 25 of the Constitution's prohibition on *ex post facto* laws.[75] In tracing this approach to the validity of decree laws, or at least those that were reissued, Alfonso Celotta cited 120 cases before ordinary judges in 12 months during 1994 and 1995 where decree laws of this genre were questioned. That could have promised a flood of references to the Constitutional Court or, worse from the standpoint of institutional standing, have allowed ordinary judges on criminal courts to act unilaterally, without direction on the issue from the Constitutional Court.[76]

The Constitutional Court followed a strategic route of self-protection from the political powers of government when confronted with questions of the constitutionality of decree laws for decades. A coherent, clearly articulated legal policy was formed that was consistent with that strategy. A point was reached, however, when if the Court had chosen to remain on the sidelines while the executive and the legislative branches sparred over dominance, its standing in the political scheme might have been pre-empted by the ordinary judiciary. The Court conceivably calculated that to remain peripheral in the dispute over reissued decree laws could result in a forfeiture to the ordinary judiciary.

Notably, the Court's status was sufficiently respected by 1996 that its dictates were followed. The Prodi government, a broad center-left coalition, had assumed office in June 1996. It issued 447 decree laws from its investiture until March 1998, and had reissued eight at the time the Court struck down the practice. Even though only 87 of its decrees had been converted, not one was reissued following the Court's decision.[77] That absolute, unquestioning compliance might not have been assured in earlier times. Whether the Court will, as it threatened, extend its reach on supervision of executive decree laws depends on the resulting configurations of power among the parties and party coalitions and on the ability of Parliament to use responsibly the prerogatives that the Court restored to it.

4
Arbitrating National–Regional Conflicts

A federal or quasi-federal system of government seemingly requires an institutional referee. Alexander Hamilton relied on that assumption in *Federalist No. 80* to justify creation of the US Supreme Court. Without an institution to exert authority over the states, he foresaw 'a hydra in government from which nothing but contradiction and confusion can proceed'.[1] This is what Alec Stone calls 'the federal logic' that 'virtually require[s] the existence of a constitutional court'.[2] Similar sentiments were voiced in the Italian Constituent Assembly by Costantino Mortati.[3] The argument that a court or courts are necessary to preserve an equilibrium between the center and the periphery prevailed not only in Italy, but also in Australia, Belgium, Brazil, Canada, Germany, India, Pakistan and Spain, not to mention the emerging democracies in Central and Eastern Europe.

The Constitutional Court's role in the Italian system of regionalism has fluctuated, depending on the topic and the time. Initially the Court tilted in favor of the national government, but that has not characterized all phases of its treatment of regionalism. Indeed, most aspects of the evolution of regional government in Italy have been non-linear. Strong local identifications were the norm for a thousand years when the Italian peninsula was dotted with city states. Centralization was, however, the path chosen by the founders of the Italian state in the nineteenth century, and that centripetal force was reinforced under the Fascist regime.[4] Representatives at the post-Second World War Constituent Assembly decided to reverse that tendency, but did so only half-heartedly. The regional governments prescribed in Articles 114 to 133 of the Constitution were implemented immediately only where separatist movements threatened, and a real regional system did not begin until 1970.

The resulting arrangement has been a source of dissatisfaction, and regional parties, some even advocating secession, sprouted in the 1990s. The system, despite tinkering by the politicians and definition by the Constitutional Court, has over two decades remained something less than federal but more than unitary – but what, precisely, is not clear. By the time the Bicameral Commission met in 1997 to propose constitutional reforms, President of the Commission Massimo D'Alema described resolution of the federal issue as forming the essential architecture for all of the other reforms.[5]

This chapter evaluates the role the Constitutional Court played in the regions' birth and development. Evaluating or interpreting the constitutional partition of powers is perhaps more complicated in Italy than elsewhere because there are not just two or even three levels of government, but rather four. In the deliberations of the Constituent Assembly 'provinces' was inserted between regions and communes in what would become Article 114. Hence, there is a four-tiered government structure, with the last two described in subsequent articles as constituencies of the regions.[6] Some textual confusion in Articles 114 to 133, compounded by shifting political agendas, made clarification, application and interpretation of the boundaries of regional government prerogatives difficult. The Constitutional Court chose generally to follow the lead of the national political elites and supported centralizing tendencies.

Early political choices

Cross-cutting motives were at work in the Constituent Assembly when it considered decentralizing the machinery of government, and the different inclinations were all rooted in historical experience. One was a reverence for local government, which could be traced to the Middle Ages, but the opposite derived from Napoleonic traditions of extremely limited local autonomy under the direct control of the government in Rome.[7] The more recent experience of Fascism prompted both the center-right and the Socialists and Communists in the Assembly to champion decentralization.[8] The result has been called a unitary government with regional autonomy.[9] That contradiction colored attempts, both political and judicial, to locate and define an equilibrium between the center and the periphery.

Debates over demarcation of authority among the levels of government in the Constituent Assembly consumed weeks, but the issues were largely over semantics and details. A generalized resolve to limit the reach of the central government and its administration existed, but there was no small measure of confusion over the precise nature of that decentralization. At one point in the debates a representative reflected the confusion, referring to the institutions under discussion as 'provincial, regional, or whatever you call this new construction'.[10] Only Francesco Nitti repeatedly argued against dividing authority. Nitti, who had served briefly as prime minister before the advent of Fascism, extolled the virtues of a unitary system: 'The great men of the Risorgimento sought to make a cohesive, national union. After too many years of tyranny and lost wars, you now want to adopt a spirit of dissolution. ... No other country in the world wants discord after the war except Italy.'[11] His speeches were met with polite applause, but his admonitions were ignored as most present were intent on administrative decentralization.

That does not mean that there were no disagreements about the form decentralization would assume. Many votes were close and multiple amendments were presented, discussed and considered in the course of passing 20 articles to prescribe how the new tiered government should work. Two important distinctions are made within that set of articles. The first is among regions and provinces and communes. Fifteen articles address only the regions, but Article 128 defines provinces and communes as 'autonomous entities within the limits set by the general laws of the Republic', while the following article adds that they are 'also units of state and regional decentralization' and, in Article 130, have the legitimacy of their enactments controlled by a regional body. Regions are also defined in Article 115 as 'autonomous bodies' governed by principles set forth in the Constitution, yet a government commissioner acts as liaison and can, on behalf of the government, refuse to promulgate a regional law (Articles 124 and 127).

The other distinction is that made among the regions themselves: Article 116 creates five special regions having 'forms and particular conditions of autonomy' which are presumably distinct from ordinary ones. The special regions are Sicily, Sardinia, Trentino-Alto Adige, Friuli-Venezia Giulia and Valle d'Aosta. With the exception of Friuli-Venezia Giulia, these were at the sitting of the Constituent Assembly exhibiting secessionist tendencies or experiencing ethnic conflicts. What is not specified is how the special regions differ from the ordinary ones, other than that the former will have 'special statutes adopted through constitutional laws'.

A lack of clarity pervades the constitutional treatment of the regions. Numerous articles of the Constitution are devoted to devolution, but their ambiguity has been the source of many of the difficulties that have plagued regional–national relations and consequently landed on the doorstep of the Constitutional Court. Early in the Constituent debates there was a strong sentiment to leave most of the form and structure of the regions to a new legislature.[12] Ultimately, that was the decision of the assembled body and from it grew a multitude of constitutional dilemmas.

The Constitution listed the areas of regional competencies in Article 117. These include jurisdiction over the communes and local police and a long list of presumably local matters: handicrafts, fairs, markets, tourism, museums and libraries, lakes and parks, spas and mineral waters, fishing, forestry, agriculture, hunting and health. The inevitable frictions with national interests are obvious, at least in hindsight, where a national health service exists and where overlapping interests in agriculture and hunting, for example, are logical. Article 119 ensures taxing authority and financial autonomy 'within the limits established by laws of the Republic', and Article 120 prohibits interference with inter-regional commerce. Articles 121 and 122 prescribe the forms of regional governments and elections. Articles 124 to 127 describe different aspects of national prerogatives in the functioning of the regions, and Articles 128 to 130 relate to provinces and communes. All of the regions are listed in Article 131, and Articles 132 and 133 govern creation of new or mergers of existing regions, provinces and communes.

The 20 articles on the subject of sub-national governments also include some contradictions. The Italian state is defined earlier in the Constitution as unitary, but the regions are described as autonomous. The differentiation between special and ordinary regions could be read as placing the special ones on a higher plane than the ordinary ones, but not necessarily. Finally, the provinces are administrative entities located between regions and communes and yet subject in some respects to the regions.[13] Sorting all of this out, legislatively, politically and constitutionally, has not been easy, and the difficulties have become more apparent with each attempt by the politicians or the judges to resolve concrete problems.

The special regions were implemented promptly after the Constitution was promulgated by Constitutional Law No. 2, 26 February 1948. Trieste remained under Allied occupation until 1954, and the status of Friuli-Venezia Giulia as a special region was not implemented until 1963. In 1972 the regional powers of Trentino-Alto Adige were devolved to two provinces, Bolzano and Trento; the former predominantly Italian, and the latter, German speaking. By a constitutional law of

1963, the regions of Abruzzi and Molise were separated.[14] Though all special regions were given considerable authority, they were also limited to actions 'in harmony with the Constitution, the general legal principles of the state, and with the fundamental laws governing economic and social reforms and with international obligations and the interests of other regions'. Though the precise wording varied among the statutes passed for each special region, all of the special regions were constrained by national interests.[15]

Preserving centralization

'Regionalism' is an odd term in political nomenclature, neither decisively federal nor quite unitary. Italians came to regard the word as synonymous with 'anti-unitary', and hence the word carried a negative connotation for national interests.[16] The reluctance of the central government to give life to the regions might be explicable by that inference, but there were also strictly partisan reasons behind the foot dragging. The pejorative coloring might also have shaded the treatment that regions received from the Italian Constitutional Court, but other calculations, both political and juridical, were likely at work. What is beyond debate, though, is that national politicians succeeded in delaying implementation of the ordinary regions for more than two decades, until 1970, and that the Constitutional Court dictated a jurisprudential line that typically supported the national government when there was a conflict with a regional one.

Early cases before the Constitutional Court related only to the special regions and mainly to Sicily, but the substance of those decisions was maintained when all of the regional governments were functioning. Parliament had also prejudged the terms of the debate in a 1953 law billed as adding specificity to the constitutional enumeration of regional matters. That law obliterated any principle of separation or non-interference between the national and regional bodies.[17] As early as 1957, the Court lighted on the constitutional provision that would ultimately block true regional autonomy, Article 5. That provision of fundamental principles, while designed to foster decentralization, begins, 'The Republic, one and indivisible'. The remainder of the article addresses autonomy of local entities and decentralization, but the Court focused on the singular nature of national sovereignty. In a series of cases, it relied on Article 5 to block regional interference in a number of areas that it regarded as the exclusive domain of the national authorities.[18] With sovereignty located only at the national

level, the Court was able repeatedly to declare that Italian decentralization was a form of regionalism, not to be confused with federalism.[19]
The basic tenet governing the division of authority was announced by
the Court in 1957: a 'generic recognition' that whatever authority was
devolved to the regions, it was always 'framed by the unity of the State
with the regions as subordinate'.[20]

Though not unwavering, those principles dictated an essentially pro-
national predilection on the part of the Court. Because the potential
for conflicts is extensive and can be multiplied by the number of
regions, the quantity of cases reaching the Constitutional Court asserting a conflict between regions and the national government is voluminous. When challenges were brought by Trentino-Alto Adige over
actions of the national prefect, by Sardinia over an aqueduct system,
by Trentino-Alto Adige and Valle d'Aosta and later Sicily opposing
nationalization of electrical power, the Court simply rejected the
questions as unfounded.[21] When laws passed by the regional governments were brought before the Court, they were typically annulled as
unconstitutional.[22]

The Court kept the special regions on a subordinate plane, and
Parliament made no effort to implement the ordinary regions. Over
the two decades since the Constituent Assembly had met, Italy was
transformed from a largely agricultural society to an urban, industrial
one, and the economic miracle of the 1950s and 1960s changed Italian
life. The parties in power had no incentive to alter the system that kept
them there, but the left in Parliament seized the initiative in 1968 to
implement decentralization. Conservatives in the legislature staged
what amounted to a filibuster to prevent the legislation, but it was bro-
ken, and a law creating an election apparatus for the ordinary regions
was finally passed.[23] Proponents of the regions argued that completing
decentralization was necessary to reinvigorate the nation and reflect
changes already apparent in society, while those of the majority center-
right cast the issue as inevitably leading to financial and administrative
confusion.[24] Two years later, the required legislation for financing the
regions passed,[25] and preparations began for elections of the first
regional governments that would be held in 1972.

Implementing regionalism

Understanding the work of the Constitutional Court requires awareness of what was happening in the parliamentary arena, for the
two followed parallel tracks in the evolution of the regional system of

government. And, both were affected by larger conceptions of the role of the state, particularly in economic matters. In the years following the Second World War the political class in Italy accepted that establishment of a liberal market economy was uppermost, but that goal yielded in the 1960s and 1970s to a blend of free market and state intervention intended to promote social as well as economic development. Those mixed visions of the state implied to many a centralized system of management and a resistance to regional devolution. The 1980s witnessed the inception of a different view of government's role, one with a more micro-economic emphasis. In this era, according to Gianfranco Cerea, there was more room for different levels of government and even competition between periphery and the center.[26]

The distribution of authority between the national and regional governments included in the implementing legislation reflected the centralizing impulses of those in Rome. The essential differences between the special regions created earlier and the ordinary ones was the legislative format: special regions required constitutional laws, whereas ordinary regions were creations of statutes. There were some small variations among the special regions, but the whole set were more alike than different.[27] There were three types of regional powers: limited exclusive, complementary and integrative. In the first, regional councils had general power to act, but were restricted to the areas enumerated in the Constitution. Complementary powers permitted the regional councils to act only within the parameters of so-called 'framing laws' ('*legge cornici*') passed by the national government. The last powers, the integrative ones, allowed the regional councils to tailor certain national laws to the peculiar needs of their region. Only the special regions were granted any exclusive authority; the ordinary regions could act only within the frameworks designed in Rome.[28]

Though implementing legislation for the ordinary regions was passed in 1970, the task of actually effectuating the required transfers delayed the process until April 1972. The inadequacy of the entire system, even once the necessary actions had taken place, hobbled the new regional governments, which were blocked on all fronts by 'an alliance of conservative national politicians, an entrenched national bureaucracy and a tradition-minded judiciary'.[29] To counter that, a group of regionalists that spanned the political spectrum banded together forcibly to extract the required resources from Rome. They did, with the passage of Law No. 382, 1975, though the real fruits of their efforts were not realized for another two years, when Decree Law 616 was promulgated on 24 July 1977, finally accomplishing a transfer of functions from the national government to the regional ones.[30] That legislative decree and other more specific legislation transferring administrative offices to the regions were the source of the conflicts reaching the Court over the next five years.[31]

By 1990 the political climate had altered sufficiently for some significant changes in national–regional relations. The primary manifestation of that was Law No. 158 of 14 June 1990 which reordered the financial relationship between the national and regional governments. This was an attempt to rationalize and reform the 1970 laws. Regions were guaranteed their own taxes and tax offices, transfers of some investments, and authority for limited deficit financing. Some provisions were also included for special financial transfers for the underdeveloped South.[32] The reform law did not produce all of the intended results and was followed by more incremental laws over the following five years.

The increased attentiveness to regional needs after 1990 was neither solely a recognition of a different view of government's role in social and economic life nor political altruism on the part of those in Parliament. Two sets of events were compelling: first, the loss of what remnants remained of public confidence in the national government as a consequence of the 'Clean Hands' corruption investigations that began in 1992 and, second, the rising popularity of the leagues or regional parties, in particular the *Lega Nord* led by Umberto Bossi. As a consequence, another major transfer of administrative functions to the regions was made in 1998.[33]

Judicial dimension

The Constitutional Court was clearly part of the national alliance that, in 1970 and thereafter, impeded dispersal of power away from the center. Whereas the Court's decisions in a number of ways tracked those of the government and Parliament and follow a chronological development, they had four judicially developed themes. The first is the Court's treatment of conflicts of attribution or conflicts of power, a judicially fashioned doctrine to guide the Court in all conflicts between competing government powers. The next two had their basis in constitutional language and served to delineate the lines between national and regional governments, but really were limitations on actions by the regions: national interest and international obligations. The final one involves the judicial gloss placed on Article 127 which prescribes the role of the national government in specific pieces of regional legislation.

The Court's inclinations in defining the relationship between the regions and the national government have been described as self-restraint whereby the judges yielded to the will of the national legislators and trailed behind them,[34] albeit following a rather 'elastic interpretation of self-restraint'.[35] Franco Bassanini wrote, with reference to the period up to the mid-1970s, that the Court had eschewed an arbitrating role between the two levels of government and concentrated only on 'clarifying the contours' of the partition between them.[36] These varying conceptions all converge on a description of the Court as timid and deferential to the national authorities. The extent to which that characterization is valid across the decades can best be illustrated by examining each of the judicially defined thematic areas.

Conflicts of attribution

The Court is charged in Article 134 of the Constitution with deciding 'conflicts among the powers of the state and between the state and the regions...'. Key among the principles of interpretation applied to conflicts between regions and the national government is that allegations of conflicts of power should not be brought lightly, and consequently the Court only intervenes in situations of real, not just perceived, infringements of power. The variation used with reference to complaints by regional governments against the national authorities is that there has been an *invasion* of a region's sphere of competence on a recurring basis.[37] That barrier to conflict of powers cases is intentionally high, because of the inevitable stickiness of stepping between two warring political organs.

As the relationship between the regions and the national government became increasingly litigious, the high bar allowed the Court to reject most conflicts of attribution or conflicts of power as inadmissible. Stefano Grassi counted 51 such cases involving regions and the national government from 1977 to 1984; only 18 of them were admitted and decided on their merits.[38] Despite the disinclination of the Court to intervene in the conflicts, the numbers lodged continued to grow: 47 in 1984, 48 in 1985, and 31 in 1986.[39] Almost all were brought by the regional governments, as the national government has a different weapon, Article 127 that will be discussed later.

Over the decades since the ordinary regions were instituted, the Court did not waver appreciably in its handling of alleged conflicts of power between the regional and national governments. Nor has it been totally one-sided, even though the central authorities were more likely to prevail. The regional governments of Lombardy, Emilia Romagna and Liguria mounted the only successful challenge to government use of decree laws in 1983, as was discussed in Chapter 3. The Constitutional Court, in Judgment No. 307, found that the repeated reissuance of a decree law governing regional finance laws interfered with regional competencies because the terms were changed in successive versions.[40] The very next year, when three special regions, the autonomous provinces of Bolzano and Trento, and two ordinary regions (Lombardy and Liguria) mounted a challenge to the national government over the National Health Service, all but two allegations were dismissed as inadmissible, and the two that were heard concerned only the special regions and involved peculiarities in the constitutional laws that created them.[41] The ordinary regions could not successfully force their case under the more general statutory framing law by which the National Health Service was decentralized.

The more general rule was that conflicts raised by regions were set aside, sometimes on technicalities such as notification,[42] and other times on assertions that no conflict existed because collaboration was envisioned between the two levels of government.[43] Others were dismissed because of the intervention of other parties, such as the promoter of three advisory referendums in Sardinia that had been voided by the Council of Ministers. In that situation, the promoters of the referendums alleged that their constitutional rights had been abridged when the process of holding the plebiscites was halted by the national government.[44] The case was, nonetheless, ruled inadmissible. Similarly, a challenge by the Region of Tuscany to the government's annulment of the hiring of an external lawyer was deflected by the Court as raising a question that was not of 'a constitutional level'.[45] Even though the subjects and the parties varied, these examples demonstrate the Court's reluctance to decide conflicts of attribution between the regional governments and the national one and its willingness to seize on minor details to avoid considering the significant questions. Analogies are obvious to the US Supreme Court's explication of political questions and other elements of jurisdiction as a means of avoiding larger issues of separation of powers. The Italian Court tries, by limiting its interventions in conflicts between the national and regional authorities, to maintain at least the appearance of impartiality.[46]

National interest

The unitary nature of the Italian state requires, according to the Constitutional Court, that national interests prevail over regional ones when the two are in conflict. The lengthy list of regional competencies in Article 117 of the Constitution carries a number of modifiers; the regions can legislate only (1) within the limits established by national law and (2) without conflicting with the national interest or that of other regions. Even though regional authority is obviously circumscribed by constitutional language, the Court has used approaches that are, according to Giorgio Berti, at variance with 'traditional canons of interpretation'. The higher level of government typically wins, but decisions on partitioning authority between the regions and the central state vary by which national interest is involved and by the capabilities of the regional legislator.[47] The latter part of that equation involves what the Court often refers to as the 'inertia' of the regional governments, and, when that can be demonstrated, the Court has given its approval to invasions by the national government. This has occurred, not because of some dogmatic national preference, but rather because of urgent necessities in some situations to harmonize or complete legislation across all regions.[48]

Beginning as early as 1970, the Court recognized a national interest that superceded any regional concern. The Court emphatically stated that 'in principle, with regard to economic development, the particular interests of any region must be reconciled with the pre-eminent interest of the country, as represented by the State'.[49] That position was repeatedly reaffirmed by the Court over the years.[50] A corollary that extended beyond just economic development was devised also by the Court: 'to safeguard the interests of the nation and of other regions' some of the matters listed in Article 117 are handled by the national government and intended only to be *coordinated* with the regions once they are transferred.[51] No exclusive regional power was implied by virtue of the enumeration of 'matters', as they were known, assigned to the regions by the Constitution. Those two overarching provisos would color and limit a wide variety of regional actions. They were, moreover, re-emphasized as part of the transfers of power included in Decree No. 616 of 1977 that facilitated the functioning of the regional authorities. The unitary character of the state was recognized as paramount in defining the boundaries of regional activities. That came to be called the 'reserved power' of the state which defeated regional assertions before the Court whenever a public interest was involved, such as in regional regulation of fishing,[52] insurance[53] and national parks.[54]

As various functions were transferred to regional authority, the national government specifically withheld some parts. For example, though markets and fairs are mentioned in Article 117 and transferred by decree law in 1977, the government retained central government control of markets and fairs that were international. The regions of Liguria, Emilia Romagna and Apulia argued that the national government's reserve of that portion of authority interfered with their ability to fulfill their constitutional responsibilities, since there were international elements to a whole variety of those events and no rationale for uniformity of regulation. The clear wording of the Constitution dictated, according to the Court, that the reserve of international components of a subject listed in Article 117 did not 'minimize regional competencies'; and the question was rejected as unfounded.[55] Simultaneously, the Court also declared unfounded equivalent challenges to limited transfers in the areas of agriculture, healthcare assistance and hospitals, public benefits and urban planning.[56] A small glitch lay in the Court's not having offered a definition of what constituted national interests. The international dimension of fairs and markets implied that subjects extending beyond national borders rather obviously were of national concern. Otherwise, as in healthcare, urban planning, hospitals and public benefits, the Court accepted state assertions that the national interest in them could not be subdivided on a regional basis.

The Court began in the early 1980s requiring that Parliament or the government justify assertions of national interest in cases involving a national agency for classifying hotels,[57] prohibiting regional governments from creating nature reserves,[58] and national regulation of health service furnishings.[59] Though most challenges to transfers of functions to the regions that included national reserve stipulations were still deflected as unfounded, the Court began to talk of 'the equilibrium between the opposite interests of the state and the regions' and to push for national justifications.[60] The national government won when the regions challenged its appropriation of control of all scenic treasures,[61] and the regional governments also lost when they attempted to tax hunting concessions.[62] In the latter case, the Court declared taxes imposed by the regions of Lombardy and Lazio unconstitutional for exceeding regional authority under Article 119 of the Constitution. Though Article 117 grants regional authority over matters of hunting, the Court said that could not be read as carrying the grant of taxing authority in Article 119. In the same case, however, the Court rejected as unfounded a challenge to a general regional tax in Piedmont. A year later, the Court reaffirmed its earlier invalidation of regional taxes on hunting concessions, adding that the national interest in regulating hunting superceded that of the regions.[63] The Court emphasized in the last case that regional autonomy in matters of taxation were 'largely conditioned' by national legislation.

The Court was seen by some as softening its attitude toward regional actions in the mid-1980s, but there were a number of instances in which regional laws were quashed as contrary to the national interest well beyond then. For example, an attempt by the autonomous province of Bolzano to regulate artisans was found to be contrary to Article 120 of the Constitution, with the Court saying it obstructed inter-regional commerce.[64] Artisans are, notably, one of the matters included in Article 117 as a regional concern. Then, in anticipation of the 1990 World Cup Soccer games hosted by Italy, the Piedmont regional council passed a law to streamline the process of transforming non-traditional facilities into lodging accommodation for visitors, but the Court found it constitutionally invalid. The Court relied on the rather elastic provisions of Constitution Article 128 that allows lower levels of government to act only within the parameters established by national legislation, despite the Article 117 delegation of hotels and tourism to the regional domain.[65]

There was evidence, however, that in the 1990s, at least in the fields of public health and national parks, that the Court was adopting what Angelo Costanzo called a 'paradigm of harmonization' to govern relations between regional and national governments, when both a national interest and a regional one were apparent.[66] As more and more responsibilities for public health were devolved to regional administration, there was greater potential for friction. The central government began reorganizing the National Health Service in 1992, and eight regions challenged several elements of the implementing legislation. Five parts of the regional challenges were dismissed, but one provision of the national law that related to financing and administration of the reorganized system was partially invalidated by the Constitutional Court. The Court acknowledged a concurrent jurisdiction for the two levels of government and the difficulties that accompany executive implementation of legislative norms. The conflicts that gave rise to this case resided in the so-called 'details' (*dettaglio statale*) or administrative rules that implement statutes. When aspects of the National Health Service were transferred to the regions, some procedures for coordination between the two levels of government were given in the statute and then altered by the national executive. The Court found that, to the extent that provisions of Article 121 that partitioned power within the regional governments were abridged, the national law was unconstitutional.[67] The case served, more importantly, as a vehicle for elaboration of the concept of concurrent jurisdiction of the two levels of governmental authority.

The Court in 1993 used disputes over a national park area to push for greater cooperation and harmonization between central and regional governments, even where a national interest was present. National parks are rather patently national, and regional governments have no constitutional basis for regulating them. However, the Archipelago of La Maddalena and some other portions of national parks were, according to the Region of Valle d'Aosta and the autonomous province of Trento, under their jurisdictions since matters of agriculture and urban planning were granted in their special statutes. They further argued that administration of these land parcels could not be managed adequately without their involvement. That part of the national legislation that ignored regional interests was invalidated by the Court, and in doing so the Court called for cooperation to achieve harmony between national and local concerns.[68] The prevailing national interest in national parks had been consistently recognized by the Court in a line of decisions dating from 1967, with a single exception made in 1989 for the special region of Sardinia when a nationally protected sea area was created. In that case the Court spoke of the need for collaboration between the regions and national authorities.[69] That seemed to signal that the assertion of a national interest was no longer sufficient to exclude any regional interest in a matter, if both levels of government could legitimately claim interests that would necessitate their cooperation rather than an assignment of responsibility to one or the other exclusively.

International obligations

Postwar Italy was committed to international involvement and that obligation was given constitutional stature in Article 11, in which limitations to national sovereignty were anticipated as necessary to assure 'peace and justice among nations'. Italy faced, as a result, no constitutional barrier to joining the European Coal and Steel Community in 1951 that expanded to the European Communities and eventually the European Union in the 1990s. Regional assertions of prerogative in some areas would necessarily run afoul of elements of that international commitment. International obligations were from the outset regarded as an explicit limitation on the reach of regional governments. A paramount national interest holds in conduct of foreign policy and all relations with foreign powers, with only minor exceptions for promotional activities and regional activities that incidentally touched the international level.[70]

The jurisprudence of the Constitutional Court has been absolutely consistent on the point of the indivisibility of the Republic, found in Article 5 of the Constitution, and from 1975 when the issue first arose, the Court never wavered in its position that, since sovereignty resides in a single national government, it 'has exclusive jurisdiction in international affairs'.[71] That attribution of power was emphasized in the decree laws of 1977 that effectuated the first major transfer of powers to the regional governments.

That single, unequivocal statement of law might have been sufficient were it not for particular legal issues that arose from the nation's membership in the European Communities. The Court first addressed that complication in 1972, when it announced that the only avenue for the regional or local governments to participate in application of Community norms was 'when the authority was delegated in agricultural matters'. Even then, the national government could substitute its own authority when the regions did not fulfill their obligations under the delegation.[72] That judicial pronouncement was also incorporated into the decrees of 1977, in which the national authority to substitute for regional action was reserved specifically to meet Community legal requirements. Within the first decade of regional government implementation, the Court twice upheld intervention by the national government when regions failed to meet their delegated obligations. The Court sided with the national government but highlighted that despite procedural and substantive guaranties to limit the substitutive power for that of the regional governments, a 'dangerous precedent for the autonomy of the regions was established, since the ability of the national executive to intervene in actuating EC regulations' opened a door for the national executive eventually to substitute its power for that of the regions in illegitimate ways.[73] According to Beniamino Caravita, the central executive saw that opening and in a whole array of laws unrelated to the EC made transfers to the regions with an explicit reserve power for itself to substitute in the event of regional inactivity.[74]

The European Court of Justice that is charged with interpreting European Community law fashioned an important doctrine for legal integration of the Community in 1963, when it ruled that provisions of the treaties forming the European Community were directly applicable in the legal systems of member nations. That meant that the treaties were immediately enforceable in any member nation and did not permit any action by the national governments. That decision was reinforced the next year in a case coming from Italy, *Costa* v. *ENEL*. The doctrine was extended to legal instruments of the Community beyond the treaties in 1973, again in a case involving Italy. Specifically, in *Commission* v. *Italy*, the European Court declared that Community regulations also had direct effect and were effective from their date of publication.[75]

The European doctrine of direct effect was immediately implicated in the legitimacy of regional government action or, more often, inaction. The Constitutional Court incorporated the essential aspects of the European Court's decisions in 1973 when it first held that European law prevailed when in conflict with Italian law.[76] Two years later, the Italian high court clearly enunciated the doctrine of direct effect of European law in Italy. It reached that conclusion by acknowledging that, consistent with Article 11 of the Italian Constitution, Italian sovereignty was limited by the treaties forming the EC; Italian judges were therefore incapable of interpreting or nullifying European law, and 'our legislator is denied in absolute terms the ability to act to the contrary'.[77]

Specific implications of those two decisions for Italian judges and legislators were made abundantly clear by the Italian Court in 1984. In a precedent that governed all alleged conflicts between EC law and national or regional ones, the Court declared the question inadmissible. The controversy had involved customs on a shipment of Canadian pasta in which an Italian regulation and a European one resulted in two different totals for duty payment. The Italian regulation was of a later date than the European one and under the Italian legal precept that the later law supercedes the former, the Italian regulation would normally be applied. The Constitutional Court restated its earlier recognition of the supremacy of European law over national law and the direct effect of European law in Italy. To explain the inadmissibility of the case, the Court said that under the doctrine of direct applicability there was no controversy; the Italian judge at the trial level must give direct effect to European law.[78]

The 1973, 1975 and 1984 cases taken together formed a cohesive explanation of the division between Italian and European law, and the Court's other pronouncements on the national government's exclusive power in foreign affairs and authority to substitute its action when a region defaulted seemed to settle the questions of regional authority with relation to European Community obligations. As a consequence, when regional laws alleged to violate EC ones reached the Court via direct access, they were rejected as inadmissible because it was impossible for a regional law that was incompatible with a Community one to take effect. There was no conflict, because the conflicting regional law was *de jure* non-existent. That device worked in the abstract sense when cases came to the Court through direct access, but not necessarily in the context of concrete review or when cases were referred from other judges for constitutional interpretation. For a law to be implicated in a concrete case, it must have been in effect. Therein lay a jurisprudential bind.

The Constitutional Court adopted a variation on the theme of the inapplicability of a national or regional law that contravenes a Community one in 1986: if a law is in effect that violates Community norms, it can be invalidated as a violation of Article 11 of the Italian Constitution as a failure to meet international obligations.[79] A regional or national law can simultaneously violate both Community norms and constitutional ones. The Court would hear those reaching it in *via incidentale* for concrete review under that interpretation.[80] That was the course followed by the Court in rendering invalid regional laws that were inconsistent with Community ones.[81]

The European Community, now Union, presented the most frequent situations for regional initiatives to run afoul of national ones in the international arena. It was not, however, the only external entity with which a regional body might have a relationship that potentially infringed the national power over foreign affairs. When regional governments signed protocols with foreign bodies, there was also a conflict of power with the national government. For example, the region of Valle d'Aosta signed a protocol of collaboration with Mogadishu in Somalia in 1976, as did the region of Lombardy in 1986. The president of the region of the Marche signed a similar agreement with Shanghai, China in 1986, and the region of Apulia did the same with Yugoslavia, and Lazio with Sonora, Mexico. When challenges to these various agreements of cooperation reached the Constitutional Court, it simply disposed of each by saying 'it is up to the national government to determine if these actions are acceptable'.[82] In the realm of foreign affairs, the Court not only gave recognition to an exclusive prerogative of the national government, it also deferred to that power.

Preventive control of regional laws

Most of the conflict of power cases between national and regional governments were brought by the regions or were incidental to cases involving private individuals. There have been only rare instances when the central government initiated cases in this field. That is because of the special mechanism that the Constitution granted to the national government for addressing regional legislation, known as preventive control.[83] Article 127 of the Constitution stipulates that every regional law must be communicated to the central government's commissioner in the region for approval. Unless the national executive objects, the commissioner must sign the law within 30 days; urgent laws have a shorter time limitation. The national government is restricted by Article 127 to three specific grounds for rejecting a regional law: exceeding the region's power, conflicting with national interests or conflicting with the interests of other regions. If the national government objects, however, the law is returned to the regional council which may, by absolute majority, approve the law a second time. Should the regional council repass the law, the government may then take the case either to the Constitutional Court if the question is one of constitutionality or to Parliament if the question is one of judgment. That has had the effect of preventing many cases from being appealed to the Constitutional Court, but, at the same time, has required that the Constitutional Court become involved in the process of interpreting applications of Article 127.

The circumstances surrounding governmental rejection of a regional law and its subsequent repassage presented several issues for clarification by the Constitutional Court. In a series of cases in 1975 and 1976, the Court tried to facilitate a collaboration and dialogue between the national executive and the regions, by requiring that very specific reasons be supplied for rejection of a regional law.[84] But other issues remained. First, there is the question of who can reject a regional law: can the President of the Council of Ministers act unilaterally or must the decision be one of the entire Council? Shortly after the ordinary regions were implemented, the Court read Article 127 quite literally and stipulated that rejection must be a collegial action of the whole national executive.[85] Later the same year, the Court clarified the status of a regional law during the period before it has been approved by the national government. A regional law must be promulgated by the government commissioner and, therefore, has no legal effect until the whole process of preventive control has been completed.[86]

The second question reaching the Court more than once relates to the process of repassing a regional law after a national executive veto. The particular issue was that of changes introduced in a regional law when it is presented to the regional council after a government objection: is the altered law passed by an absolute majority of the regional council the same law that had already been sanctioned or is it new and again subject to review by the national government? Originally, the Constitutional Court took a very formal view and held that 'any alteration', even modest variations in the text, in the second passage renders it a new law that must again be submitted to the government commissioner and subjected to Council of Ministers' decision.[87] That ruling underwent a substantial revision in 1988, when the Court assumed a less technical stance and allowed that minor changes in the law on the second passage did not constitute a completely new law. The options available to the government were, after the second passage, limited to challenges before the Constitutional Court or in Parliament, depending on the nature of the alleged defects.[88] In a slight change of course, the Court, in 1993, for the first time seemingly admitted that the government's political motivations for rejecting a regional law were acceptable and looked to the substance, not the formalities, of consultations between the President of the Council of Ministers and Council deliberations.[89]

Anti-region or cooperative regionalism?

The Constituent Assembly failed in its attempt to create a decentralized system for the Italian Republic, and subsequent actions by Parliament, the national government and the Constitutional Court reduced regional governments to mere interstitial layers in the power scheme.[90] There have been some variations on that theme over the history of the Republic, but the flow of governmental power has been toward the center. Early decisions of the Constitutional Court were labeled as anti-region,[91] but some shift in the Court's treatment of regional government appears over time. Martines claims that the eventual model is one of 'cooperative regionalism', but he bases his assessment on decisions of all three branches of the national government, not just the Court.[92]

Clearly there is some interest in seeing the regional governments succeed, and a number of scholars have found positive perspectives in the regional–national balance. Modern regionalism focusing on increased national–regional cooperation was hailed by Cassese and Serrani as early as 1980, but their analysis was based largely on anticipation of what steps Parliament might take.[93] A form of 'neo-regionalism' was predicted as a consequence of constitutional reforms debated, but never enacted, in 1993.[94] Even a more dispassionate analysis of the success of the regional experiment, taken as a whole, is that there are wide differences from region to region in how effectively the powers and authority, meager though they may have been, were used.[95] The optimism expressed by some supporters of regionalism and regional governments generally exclude assessments of the work of the Constitutional Court. Though a 'new role' for the Court was predicted in the 1980s, one that would give greater credence to regional authorities,[96] the reality is that the Court has largely chosen to remain on the margins of the conflict. Its primary strategy when dealing with the special regions, beginning in the 1950s, and continuing through the next three decades, has been to reject cases involving regional–national government disputes as unfounded or inadmissible.[97]

The Court's jurisprudence on the balance between regional and national governments has tilted toward the central government, though there have been some minor deviations worth recalling. In the field of preventive control, the Court has favored national prerogatives, but has facilitated some regional legislation by allowing at least that small changes are permissible in the text of a law when presented for passage after national rejection. Also, in its decisions delineating where the national interest prevails, the Court, though consistently supporting real national interests, has recognized some areas of concurrent jurisdiction, at least with regard to the health service and some aspects of national parks.

Even when not siding with the regional entities, the Court has encouraged cooperation and harmonization over litigation between the two levels of government. Overall, however, the regional governments have not always received a sympathetic hearing before the Constitutional Court. That is most apparent in the Court's rulings on international obligations, but the Court would seem to have little room to maneuver in that field; national sovereignty requires a single voice in foreign policy and foreign affairs, and the Italian Constitution placed that power rather squarely with the national government. The jurisprudential field where the Court would seem to have the greatest latitude for fostering regional interests is in that of conflicts of power. The Court has, with reference to the regions, behaved no differently than it has tended to act toward all conflicts between organs of government: it has chosen whenever possible to avoid deciding through the mechanisms of inadmissibility and unfounded questions. Notably, when conflicts have arisen between two organs, the Court has used a standard of real rather than perceived incursions of power. It instituted a higher barrier when considering challenges from the regions – *invasions* of authority on a recurring basis.

The degree of consistency in decisions by the Constitutional Court on national and regional conflicts points strongly toward a conclusion that the Court was pursuing good law. The Court's first readings of the constitutional text were applied with minimal variation to subsequent legislation and were assumed to lead to a single legal conclusion. That may well be the answer. However, judicial independence as gauged by recruitment of the judges to the high court may have provided a political expedient to reinforce that outcome. The judges on the Constitutional Court are clearly part of the national political elite, owe their judicial appointments to that elite, and likely may have their post-Court careers determined by members of the political class at the national level. An objective assessment reveals no apparent benefit to the judges individually or to the Court as an institution in favoring regional over national authorities. The Court's treatment of regional disputes with the central authority has been consistent with what the legal model would predict, but its avoidance of questions and its inclination to favor national powers also have dimensions of good policy.

New partitions of power between the two levels of government continue, with the most recent in 1998, but changes have and will continue to emanate from sources other than the Constitutional Court. There are strong voices calling for more devolution, a form of fiscal federalism or even real federalism. Umberto Bossi even went so far as to declare the independence of the so-called nation of Padania North of the Po River and led a 'March to Venice' in 1996.[98] His theatrics and those of his followers often serve as a source of amusement, but they also reflect a genuine dissatisfaction, particularly – though not exclusively – in the North, with the limited degree of decentralization. That was accentuated even more as revelations of scandals bolstered long held perceptions that the central government in Rome was corrupt. Federalism or a system of greater regional authority was a major theme in the 1997 Bicameral Commission on Constitutional Reform.[99] If a major redistribution of authority between the regions and the national government occurs, it will be a result of decisions made in Parliament and the national executive, not by the Constitutional Court. The line of development of relations between the two levels of government has, over four decades, been determined by the most political bodies, and their decisions have conditioned reactions of the Court.[100]

5
Impeachment: the Lockheed Corruption Trial

European constitutional courts are often assigned auxiliary tasks that can best be classified as monitoring functions and are more political than judicial in character. The Italian Constitutional Court was given the quasi-judicial job of trying accusations against the President of the Republic, the prime minister and other ministers. Only once, in the Lockheed scandal of the 1970s, has the Court been called upon to do so. In that context the Court found itself moving between its normal role of interpreting the applicable constitutional provisions and statutes and another of actually conducting a trial layered with political implications. The ambiguity of the procedure and the Court time involved led to a constitutional amendment in 1989 that limited the Court's future role as a trier of accusations only to those cases involving the President of the Republic.

The Court sits astride a political–legal divide when it acts as a trier of facts and interpreter of law. That would seem to be precisely what every Anglo-American trial judge is called upon to do, but, in the case of a procedure that is closely akin to an impeachment, the position of the defendant and the nature of the 'crime' impose a distinctly political quality with strong partisan subtexts to the proceedings. Costantino Mortati had argued in the Constituent Assembly for adding lay judges to the panel of constitutional judges precisely because of the inherently political character of the proceedings. Actions that might trigger the procedure are not, he claimed, of the normal criminal variety and require an evaluation different from what judges are normally called upon to do.[1] Gustavo Zagrebelsky later described the process as an example of 'political justice' distinguished from 'solemn and impartial justice'.[2]

The Court's responsibility for the trial of accusations against the President, prime minister and other ministers was initially found in four different constitutional provisions. Article 90 held and still holds that the President of the Republic is not responsible for actions in the exercise of his office, 'except for high treason or plots against the Constitution', and in that event can be charged by an absolute majority of the membership of both chambers of Parliament in a joint sitting. A similar joint sitting of the two houses was prescribed in Article 96 to accuse the prime minister or other ministers of 'crimes committed in the exercise of their duties'. These two articles assumed that the process follows the Anglo-American model of impeachment and is separated from the actual trial. The specifics of implementation are included in the sections describing the Constitutional Court. Article 134 states that the Court tries accusations, and Article 135 provides that such trials are to be conducted by the 15 judges plus 16 laypeople whose names are drawn by lot from a list compiled by Parliament, using the same procedures it follows to elect the judges to the Court. The laypeople must meet the eligibility requirements for election to the Senate, that is they need to be citizens, 40 years of age or older, and are elected in a joint sitting of the two houses every nine years.

Earlier political choices

Statuto Albertino that governed Italy until the advent of the Republic provided for an impeachment mechanism that closely paralleled the British model. Article 47 of that document stated that the Chamber of Deputies could bring accusations against ministers and transmit them to the Senate, that, according to Article 36, was the High Court of Justice for trial. The Senate's role as High Court of Justice extended also to trials for treason or attacks on the security of the state.[3] The Senate was called by decree of the King to act in that capacity only four times: on the occasion of the attack on King Umberto I and to consider allegations against Giolitti in 1895, Crispi in 1897 and Nasi in 1907.[4] In the case of Giolitti, Parliament was closed before any action could be taken.[5]

Not surprisingly, the Constituent Assembly's inclination was to follow the approach that was familiar in Italian history. The Commission of Seventy-Five that presented the initial draft of the Republican Constitution proposed making the President of the Republic liable only for 'high treason and violations of the Constitution'. Charges would be brought by an absolute majority of the Chamber of Deputies[6] and would be followed by trial in the Senate acting as a high court.[7] That original text was altered in two ways by the Constituent Assembly.

First, since both chambers sit together to elect the President, by reason of parity, both should be involved in any move to accuse him formally.[8] That shifted the responsibility for actual trial to the Constitutional Court, which would presumably be more insulated from political pressures.[9] Second, 'violations of the Constitution' was replaced with 'attacks or plots against the Constitution'.[10] With those modifications, the text was approved rather expeditiously.

The draft presented by the Commission of Seventy-Five relating to the prime minister and other ministers was different, providing that they could be accused (impeached) by the two chambers sitting jointly for a broad range of actions, any 'committed in the exercise of their duties'.[11] Since most of the ground regarding accusation and trial had already been covered in the debates about the President of the Republic, the only amendment offered and approved was to make 'actions' more narrow, by substituting the word 'crimes'.[12]

Some six weeks later, when the Constituent Assembly debated provisions about the Constitutional Court, the final elements of the process were resolved. At this stage, there was concern about the appropriateness of the Court's role as trier of fact and several amendments were offered to shift the responsibility back to Parliament, where the two chambers would jointly serve as a high court of justice or where the Chamber of Deputies would bring allegations and the Senate would try them.[13] Costantino Mortati offered an amendment, one that was readily accepted by the Commission of Seventy-Five. Because he considered a trial of the President and ministers had political connotations, it could best be served by supplementing the 15 judges on the Court with 16 other citizens, whose presence could moderate any biases that the judges, particularly those appointed by the President, might have.[14] The Mortati amendment carried.[15]

The Constitution only outlined the process, and specifics had to be added through implementing legislation. Constitutional Law No. 1 of March 1953, which was crucial in delineating the Court's scope, also fleshed out the accusation and trial process. Parliamentary procedures for bringing allegations were clarified, and the Constitutional Court was granted authority to suspend the President from office during the parliamentary phase. Parliament was also authorized to name one or more of its members to serve as commissars to prosecute the case before the Court. Finally, the implementing legislation granted the Court power to sentence a minister or the President if found guilty.[16] Subsequently, in 1962, another law was enacted further elaborating the process, most notably by providing that deliberations of the chambers would be secret, but trial before the Court would be public.[17] The 1962 legislation lent considerable detail to the mechanism and was even described as a 'little code of criminal procedure for crimes by the ministers and the President of the Republic'.[18] There remained, even so, no small number of issues that the Court itself would have to resolve when confronting an actual case. Following one experience with a trial, moreover, both of these laws were amended, first, in the midst of the Lockheed case in 1978 and again in 1989.

Under the old procedures, those in effect before the Lockheed case, the first step once an accusation had been brought was the formation of an inter-parliamentary commission, composed of ten deputies and ten senators, elected by their respective chambers. This commission was, in reality, a pre-investigation body, for it decided, among other things, if the actions alleged actually qualified as 'crimes'. They also served as the first investigatory body, somewhat like the initial prosecutor in the Italian criminal system. Their findings were determined by a majority vote and then presented to the two chambers of Parliament, meeting together and behind closed doors. The joint sitting of Parliament could result in a dismissal or '*archiviazione*', a term that implies less than a final determination but rather a decision not to proceed further at the time. If the outcome of the deliberation was a formal accusation or impeachment, approved by an absolute majority of the two houses, then the president of the Chamber of Deputies transmitted that finding to the Constitutional Court. The Court retained, however, the power to modify or even to revoke the accusation brought by Parliament.[19]

The Lockheed case: Tanassi and Gui

The first experience in the Republican era with the new system of accusation came in 1965 and involved ex-minister of finance Giuseppe Trabucchi, who was charged with corruption. More specifically, he allegedly accepted bribes that went, not to him personally, but to the Christian Democrat Party.[20] Those charges did not go beyond the parliamentary stage, since the vote in the joint sitting of the two chambers for the accusation was not passed by an absolute majority of the two houses.[21] In actuality, constitutional language requiring that majority was only for cases involving the President of the Republic and not ministers, but since there is no appeal from the parliamentary decision, the impeachment of Trabucchi was ended.

Parliament and the Court were both drawn into the later case of ex-ministers Mario Tanassi and Luigi Gui, and the process engaged the

Constitutional Court from April 1977 until March 1979. Both men were former ministers of defense and accused of corruption for events that had occurred several years earlier. Luigi Gui, a Christian Democrat, had begun, while serving as Minister of Defense, the process of acquiring 14 C-130 Hercules long-range aircraft from the American Lockheed Corporation. In 1964 a technical agency of the government had recommended against the Hercules for the Italian military and made the case instead for a transport plane with a short to medium range that could be built by an Italian company. Indeed, by 1969, Fiat had finished research and development for its G-222 plane to meet precisely the specifications made in the 1964 report. Simultaneously, a bid for the C-130s arrived from Lockheed. Almost immediately, Italian Gen. Duilio Fanali of the Italian joint chiefs, who was subsequently charged along with Gui and Tanassi, began arguing that the existing Italian aircraft were obsolete and inappropriate for the nation's NATO role. He demanded that they be replaced immediately with the Lockheed aircraft, since the Fiat version would take too long to manufacture.[22]

Defense Minister Gui met with Lockheed officials in November 1969, and the Lockheed representatives requested a letter of intent for the purchase by mid-January; Gui provided it. He met again with Lockheed personnel on Christmas Eve and, three days later, with Gen. Fanali. That day Gui also contacted Prime Minister Mariano Rumor, who had already given his approval to the project, to emphasize the necessity for proceeding rapidly to lock-in the price. A crisis in the Rumor government resulted in Gui's being replaced as Defense Minister by the secretary of the Social Democratic Party, Mario Tanassi; Gui remained, even so, very interested in the airplane project and its financing. A new letter of intent was then required by Lockheed; Tanassi complied and, eventually, signed the purchase contract with Lockheed. Gui had touted the project's value in terms of price, terms, and even offers of some compensation for the losing Italian firm. Yet, when the contract was finalized over Tanassi's signature, not only were all of those elements omitted, but also the soundness of Lockheed's own financial condition was uncertain.[23]

Suspicions surrounding the Lockheed contract did not evaporate once the deal was completed. Allegations that money had changed hands prompted a parliamentary inquiry, and an inter-parliamentary commission to investigate was formed in 1976. That inquiry reached the prime minister, a number of former ministers, the President of the Republic and some non-political figures. In a public session of the commission on 29 January 1977, former prime minister Mariano

Rumor was exonerated by a bare majority vote of 11 to 10. Ex-ministers Gui and Tanassi and a number of other participants did not fare so well, and the commission's allegations were forwarded to the two chambers for deliberation in a joint meeting. The joint session, held behind closed doors, lasted from 3 to 11 March, and the final vote was for charging Gui (487–467) and Tanassi (513–441).[24] Those decisions were forwarded to the Constitutional Court by presidential decree on 14 March.[25]

The Constitutional Court would face a host of previously unasked questions in its conduct of the Lockheed case. In anticipation of the accusation, the Court in January, even before the parliamentary phase was completed, began to grapple in council chambers with the issue of the laypeople who would join them to try the case. The Court issued two ordinances in March relating to anticipated issues of selection and eligibility of those on the list of laypeople, and three were disqualified.[26] What the Court did was to divide responsibilities thereafter between the 'integrated Court' or the 31 judges, both lay and regular, and the 'ordinary Court', which continued to decide questions of constitutional interpretation. The panel of laypeople, who would supplement the 15 constitutional judges to form the integrated Court was drawn on 28 March. A quorum for hearings and deliberations of the integrated body was 21, and by the conclusion of the trial, the full body had been reduced to 29 by virtue of the illness of two of the laypeople on the panel.[27] The full integrated Court was called for its first meeting on 21 April.[28]

One of the first issues to be resolved was that of the Court's jurisdiction over nine defendants who were not in the government and had never held a government ministry, the so-called 'non-political' ones. No constitutional provision or law had anticipated that contingency, and, indeed, two constitutional provisions appeared to run counter to the notion of trying non-political defendants. Article 25 specifically held that no one could be brought to trial except 'before the proper judge who has jurisdiction over his case', and Article 102, in describing the ordinary judiciary, clearly stated that 'the judicial power is carried out by permanent judges', a criterion that no one on the integrated Court met. That article also explicitly prohibited special or extraordinary courts. The Court in its normal constitutional capacity dispensed with the question by concluding that the non-political defendants' culpability was directly connected to that of the political ones and raised the jurisdiction of the integrated Court to that of a judge *a quo* or trial court.[29] The same day, the Court revoked arrest warrants on two of them, and without directly acknowledging arguments by the non-political defendants that they could not be denied their constitutional right to travel (Article 16) seized their passports; the passport of General Fanali was, however, restored.[30] Those warrants were, incidentally, re-instituted on all within months.[31]

The other major constitutional issue that had to be resolved was that of the apparent conflict between the provisions for accusation and trial (Articles 90, 96 and 134) and those embodied in Articles 25 and 103. A portion of the former had already been addressed by the Court in its handling of the non-political defendants, but Article 25 provided not only that one must be tried by a proper judge, but also prohibited trial in the case of *ex post facto* laws. Article 103 addressed military justice, and General Fanali invoked it as requiring that he could be tried only by a military tribunal. The Court side-stepped all of these questions, rejecting them as unfounded. Their reasoning was simple – the special circumstances of impeachments and trial were not bound by either article. The *ex post facto* quality was dismissed in these cases because normal criminal laws easily covered the charges that were lodged against all of the defendants. Were the President of the Republic the subject of the charges, the actions that might bring him before the Court could have a more conceptual quality, but even if that should occur, the triggering behavior would have to be, according to the Court, legally pre-determined. That question was not, however, directly posed in the Lockheed proceedings.[32]

Other questions that the Court had to confront, in its capacity of constitutional court, were applications of the various pieces of implementing legislation, such as the laws of 1953 and 1962 that covered impeachment trials and applicable portions of the criminal code. The Court applied an adversarial model, even though Italy then used a more inquisitorial system for criminal proceedings. At the same time, it adhered to normal Italian criminal procedures by appointing an examining judge in the case, in this case an ordinary court magistrate, and granted to the parliamentary commission or the 'commissars' the attributes of public ministers or prosecutors.[33]

Before any testimony was ever heard by the Court, Parliament amended the statutes governing the parliamentary phase of future impeachments. Law No. 170, 10 May 1978 amounted to a total revision of the parliamentary stage of an impeachment and repealed 16 articles of the 1962 law that had governed the process. It had the effect of limiting the powers of the parliamentary commission of inquiry that preceded a calling of a joint meeting of the two chambers. Most importantly, the revision altered the commission of inquiry from a body with the powers of a public minister to one with simply the powers of investigation.[34]

The integrated Court held its sessions in Palazzo Salviati, because the facilities in the Constitutional Court's normal home in Palazzo Consulta could not accommodate more than double the number of judges. For 51 days, from September 1978 until March of the next year, the integrated court heard testimony and arguments, along with the presentation of other evidence. The accused, besides Gui, Tanassi and Fanali, included Camillo Crociani, an executive with a state holding company, who fled, and the brothers Ovidio and Antonio Lefebvre, the latter a university professor of maritime law who had access to the major power centers. The others were Luigi Olivi, Bruno Palmiotti, Maria Fava and Victor Max Melca and the representative of Lockheed, Vittorio Antonelli.

The three commissars from Parliament, each designated by their parties, could not fully agree on prosecution strategy. Professor Marcello Gallo, who was named by the Christian Democrats, registered his dissent to the accusations against his fellow Christian Democrat, Luigi Gui. That was a rather vital disagreement, but was accommodated by a division of presentation of the charges among the three. Alberto Dall'Ora, a lawyer from the Socialist Party, presented the general design of the allegations. To emphasize the severity of the crimes, he claimed both the bribe-offering and the bribe-accepting defendants 'had damaged the international reputation of the nation' and had sold the country's prestige. The bribes, both offered and taken, showed that private interests superceded public ones and constituted a betrayal of the nation. Dall'Ora also outlined the strategy that Lockheed had adopted, not only in Italy, but also in the Netherlands, Japan, Turkey and elsewhere, of recruiting so-called 'consultants' who happened to work at levels of government that enabled them to affect contract decisions.[35]

Carlo Smuraglia, a professor named by the Communist Party, developed the motive for the crime. His part of the prosecution mapped out the crucial and not, he emphasized, coincidental dates for letters of intent and contracts. He argued for linking the actions of Gui and Tanassi, as one replaced the other as minister of defense, and highlighted the earlier recommendations against the Lockheed aircraft in favor of a shorter range one. In his presentation of the charges against Christian Democrat Gui, Smuraglia explained that the ex-minister was not involved in the plot for money for himself, but rather for his party. The Christian Democrats received, according to Smuraglia, $2 020 000 from Lockheed through Ovidio Lefebvre in December 1969. This was supposedly the third installment paid. The first had been in cash and could not be traced, but followed the second letter of intent signed by Tanassi. The second payment was made, according to the prosecutors, to a special interest of Tanassi after the contract was signed. The timing of each stage of the sale paralleled, according to the Communist prosecutor, payments by Lockheed.[36]

Questioning defendants and presenting evidence, including wiretapped phone conversations, continued until late September 1978, and then the defense for each accused was presented individually. Throughout the testimony, references were made repeatedly to the President of the Republic, Christian Democrat Giovanni Leone. Though he was not officially charged, Leone resigned six months before the end of his term, in June 1978, citing health considerations. The case was not without a number of complications, ranging from attempts to discover the identity of the mysterious middle-man referred to only by the codename 'Antelope Cobbles', to the early disappearance of defendant Crociani and the later flight by Olivi to Brazil. Documents provided by the US Securities and Exchange Committee were introduced, and an examining magistrate was sent to Brazil to interrogate Olivi, while the Court attempted to have him extradited. The trial concluded in February 1979.[37]

After completion of the public phase, the integrated Court met behind closed doors for deliberations lasting some 23 days. Their decision was announced on 1 March 1979, but a complete explanation of it was not filed until 2 August. Of all the defendants, only Gui was completely absolved. In two other instances, those of Maria Fava and Vittorio Antonelli, the Court concluded that the actions with which they were charged did not constitute crimes.[38] The verdict regarding Gui may seem to be an anomaly in light of the evidence, but is not surprising in light of the implications of his involvement for the Christian Democrat Party. At that time, all presidential appointments to the Court had been made by Christian Democrat Presidents of the Republic, two-fifths of the parliamentary appointments had gone to Christian Democrats, and surely a significant proportion of the laypeople named to the directory for service on impeachment trials, such as this, were supporters of the Christian Democrats, though that proportion might have been more or less as a consequence of the random drawing of names from the list for this panel.

In the United States, the penalty for one impeached and convicted is removal from office and at most prohibition from holding other public offices. That is not the case in Italy, where the Court not only found defendants guilty, but also actually imposed criminal penalties. Ex-Defense Minister Mario Tanassi was found guilty of aggravated corruption for acts in his official capacity and was sentenced to two years and four months in prison and fined 400 000 lire. Tanassi was at the time a sitting member of Parliament and, therefore, had immunity from prosecution. The Court referred its decision of guilt to the Election Cabinet of Parliament that on 7 March revoked Tanassi's parliamentary mandate. Luigi Olivi and Victor Max Melca were not found guilty per se on the grounds that the facts alleged were not sustained; the Court's inclinations, though, were transparent when it transmitted their cases to the Public Minister for further investigation.[39]

Fugitive Camillo Crociani was found guilty *in absentia* and sentenced to two years and four months in prison and assessed a fine of 400 000 lire, the same punishment as Tanassi. General Duilio Fanali, Bruno Palmiotti and the Lefebvre brothers were all declared guilty of corruption and given prison sentences together with fines. The six guilty parties were also required to compensate the state both for cost of the trial and for their maintenance in prison.[40]

Revisiting and revising

The Lockheed Affair ended with the conviction of six people, the resignation of the President of the Republic, and questions about finances of the Christian Democrat Party. The last would again be spotlighted in the 1992 'Clean Hands' prosecutions, along with the parallel practices of other leading political parties. The process itself was a casualty of this first experience with a trial of government ministers. Then President of the Court, Leonetto Amadei, requested that Parliament reconsider and revise the process.[41]

The Italian Parliament has never been known for moving rapidly, and despite the obvious interest in a revision of the system for bringing charges and trying accusations against officials of the Republic, the issue receded into the background. Joint sittings of the two houses were required on several occasions in the next few years to consider charges of corruption against ministers: Prime Minister Francesco Cossiga in 1980, Prime Ministers Giulio Andreotti and Mariano Rumor and Minister of Defense Tanassi in 1982, Minister Andreotti in 1984, Minister for the Mezzogiorno Giacomo Mancini in 1984, 1985 and 1986, Minister of Finance Salvatore Formica in 1988, Ministers Franco Nicolazzi, Clelio Darida and Emilio Colombo in 1988. During this time, there were also parliamentary commissions of inquiry into the sale of ships to Iraq in 1988 and scandals regarding the state hydrocarbons agency, ENI, in 1983, 1984 and 1985.[42] These sittings were behind closed doors and never ended in formal accusations that would carry the cases to trial before the Constitutional Court.

Parliament may not, in fact, have ever taken up the question of reform had it not been for a referendum called in 1987. The referendum was provoked in part by the seeming inability of Parliament to bring charges against ministers, whatever the apparent evidence or the severity of the allegations. A referendum may be called upon a petition by voters that must also pass the scrutiny of the Constitutional Court. The specifics of the process will be discussed in Chapter 6, but for present purposes, the requisite signatures to repeal the legislation governing aspects of the of existing impeachment process were presented in July 1986. The highest ordinary court, *Corte di Cassazione*, validated the signatures that December, and the Constitutional Court certified the referendum as admissible the next January.[43] The President of the Republic set a date for the referendum, that would be held along with several others, but later had to defer the election when Parliament was dissolved and parliamentary elections called. The referendum to abrogate 'the new laws governing procedures of accusation' was finally held, along with four others, in 1987.[44] An overwhelming majority of 85 per cent of the voters called for abrogation of portions of the 1962 and 1978 laws that governed the process of accusation.[45]

When a law is repealed or abrogated by a referendum, Parliament is required to rewrite the legislation, but is guided only by the rather obvious requirement that the replacement statutes be consistent with the spirit of the referendum. The first parliamentary reaction to the referendum was to pass a constitutional law that rewrote Article 96 of the Constitution regarding the criminal liability of government ministers. The new text specified that even after their resignation from office, ministers were subject to prosecution under *normal justice,* or in the regular criminal courts, and, therefore, clarified that ministers were answerable only for crimes recognizable in the criminal law. The sole special requirement to proceed against a minister or former minister was that permission must be granted by either the Senate or the Chamber of Deputies, as would already be required by provisions governing parliamentary immunity, should the minister or ex-minister currently hold a seat. Thus, prime ministers and other ministers were no longer subject to the impeachment process. The language of Article 90 applying to the President of the Republic was left unchanged.

Alterations were made to the language of Articles 134 and 135 that described the powers and duties of the Constitutional Court to bring them into line.[46]

In addition to the constitutional revisions, Parliament also rewrote the statutes governing accusation procedures. Five articles of the 1962 legislation, as already amended in 1978, were rewritten. The most important of these limits the Court's ability to consider 'connected crimes' and 'connected defendants' without parliamentary authorization. The new law also clarified that ordinary or administrative courts could impose sanctions against an accused President of the Republic only if the Constitutional Court had not.[47] To complete the revisions, both chambers of Parliament, in June 1989, revised their own internal rules for hearing accusations.[48] None of these revisions addressed the cognate question of parliamentary immunity from any prosecution without authorization from the relevant chamber.[49]

Under the revised procedures, Parliament remains involved in prosecutions of both the President of the Republic and of any ministers. Because the latter no longer implicates action by the Constitutional Court, it can be disposed of briefly. So-called 'ministerial crimes' committed in office are handled by the ordinary judiciary like other criminal accusations, with the single exception that Parliament must authorize the investigating magistrate to proceed. Only one chamber need be asked for this authorization, and, quite obviously, that chamber may simply grant permission or withhold it, at least for the moment. But, there is another wrinkle in the possibilities: the chamber may determine that indeed a crime was committed, but that it was justified because the minister was acting on a 'superior interest'. If that should be the finding, the minister cannot be prosecuted at that time or at any future date. However, to deny authorization for prosecution requires, not a majority vote of a single chamber, as in the case of a grant, but rather an absolute majority of both houses.[50]

The impeachment of a President of the Republic still involves both chambers and, if Parliament votes an accusation, also the Constitutional Court. The grounds and mechanisms remain in the realm of academic speculation since no accusation has ever achieved the required majority vote. The initial investigation of the accusations is undertaken by a committee consisting of the leadership of each chamber. That committee can find that there is insufficient evidence to proceed or that Parliament is not competent to act, because the crime is not one of those included in the Constitution. Their findings are, if warranted, presented to a joint meeting of the two chambers that may, after closed

door deliberations, vote by absolute majority to forward the impeachment to the Constitutional Court. If that is done, then one or more
'commissars' are elected to prosecute the case before the integrated
Constitutional Court. None of the procedures of the Court were changed
by the 1989 revisions, and only the Court's jurisdiction over 'connected crimes' or 'connected defendants' was affected.[51]

The blurred areas that linger are definitions of what might constitute
high treason or attacks on the Constitution, those acts for which the
President of the Republic may be impeached and tried. These terms,
like 'high crimes and misdemeanors' in the US Constitution, lack preci-
sion and are capable of quite elastic interpretations. Most authors have
focused on high treason and suggested that it refers to acts against the
personality of the state or violations of the President's oath of office,
while others have concluded that such an accusation could be trig-
gered only if the President acts to compromise the state in an international context, such as supporting a foreign nation against Italy.
Another line of interpretation holds that a President can run afoul of
the Constitution if he abuses his office or violates the duties and responsibilities of the office. Since most constitutional commentators in
Italy are trained in the law, not surprisingly some argue that there is no
need for elaborate interpretation, since high treason is clearly defined
in the Code of Military Procedure and attacks against the Constitution
are covered in the criminal code. If the nature of the crimes for which
a President of the Republic may be accused are vague, the conceivable
punishments that might be imposed are even more obscure.[52]

Much of the imprecision of the new, as with the old, procedures
would be resolved, it was assumed, on a case by case basis. That did not
require a lengthy wait. Within days of revising the internal parliamentary procedures in 1989, formal charges were made against a minister,
Remo Gaspari, but the requisite majority vote was not obtained and,
therefore, authorization to proceed with a prosecution was not forthcoming. The next month, on 20 July, the Chamber allowed a criminal
prosecution of Minister and Secretary of the Social Democrat Party
Franco Nicolazzi to proceed without ever taking a vote. The logic was
that the prosecution of a minister of government could be barred by a
parliamentary vote, but if there were no vote, the prosecution could
continue its natural course.[53]

At least some precedents have, therefore, been established, however
inexactly, regarding criminal proceedings involving ministers. There
has been far less activity that might resolve some of the ambiguities
surrounding impeachment of the President of the Republic. But, there

has been some. Twice during the tenure of President Francesco Cossiga (1985–92), charges were brought against him. The first was on 26 July 1989 when the joint committee of the two houses voted to archive (dismiss at least for the moment) the charges. A second followed on 4 January 1991, when Cossiga was again accused by two deputies of attacks on the Constitution. The recorded debates on that accusation suggest that the committee concluded that accusations must have some grounding in demonstrably criminal acts and did not reach to more vague allegations that the President endangered the constitutional order through a pattern of questionable activities. Cossiga had launched public attacks on the judiciary and the whole of the party system, clearly angering more than a few.[54] The subjective quality of the charges, however, lost to the desire for a more tangible and objective accusation, which was not forthcoming. The charges against Cossiga were archived a second time.[55] An article in the daily *Il Mattino* later that year more clearly outlined the not infrequent calls for Cossiga's removal. At issue was not 'violations of the constitution, pure and simple', but rather 'the existence of actions (and omissions) that objectively demonstrated his intention to alter the Constitution and its form of government ... [and give] the impression that the President of the Republic acts as though the reforms of the presidency that he advocates had already taken place'.[56] Cossiga resigned in April 1992, two months before the end of his term.[57]

Assessments

The Lockheed scandal is regarded by most Italian constitutional scholars as a mere historical footnote, an event that will never be repeated. That assumption is predicated not on a belief in the absence of corruption in Italian political life, but rather on the constitutional modifications that now make only the President of the Republic susceptible to parliamentary accusation and trial before the Constitutional Court. The single event some two decades past remains important, nonetheless, for understanding the behavior of the Italian Constitutional Court.

The process of accusation and trial deviates from more normal institutional activities of the Constitutional Court and is a mere auxiliary function of this or other, similar courts. Whereas the procedure is clearly an exception in a number of ways, the processes for judging the goals of the Court can still be viewed through the same lenses as other, more standard functions. What is most distinct about the trial of government ministers is that the constitutional judges had two different capacities, constitutional interpretation when acting as the ordinary court and weighing factual evidence when joined by the laypeople as the integrated court. In the former, the Court seems to have been more jurisprudentially oriented, while in the latter, perhaps more inclined toward reaching a politically desirable outcome.

As constitutional interpreters, the judges were confronted with a jurisdictional issue relating to the non-political defendants. Conflicting constitutional provisions were reconciled by saying that sorting out the guilt of the office-holders would be difficult without reference to the deeds of the non-political defendants. The second constitutional dilemma was that of application of *ex post facto* laws, prohibited by Article 25. The acts with which they were charged were covered by the criminal code and, therefore, hardly retroactive laws. For both issues, constitutional mandates were not clear, but the judges' resolution of them appears to have served no end save achieving legal clarity and legal accuracy.

The outcome of the actual trial, resolving the factual issues, may have involved extra-legal influences. Whatever the individual attitudes of the 15 judges may have been toward the crimes alleged and the partisan affiliations of the accused, they were masked and filtered by the single result from the Court. The addition of laypeople to the process of ascribing guilt or innocence could obviously modify the normal interactions among the judges. Therefore, pivotal aspects of the Court's role were different in some ways, but also still susceptible to the same influences as with constitutional cases. The independence of the judges appears to be a crucial explanatory factor. Despite the limited tenure of the judges, their discretion in resolution of the Lockheed case may have been colored by their concerns for the various audiences to whom they were playing. Remember that Christian Democrats had dominated parliamentary appointments to the Court, and all Presidents of the Republic were likewise members of that party. The importance of that affiliation was strongly highlighted when even the Christian Democrat commissar, Marcello Gallo, refused to concur in the prosecution of his fellow Christian Democrat, Luigi Gui. The calculation that a majority or almost one of the 31 members of the integrated court had some tie to the Christian Democrats is noteworthy. Future political prospects and acceptance of decisions by political audiences of the judges would seem relevant in understanding the Court's exoneration of Gui, particularly since the Social Democrat Tanassi, accused alongside him, was convicted.

The structural role of the Court was also different for trial of the Lockheed defendants. The trial came to the Court directly from

Parliament, as a result of an extraordinary joint sitting. The parliamentary decision taken by majority of both chambers could easily have biased the process. That decision in 1977 to forward the case against ex-ministers Gui and Tanassi must have had some political motivations, particularly in light of the decision *not* to forward accusations against ex-prime minister Rumor at the same time. The Court's entire role, both legally and within the political scheme, was dramatically altered by the very nature of the 'trial', in which the Court acted as judges of first instance to decide the facts in a political case. The Court's place was transformed when it was expected to decide concrete issues of guilt in an impeachment trial. That position and possible politicization were accentuated when judging the facts of the case, ones that here were at the core about how political parties were financed. Trying such a case is undeniably political and could not be otherwise when the most important defendants are politicians and office-holders charged with betrayal of the public trust, even though the precise allegations were those of corruption as defined in the criminal code.

Was this a case of good law or good policy? The outcome of the trial points to one quite plausible conclusion. Nine men were tried, and only six convicted. None convicted were Christian Democrat office-holders, but rather the one who had fled, General Fanali, Social Democrat Tanassi and three non-political defendants. Even Tanassi's conviction could be seen as a political expedient: his status as a parliamentarian dictated that Parliament decide the issue ultimately when choosing to lift his immunity and allowing the penalties to be imposed. Whether the outcome was a compromise solution, a conscious decision to preserve the prevailing status quo of DC dominance, a manifestation of party loyalty, or protection of the judges' future interests is hidden beneath the veneer of a single unified decision, both as to the verdicts and the legal explanation.

From a longer term view, the Court's single experience with a trial of ministers prompted an eventual rewriting of both laws and the Constitution. The 1987 popular referendum and the legal changes that followed made accusation, trial and conviction of ministers, including the prime minister, easier and shifted those decisions to magistrates on the ordinary courts. Parliament retained a hand through its ability to withhold authorization to proceed, but the interpretation that Parliament's inaction signaled its agreement with a prosecution relegated the most overt political protection afforded to corrupt officials to a reactive one. Criminal prosecutions no longer relied on the difficult process of obtaining a vote for prosecution through an absolute vote of the two chambers.

The concentric circles radiating out from the Lockheed case and the Court's handling of it are potentially quite wide. Sorting out a chain of causation would require, however, major inferential leaps. What is clear is that subsequent to the Lockheed scandal, laws and policies were rewritten by Parliament. Not only was the legislature's authorization to proceed against a minister made easier to obtain in 1989, but the criminal law's ability to reach parliamentarians was affected by constitutional amendment in 1993. Constitutional Law No. 3, of 29 October 1993, amended Article 68 of the Constitution regarding parliamentary immunity. Under the old provision, parliamentarians were immune from arrest, detention and criminal prosecutions unless apprehended in the act of committing a crime. Moreover, they were even protected from execution of previously issued judgments. Under the 1993 version, that last protection was dropped.[58] There were a variety of reasons offered for the modification. One was that the old version was too ambiguous and another was that both chambers of Parliament repeatedly denied authorization to proceed by claiming that the alleged misdeed was part of the 'parliamentary function'.[59] The unfolding saga of 'Clean Hands' investigations was undoubtedly the proximate cause of the 1993 change, but the 1988 decision of the Constitutional Court that redefined the relationship between the ordinary judiciary and the legislative branch when authorization to proceed was denied by the appropriate chamber, may also have been implicated.[60] Prosecutors were able, though not always with ease, to investigate and try public officials.

The Lockheed case was neither the first nor the last of the public corruption scandals in postwar Italian political life. *Tangenti* or bribes became a normal part of business in Italy. Antonio Gialanella argues that corruption in Italy results from a particularly Italian set of options at the foundation of society and institutions and the relationship between work and life.[61] His left-leaning brief places the blame on capitalism, but undoubtedly the right side of the political spectrum could muster an argument for the culpability of the social welfare state and the massive quantities of money appropriated and available for government projects. Whatever the source, Italy has experienced no small measure of public airing of political corruption scandals, much with its origins in 1992 with the 'Clean Hands' operation.[62] By the end of Parliament XI in 1992, various parliamentarians were charged with violations of 108 articles of the criminal code, five of the civil code, four of the military code, and four of the navigation code.[63] A twist on the revision of parliamentary immunity that permitted the widespread investigations was the suggestion that maybe the immunity that judges on the Constitutional Court enjoy should likewise be lessened.[64]

The Constitutional Court worked its way through the Lockheed case by making up many of the rules on an *ad hoc* basis, but that single trial, whether the case was rightly decided or not, gave the first impetus to revision of the process. Without the 1987 referendum, Parliament might have delayed even longer, but the system that finally replaced the old one makes the trial of accused ministers and parliamentarians easier and the possible crimes clearer. Those modifications may, at some point, serve as sufficient deterrents, and perhaps the investigation and trial of politicians will cease to be commonplace.

6
Gatekeeper to the Public: Referendums

The referendum process is the second quasi-judicial activity with political overtones that falls to the Italian Constitutional Court. Referendums of some kind are mentioned in the constitutions of 13 Western European countries,[1] but their use is rare and typically 'invoked to solve a particular problem or to justify a particular solution'.[2] The main exceptions to that general trend are Switzerland, where referendums are annual events, and Italy, where the frequency of referendums is approaching the Swiss record. Italian voters have faced 45 questions in less than a quarter of a century (1974–97). Courts are not normally part of the referendum system, but in Italy, the Constitutional Court is the primary institution that can block plebiscites. A similar judicial hand in the process can otherwise be found only in some American states.[3] The Court's gatekeeper position has raised popular awareness of the Court and testified to its political nature.

Referendums are essentially a device for direct democracy, whereby legislative enactments can be overridden by popular vote. Those who oppose them usually cite the 'thin-edge-of-the-wedge' logic: 'If you consult the people on this question, how can you refuse a referendum on a host of other issues?'[4] Are the voters to second guess everything that their elected representatives do? Those and similar arguments combined with partisan desires to avoid diluting the power of the ruling coalitions delayed implementation of the referendum until 1970. The new device debuted cautiously, with the electorate asked to revoke two of Parliament's most controversial laws, those to permit divorce and abortion. In both cases, the legislation was sustained.

Thereafter, however, the Italian experience validates 'thin-edge-of-the-wedge' arguments and in the 25 years since 1972, when the first referendum question reached the Constitutional Court, one hundred others followed. The questions presented ranged quite literally from the sublime (the role of the Roman Catholic Church) to the mundane (timing of commercial breaks on television). Faced with the barrage of questions, the gatekeeper role of the Court was quickly apparent, and it has rejected 46 over the years. Some questions the Court admitted were rendered superfluous as a consequence of parliamentary responses to the proposals or other events that prompted their withdrawal. The issues proposed range from abortion, divorce, life imprisonment, state financing of political parties, media pluralism and electoral reforms to hunting, environmental issues, shop closing hours, wages, pensions, house arrest, extra-judicial roles for magistrates, and more. As the Court navigated among the requests, it broke from simply verifying the specific constitutional prohibitions and fashioned a coherent jurisprudence to limit the subjects. Then, it began to apply its own rules more and more elastically to accommodate a political agenda. As if to underscore the political nature of these activities, Presidents of the Court regularly called press conferences to explain decisions. As the gatekeeper to the referendum process, the Court has been increasingly acknowledged as a political force in Italian politics.

Early political choices

A form of referendum was used in Italy during the unification process in the mid-nineteenth century to gain approval for annexation of new territories. Those early referendums were widely regarded as suspect, and their presumably fraudulent character was captured in Giuseppe di Lampedusa's novel, *The Leopard*. After the Second World War, an institutional referendum was held to determine whether Italy would be a monarchy or a republic. Through that referendum in 1946 a republic was chosen, but in a relatively close vote.[5]

Prior experience with the referendum made the mechanism a rather obvious topic for discussion in the Constituent Assembly in 1947. The argument for inclusion of a means of direct democracy was made by Costantino Mortati to the subcommission that wrote the first draft of the Constitution:

> The referendum has a function more penetrating, more important ... in that it [permits] resolution of conflicts, gets a sense of the people, and is able to live with a parliamentary regime .... The people are allowed to participate not just with a yes or a no, but also in the debate of the questions.[6]

Within the subcommission, a number of objections were raised – interference with the power of the President, potential for a small party to use the device to sabotage Parliament, conflicts with the system for passing laws, and the availability of public opinion polls to accomplish the same thing – but three forms of referendum were included in the draft that was presented to the full assembly.[7] Because the proposal was among those most basic to the constitutional structure, referendums were debated early in the Constituent sittings, and three full days in January 1947 were devoted to discussions. The Swiss experience and that of some American states were invoked as examples of the positive results that could be anticipated, but the contradictions of having democratic will expressed in Parliament and then subjected to separate popular votes were also noted. Numerous amendments and proposals were offered and subjected to votes, but only principles were settled until the subject was revisited in autumn of that year. After considerable tinkering and modification, inclusion of an abrogative referendum was approved, but by a relatively close vote.[8]

Actually, several types of referendum are permitted by the Constitution: one to repeal constitutional amendments (Article 138), another to merge or otherwise alter regional boundaries (Article 133) and, finally, one whereby laws passed by Parliament may be repealed through popular vote (Article 75). The last of these is the one that has proved to be politically charged, and its application has resulted in more than one hundred issues before the Constitutional Court. Article 75 provides that, upon petition by 500 000 voters or five regional councils, an election will be held to repeal all or part of any law. The referendum is valid only if a majority of eligible electors vote, but then a simple majority is sufficient to revoke the law. The final sentence in that article requires that implementing legislation specify procedures. The referendum process became a political football, seen as a means of diminishing central authority, and the necessary legislation for its activation did not come until 1970 and then only as part of a larger political compromise.

The Christian Democrat-dominated government, once entrenched, was reluctant to devolve any power – to the Constitutional Court, to the regions, or even to the people. Regional governments and the referendum were effectuated only after major political disruptions, beginning in 1969, affected the inner workings of the party itself. More and more factions developed and were reflected in one short-lived government after another. Implementing legislation for referendums was approved as part of a compromise in the passage of the law permitting divorce in 1970. Christian Democrat President of the Chamber of

Deputies Giovanni Leone consented to passage of the divorce law, with the expectation that it would then be abrogated through a referendum. That was a major miscalculation. As a consequence, however, another major step toward decentralization was put in place.[9]

Legislation implementing the Constitutional Court included an additional role in the sphere of the referendum, charging the Court with adjudicating the constitutional legitimacy of proposed questions. The 1970 law implementing referendums elaborated more completely the steps a referendum must follow before reaching the voters. The *Corte di Cassazione* or highest ordinary court serves as the Central Office for Referendum, verifying signatures on petitions and forwarding certification to the Constitutional Court, which must hold deliberations on the proposal before the next 20 January. The Constitutional Court was not required to hold a public audience, but rather the government and sponsors of the referendum submitted written arguments and the judges met in chamber to decide admissibility. Recently the Court began hearing oral presentations by the sponsors and the government, but in chamber and out of the media glare. If a referendum question is admitted, the President of the Republic must set a date for the vote between mid-April and mid-June. If Parliament is dissolved and elections called, however, the President must set the referendum polling day one year later.[10]

Judicial self-restraint

If the Constitutional Court is to decide which referendum questions are constitutionally admissible, what are the constraints on their constitutionality? Article 75 stipulates that issues of taxes, budgets, amnesties and indulgences and the ratification of international treaties are beyond the scope of a referendum. Initially, the Court limited its role to verifying that no referendum transgressed those four categories, but as the number of proposed referendums grew, so did the subjects that they addressed, and the constitutional judges extended their requirements for admissibility. The first referendum to achieve the requisite signatures and pass inspection of the highest ordinary court proposed to repeal the divorce law, and the ones that followed immediately also addressed major political controversies.

The same student and worker movement that was the catalyst for decentralizing governmental power also voiced the concerns of women. Many of the laws women found objectionable were of Fascist origin and a direct consequence of the special position the Roman Catholic

Church had been granted by Mussolini in the Lateran Pacts. The privileged place of the church in a host of areas was absorbed into the republican Constitution by Article 7 and included, among other things, marriage. Specifically, according to Article 34 of the Lateran Pacts, 'cases concerning annulment of marriage and dispensation from marriage ... are reserved for ecclesiastical tribunals and their departments'.[11] That translated into the reality that civil divorce was impossible in Italy. That divorce – or more accurately, no divorce – law was a target of both feminists and the worker-student coalition in the late 1960s.

Socialist Loris Fortuna and Liberal Antonio Baslini introduced a law legalizing divorce in the late 1960s that passed the Chamber of Deputies in 1969 by a vote of 325 to 283, with opposition coming solely from the Christian Democrats and the neo-fascist Italian Social Movement. It passed the Senate the next year and became law in December 1970.[12] The Catholic Church used every option available to reverse it, taking constitutional questions to the Court and being rebuffed on five occasions. The other route for repeal of the law was the referendum, and Pope Paul VI and the Italian Episcopal Conference mobilized Catholic organizations and the Christian Democratic Party to gather the required 500 000 signatures.[13] The *Corte di Cassazione* declared the validity of the requisite signatures on 6 December 1971, and the Constitutional Court deliberated in chamber on 11 January 1972. The Court issued only a six paragraph decision saying succinctly that Constitution Article 75 lists only taxes, budgets, amnesties and indulgences and international treaties as beyond the scope of a referendum; obviously, 'the law to which the referendum refers, in its complete and sole disposition, does not concern a matter excepted by the Constitution'.[14] The referendum question was declared admissible and, on 12 May 1974, the referendum was held in which the law permitting divorce was upheld by a majority of almost 60 per cent of those voting. Voter turnout neared 90 per cent, a level that would rarely be attained in a subsequent referendum.

The next referendum question to reach the Court was a challenge to the Fascist era criminal code that made abortions illegal. Together with that initiative was another that challenged an element of the 1974 law governing public financing of political parties and the number of subscribers a party must have to qualify for government subsidies. The ultimate fate of those initiatives illustrates the complex political maneuvering that a referendum request can set in motion. Signatures of both had been verified by the highest ordinary court in November 1975. They were then passed to the Constitutional Court that declared them constitutionally admissible. In doing so, however, the Court limited the function of the ordinary court. The *Corte di Cassazione* could validate and count the signatures, but the Constitutional Court held exclusive power under the Constitution to decide admissibility.[15] In May, Parliament was dissolved and new elections scheduled, thus postponing any referendum until the following year. Two years later, with the referendum still technically alive, Parliament passed legislation governing abortion that accomplished some of what the referendum had intended, and the highest ordinary court declared that the motives for the referendum were met. The abortion referendum sponsors countered with an allegation of conflict of powers, since only a watered-down version of what they had wanted was embodied in the law. They lost that bid before the Constitutional Court in March 1980.[16]

Even though the law that made abortion criminal was rewritten, clearly in response to the referendum, the new law was unsatisfactory to either side of the issue and would appear again on the referendum agenda. Similarly, the law governing state financing of political parties was altered slightly to conform to the challenge, but dissatisfaction with it persisted. Referendums would often be the stimuli to spur politicians into action, but parliamentary responses were too often merely diluted versions of what the referendum sponsors were seeking. Parliament tried in this fashion, though, to regain control of issues and to blunt potentially more radical changes.

Judicial gloss

The Court read Article 75 quite literally and found only four exceptions to laws that were subject to repeal by the voters. Scholarship was already suggesting that some other subjects might be barred 'through cautious analogy' to those mentioned in the Constitution.[17] A pool of requests in 1978 presented the Court with the opportunity to do just that and to apply the first judicial gloss to the words of the Constitution. In a single opinion, announced on 2 February 1978, the Court disposed of requests for eight different referendums on quite diverse topics: two on the military judicial code, and one each on state financing of political parties, parts of the Lateran Pacts, state responsibility for the insane, various parts of the criminal code, the 1977 anti-crime act and commissions of inquiry for impeachments. The complexity of the issues raised by some of these proposals is best captured in the proposal to repeal parts of the 1930 criminal code. That proposal included repeal of articles addressing life imprisonment, legitimate use of arms to resist authority, crimes involving publications, designation of 'socially dangerous' criminals, juvenile crimes, state secrets and more – a total of 97 articles of the criminal code! A wholesale reform of the code was implicated in a single proposal.

For each of the eight proposals, the government presented arguments that managed to wedge the questions into one of the proscribed subjects for referendums listed in Article 75 of the Constitution. For example, the state law on financing political parties was deemed a budget bill and the Lateran Pacts were a treaty. The Court chose, though, not to accept that view, but rather to elaborate for the future 'the fundamentals, scope and criteria that will judge the admissibility of referendums'.[18]

The Court then enunciated four separate reasons whereby a proposal would be considered constitutionally inadmissible. All four were, according to the Court, 'inherent in the essential character and necessities of the institution of referendum'. First, a proposal may not contain multiple and heterogeneous questions. That prohibition was necessitated, according to the Court, to preserve the democratic principle: you cannot ask people to make a single vote on issues that cannot be reduced to a single unifying question. To do so would, according to the Court, violate the liberty of the ballot. The second was that a proposal could not involve or implicate any part of the Constitution or a constitutional law (amendment). Referendums that involved the Constitution or constitutional laws were governed by Article 138 of the Constitution with its own very different requirements from ones brought under Article 75. The third disqualifying feature was if the proposal's central intention could be attained only by injuring the Constitution or other laws. And, last, a proposal could not fall under any of the categories listed in Article 75 as being beyond the reach of a referendum.[19]

That formula, when applied to the eight proposals before the Court, rendered four admissible and four not. Altering the Lateran Pacts amounted to altering the Constitution, since Article 7 had incorporated them. Repealing 97 articles of the criminal code presented multiple and heterogeneous questions, and the two modifications of the military judicial code were also 'thematically too different' to constitute a single question. The remaining four were, however, certified as admissible.[20]

Of those, only two reached the electorate. In advance of the June referendum, Parliament enacted a new law governing treatment and commitment of the insane, and the referendum was declared moot by the *Corte di Cassazione*. Also, that May, Parliament passed a new law covering questions on commissions of inquiry and, thereby, avoided the referendum process. The remaining two were presented to the voters in June 1978, who upheld the anti-crime law by a vote of almost four to one and the law on state financing of political parties, but by a closer margin (56 to 44 per cent).[21]

In the course of the 1978 referendums reaching the voters, the Court made two other relevant decisions, though not on the admissibility of a specific proposal. The Court used that opportunity also to assert its authority by limiting that of the *Corte di Cassazione* in its capacity as the Central Office for Referendum. The sponsors of the referendum on the anti-crime law that the Court had deemed admissible in February, filed for a conflict of powers hearing before the Court in May. They alleged that the *Corte di Cassazione* had exceeded its power when authorizing the referendum proposal by removing one challenged portion of the law from it. The ordinary judges had claimed that a 1977 amendment to the law had superceded the deleted provision. Promoters of the referendum argued that the existence of the proposal blocked any action on the part of the legislature to modify the challenged law. The Court upheld the power of the legislative branch to act in advance of the actual referendum, but it invalidated that portion of the 1970 law implementing the referendum that allowed the highest ordinary court to remove any part of a referendum proposal that was integral to the overall sense of the referendum.[22]

That decision was followed within a week by another involving the same parties. The sponsors objected to the highest ordinary court's substitution of the new language of the 1977 amendment instead of the original 1975 law. The Court again annulled the decision of the *Corte di Cassazione* and invalidated the part of the referendum implementing legislation that allowed the ordinary court to review a proposal's content. Citing its authority under Article 75, the Constitutional Court claimed that it alone could determine the substance and admissibility of referendum questions.[23]

With the ground rules somewhat clarified, another group of proposals began working their way through the system, and their admissibility was decided by the Constitutional Court in January 1981. A total of 11 referendums were decided by the Court that February, and six were found admissible. However, application of the Court's criteria seemed rather arbitrary when applied to the diverse questions. A challenge to the 1979 emergency anti-terrorism legislation, prompted by the rise of terrorism generally and by the kidnapping and assassination of former prime minister Aldo Moro, was permitted. The Court reasoned that the proposal spanned a number of elements, but had a common, unifying principle.[24] A challenge to the existing law governing capital punishment was also found to raise a single homogenous question.[25] A referendum to limit the circumstances whereby one could obtain a license to carry a weapon was also allowed by the Court,[26] as was the proposal to repeal a single article of the code governing the military judicial system.[27] Two separate proposals relating to the 1978 law legalizing abortion, one to repeal the law and another to repeal certain articles and thereby liberalize its effect, were also admissible.[28] However, a proposal to restrict hunting was found to implicate other laws and was blocked,[29] and a proposal to repeal legislation on crimes of opinion was declared too heterogeneous to qualify.[30] Similarly, proposals to repeal certain articles of the law governing the Financial Guard[31] and personal drug use[32] were not sufficiently homogenous to pass scrutiny. Finally, a proposal to restrict nuclear generating plants was said to implicate the EURATOM Treaty and was, consequently, beyond the scope of a referendum.[33]

An obvious dividing line is difficult to discern, with the possible exception of the distinction between proposals that addressed a single article of a law versus ones that included multiple articles. The charge of excessive judicial discretion carries some weight when the 11 proposals are viewed together. Parliament intervened in only one instance, that of the military judicial code, to revise the targeted provision in advance of its submission to the electorate. Perhaps more interestingly, all five challenged laws that reached the electorate were sustained. The Court perhaps sensed which would prevail and which would fall if allowed to reach the voters.

Over the next two years, the Radical Party, which had sponsored some of the earlier referendums, accelerated its recourse to the plebiscite as an avenue for reform. One initiative was presented in 1981 to reform the Worker's Rights Law of 1970, but the Court rejected the constitutionality of the proposal under its 1978 criteria.[34] On the same day, however, another on the wage indexation scale, was declared admissible.[35] Parliament revisited the wage index and in May passed legislation that the highest ordinary court said met the objective of the referendum. That was insufficient in the eyes of the referendum sponsors, who filed for a conflict of powers hearing before the Constitutional Court; their claim was rejected.[36]

Was the Court protecting the values of the political regime and blocking popular will? Allegations to that effect were blunted when the Court, in 1985, permitted a highly charged referendum to pass to the voters. In the face of sky-rocketing inflation, the Craxi government had issued a decree law in 1984 to cut the mandatory wage indexation scale. The so-called *scala mobile* automatically raised wages for employees of both public and private enterprises to compensate for inflation. After Parliament converted the decree, the Communist Party immediately began acquiring signatures to force a referendum. The requisite petitions were confirmed by the *Corte di Cassazione* in December 1984, and the constitutional issues were decided by the Court early the following year.

The law in question reduced the wage escalator clause for only two trimesters of 1984, but the referendum proposal addressed only the first of those trimesters. The *Corte di Cassazione* questioned the validity of admitting a referendum whose subject matter was wholly in the past or would have a retroactive effect. The constitutional judges saw it differently: to diminish the escalator clause for one trimester effectively lowered all subsequent wage increases, since each percentage increase builds upon the preceding ones. The Court dismissed the *Cassazione*'s reading and relied on the 1970 implementing legislation that limited the *Corte di Cassazione* to examining proposals 'for conformity with the law, *exclusive of determination of admissibility'* [emphasis mine]. The Court emphasized again that it alone could 'in its own time' decide 'the typology of abrogative referendum that the Constitution defined and permitted'.[37]

The government's argument against the referendum proposal rested on the text of Article 75 of the Constitution, that the challenged provision was a budget law, prohibited by constitutional language. The limits on salary increases obviously had implications for government finances, since they simultaneously affected both government salaries and tax revenues. The Court was not, however, persuaded. Undoubtedly the law had economic dimensions, but the Court said that changes to the indexation rate predated the 1984 financial law, and its consequences had been anticipated in formulation of the budget. The Court concluded that the issue of homogeneity was the only criterion that remained, and the question was straightforward: 'were salaried workers to make the economic sacrifice involved in the law?' And, the Court added, that question 'is only up to the electorate, not this Court, to decide'.[38] On 9 June 1985, following a hotly contested campaign, the voters sustained the law by a vote of 54.3 per cent, a narrower margin than even in the divorce referendum.

Political judgments

Every referendum until 1985 that reached the public had resulted in a victory for the government. That changed in 1987 when five laws were repealed through the referendum process. A total of eight separate referendum proposals were considered by the Court on 16 January 1987, with three declared inadmissible. The five that passed called for repeal of laws on civil liability for judges and prosecutors and parts of the law governing trials of government ministers, plus three on various aspects of nuclear power. The three unsuccessful proposals would have asked the voters to alter the method of selecting members of the Superior Council of the Magistrature (the body that manages the careers of judges and prosecutors), to repeal all of the laws governing hunting so that a wholly new law could be designed, and to revoke the law giving hunters access to agricultural properties without owners' permission. The distinctions between which fell on the admissible versus inadmissible sides of the line were blurred.[39] The referendum on naming members of the Superior Council of the Magistrature was rejected as being too intertwined with other laws. The Court also claimed, for the first time, that the Constituent Assembly had intended to insulate elections from the Article 75 referendum. That was, however, a subsidiary legal point for rejecting the proposal.[40] Both of those on hunting were rejected for lack of homogeneity, clarity and consistency.[41] One hunting proposition could easily result in two distinct interpretations: to eliminate hunting totally or to drastically limit hunting. The other hunting proposal was rejected because the Court said that it addressed two 'distinct matters', hunting and fishing, The Court relied on a technical reading of the question, instead of seeing the intent as one of general environmental protection.[42]

The set of 1987 decisions was a turning point in judicial interpretation, not because of the legal justifications, but rather because the electorate supported the proposals that passed the Court's scrutiny.[43] Also the Court had appropriated to itself almost total discretion, since 'homogeneity' and 'laws intertwined with others' could readily be manipulated by the judges to block or admit all kinds of referendum questions.[44]

Though referendums on hunting had been rebuffed previously by the Court, sponsors wishing to limit or prohibit the sport did not give up, and in 1990 the Court was presented with two additional initiatives for referendums. One was directed at severe limitations on when and what wildlife could be hunted, and the second attempted simply to prevent hunters from entering private property without the owner's permission. The two were considered jointly and both were upheld as constitutionally permissible. The former, the more far-reaching, was challenged as interfering with European Community agreements, infringing on regional power and affecting government finance laws because of the taxes on hunters' licenses. The Court found that all of the relevant international conventions allowed for implementation of more stringent limitations on hunting, that there was no conflict with regional authority and that taxes and hunting licenses did not constitute the constitutionally prohibited category of budget and finance laws. Turning to its own 'implicit limitations', the Court found the proposal capable of public comprehension. The more limited second referendum was acceptable by analogy to the first and was 'clear, homogenous and unequivocal'.[45]

Fates of two other proposals were decided by the Court the same day, one to limit the use of pesticides in food products and another to repeal business licensing requirements for agencies employing fewer than 15 people. Both were admissible. The proposal relating to pesticides was challenged on grounds of international obligations relating to the European Community, but the Court found that implementation of the proposal, were it to pass, was clearly within the power of the Ministry of Health. It also met, according to the Court, 'the other profiles' and was, therefore, admissible.[46] A challenge to one section of the Worker's Statute was also disposed of by the Court rather simply: it violated none of the prohibited categories and was homogenous and clear.[47]

The last proposal never reached the voters, since Parliament passed a law in May that accomplished its intent. When the *Corte di Cassazione* declared the object of the referendum met by the new law, the sponsors filed for a conflict of powers case with the Constitutional Court. They alleged that the new law fell short of the intent of the referendum, but the Court rejected their claim as inadmissible.[48] That decision was consistent with the Court's 1978 conclusion that initiation of a referendum does not preclude subsequent legislative action toward the same end. The decision struck, in other words, a balance between representative institutions and those of direct democracy.[49]

All three remaining initiatives were supported by environmental groups, but the hunting lobby was so strong in Italy that only the Communist Party and the fringe left Radicals, Greens and Democratic Proletarians joined environmentalists in campaigning to repeal the laws. The other political parties either opposed repeal or called for a free vote and endorsed no position. The largest licensed hunting group, representing 1.5 million hunters, adopted a rather novel approach to the referendums: they campaigned for abstention.[50] Since Article 75 requires that a majority of the eligible voters must participate for a referendum to be valid, this was a clever strategy. The hunters' lobby campaign, the apathy of the parties and the particular questions combined to make the three 1990 referendums the first to be annulled for lack of a quorum. Only 43 per cent of the voters turned out, and the referendums were void, despite the overwhelming vote to repeal the laws.

In 1991 another set of controversial referendums were certified by the highest ordinary court and sent to the Constitutional Court for adjudication. All addressed elections, those of the Senate, the Chamber of Deputies and communal councils. That all were intended to strike at the core of the system of *partitocrazia* or government by parties was apparent and made their outcomes extremely important both to those in power and to those seeking reform. A wholesale revision of Senate elections was proposed, and a more modest one for the Chamber of Deputies. The Chamber proposal asked for elimination of preference votes. Chamber of Deputies elections were based on strict proportional representation of the political parties, with no threshold, but preference voting was introduced in 1957 to allow the electorate to select specific candidates on the party list by ranking them. Preference voting had been introduced to personalize the selection of representatives, but had long been viewed as a way for parties to manipulate outcomes, even fraudulently. Communal elections, also using proportional representation, were governed by a 1960 law.

The three were, because of their related subject matter, considered jointly by the Constitutional Court, but only the challenge to preference voting in the Chamber was found admissible. The Court's reasoning was particularly creative. The first point of law discussed the claim that the Constituent Assembly had passed an amendment to add the words 'election laws' to the list of subjects proscribed for referendums, but that amendment was somehow omitted when the final document was drafted. That point had also been mentioned, but was not determinative, in the 1987 decision relating to elections for the Superior Council of the Magistrature. The Court also argued that referendums could not interfere with constitutional organs or processes whose alteration could paralyze the process of government. The Court also considered homogeneity, clarity and confounding questions and the need for a single common unifying question.[51]

The Court ultimately concluded that too many diverse elements were involved in the proposal to alter senatorial elections – limiting a candidate to one district, winning 65 per cent in that district, and having a quorum of voters participating. The proposal was 'imprecise and too generic'; two different outcomes were possible if the question were passed. Therefore, it was denied. Use of preference voting for the Chamber of Deputies was distinguished, however, as presenting a single, clear and unified question and was admissible. Communal election questions were, on the other hand, susceptible to different interpretations, making them impractical to implement and therefore not admissible.[52]

The complexity of the decision and the hairsplitting distinctions were met, not surprisingly, with suspicion. What were seen as the two most important challenges to the system of *partitocrazia* were blocked by the Court, but the stage was set, even so, for the public to record its displeasure with the state of national politics.[53] Potential implications of the remaining referendum, that on preference voting for the Chamber, placed the parties in an uncertain position. The dominant Christian Democrats declared a free vote, meaning that they took no official position, and the Socialists advocated the strategy that hunting advocates had used so successfully – abstention. The Democratic Party of the Left (reformed Communists), neo-fascist Italian Social Movement, Republicans, Liberals, Refounded Communists (unreformed) and Greens advocated a 'yes' vote.[54] Voter turnout neared two-thirds, and the referendum passed by an overwhelming majority of 95 per cent, the highest in the history of referendums in Italy. That referendum was the first step in what would eventually amount to dismantling the way political business was conducted in Italy.

The results of the 1991 referendum signaled the beginning of change in Italian politics, but that might have come to naught had the Milan magistrates not begun their 'Clean Hands' investigations the next year. As more and more of those in the political class were charged with corruption and schemes to extort the nation's finances were exposed, public rancor increased. One avenue that frustration took was the referendum, for through it those not in positions of power could initiate reforms and go directly to the voters, if, of course, they could get their proposals past the Constitutional Court.

Nineteen referendum proposals confronted the Court in January 1993. These were different, in some ways, from previous ones. First, five of them were sponsored not by voters, but by regional councils seeking to break central government control of some areas of governance. Also in this set were two referendum proposals that had previously been rejected by the Court. The judges reconsidered their former decisions, but argued that the questions presented were distinct and separable from the earlier ones. The Court's willingness to backtrack on two major electoral issues strongly suggests that it was not impervious to the public mood, a mood that was anti-system and anti-politician.

Article 75 provided that a referendum could be sought by petition of five regional councils, but this was the first time any of the regional governments used that mechanism. Their strategy was a solid one, for the two that reached the voters won; three did not, however, survive inspection at the Constitutional Court. All five of the regionally sponsored proposals called for the elimination or significant modification of a central government agency. One, calling for the elimination of the Ministry of Agriculture, was sustained by the Court as 'congruent, coherent, clear and homogenous' and contravening none of the constitutionally proscribed subjects. Even though aspects of the European Community were implicated, the Court noted that there was no necessity for a cabinet level office to exist to meet EC obligations.[55] Similarly, the referendum request for elimination of the Ministry of Tourism and Entertainment was pronounced admissible. The Court even said that 'no one could doubt the admissibility', since it fulfilled requirements of 'clarity, unity and homogeneity' and amounted only to the 'elimination of a bureaucratic and administrative apparatus'.[56]

Others directed at eliminating the National Health Service, the Ministry of Industry and Corporations, and the National Agency for Tourism were poorly drawn and technically flawed. The request to ask voters to eliminate the National Health Service isolated the 1958 law that created it, but ignored all of the subsequent legislation that also involved the agency. The Court said that it lacked clarity, was intertwined with other laws and was insufficiently clear for the electorate to cast its votes knowledgeably.[57] The proposal to modify the Ministry of Industry and Corporations ignored the reality that the designation involved a complex organization, many offices and organs; the proposal was 'incoherent and contradictory'.[58] The proposal addressing the National Agency for Tourism was deemed inadmissible for lack of homogeneity and clarity. It was connected to a whole list of other state offices and had implications on both the national and international levels.[59]

In that group of referendums, the Court also approved ones that would decriminalize personal drug use,[60] eliminate the Minister for Public Works (whose job was increasingly less necessary in view of the move to privatization),[61] change the method for distributing public funds to political parties,[62] remove some local environmental issues from the National Health Service,[63] and shift the power to name the president and vice president of the savings bank away from the Minister of the Treasury.[64] For each, the Court repeated that they fell into none of the prohibited categories and were sufficiently coherent, simple, clear and homogeneous. Even the proposal to eliminate the special funding for projects in the Mezzogiorno (South of Italy) survived the Court's review. The judges noted that the law was exceedingly complex, but that the referendum question was 'reducible to a single rational principle, essentially to halt the special funds'.[65] Notably, Parliament acted as it had previously and passed a new law governing funding for the poor southern region of Italy, but it did not meet the intent of the referendum. The Court acted, in an unprecedented way, to sustain the referendum in spite of the new legislation.[66] Parliament had to act a second time to avoid submission of the question to public approval.

The remaining two proposals were aimed at elections and both were essentially the same as ones brought to and rejected by the Court in 1991. One proposed transformation of senatorial elections, by making three-quarters of the seats subject to majority vote in districts and leaving one-quarter to be selected through proportional representation and therefore subject to partisan lists. The Court cited its earlier decision that prohibited allowing a referendum on election of constitutional organs and then said the former case is 'analogous to this one, but in different terms'; the 1993 referendum offered a 'coherent modification' and was admissible.[67] A similar tactic was applied when changing communal elections from proportional representation to majoritarianism was considered the second time. The judges said that the 1993 version was a 'new formulation' in which 'there is a single rational motive that is presented in a unified fashion and can be clearly understood by the electorate'.[68]

In all, only three of the 19 proposals were blocked by the Court, but Parliament successfully staved off eight of those. The remaining eight that reached the voters were all successful. Voter turnout was high, and the vote was close only on the question of decriminalizing personal drug use (55.4 to 44.6 per cent). Public sentiment was, at that time, so anti-government and anti-political status quo that any proposal for change would likely have won public approval. Voter turnout, which had been in steady decline since the first 1974 referendum, had turned around and more than three-quarters of eligible voters participated. As can be seen in Table 6.1, the 1993 referendums were the last, however, to capture public interest.

Table 6.1   Italian referendum results (1974–97)

Subject	Year	% Yes vote (Repeal law)	% No vote (Sustain law)	% Voter turnout
Divorce	1974	40.7	59.3	87.7
Public order/ Anti-crime	1978	23.5	76.5	81.2
Financing political parties	1978	43.6	56.4	81.2
Public order/ Anti-terrorism	1981	14.9	85.1	79.4
Life imprisonment	1981	22.6	77.4	79.4
Carrying weapons	1981	14.1	85.9	79.4
Abortion (Liberalize)	1981	11.6	88.4	79.4
Abortion (Restrict)	1981	32.0	68.0	79.4
Wage indexation	1985	45.7	54.3	77.9
Civil liability of magistrates	1987	80.2	19.8	65.1
Impeachment of ministers	1987	85.0	15.0	65.1
Nuclear power sites	1987	80.6	19.4	65.1
Nuclear power subsidies	1987	79.7	20.3	65.1
Nuclear power abroad	1987	71.9	28.1	65.1
Prohibit hunting	1990	92.2	7.8	43.4
Restrict hunting	1990	92.3	7.7	42.9
Limit pesticides	1990	93.5	6.5	43.1
Chamber of Deputies preference vote	1991	95.6	4.4	62.4
Environmental powers-local	1993	82.6	17.4	76.9
Public financing political parties	1993	90.3	9.7	76.9
Personal drug use	1993	55.4	44.6	76.9
Ministry for State Enterprise	1993	90.1	9.9	76.9
Central Bank appointments	1993	89.8	10.2	76.9
Senate elections uninomial	1993	82.7	17.3	77.0
Ministry of Agriculture	1993	70.2	29.8	76.9
Ministry of Tourism	1993	82.3	17.7	76.9

Table 6.1   (Continued)

Subject	Year	% Yes vote (Repeal law)	% No vote (Sustain law)	% Voter turnout
Union negotiating powers	1995	50.0	50.0	57.2
Limits on union negotiations	1995	62.1	37.9	57.1
State sector unions	1995	64.7	35.3	57.3
House arrest for Mafia suspects	1995	63.7	36.3	57.2
Privatize radio-television	1995	54.9	45.1	57.4
Local shop regulations	1995	35.6	64.4	57.2
Union dues deductions	1995	56.2	43.8	57.3
Elections for mayors	1995	49.4	50.6	57.4
Shop hours	1995	37.4	62.6	57.3
Limit TV channel ownership	1995	43.0	57.0	58.0
TV advertising	1995	44.3	55.7	58.1
Limit TV ads to 2 channels	1995	43.6	56.4	58.1
Privatization of state industries	1997	73.9	26.1	31.9
Conscientious objectors	1997	72.5	27.5	31.4
Hunting on private property	1997	81.6	18.4	32.2
Seniority for magistrates	1997	83.7	16.3	29.8
Journalist credentials	1997	65.5	34.5	29.9
Extra-judicial jobs magistrates	1997	86.1	13.9	30.6
Ministry of Agriculture	1997	67.4	32.6	30.2

Note: Data for 1974–95 are from Servizi Studi Camera Deputati; for 1997, from *La Repubblica*, 16 June 1997, p. 3.

Trivializing the process

Nineteen more referendums would be held over the next four years, and the Court would face 48 additional requests in that brief span.

Though some important issues, most notably that of media pluralism, would be involved, public attention steadily waned. The seven referendums held in 1997 were annulled when the 50 per cent of voters necessary for a quorum was not met. The Court's turn around in 1993 that allowed previously barred questions striking at the core of the political system seemingly signaled a weariness on the part of the judges to act as the barrier protecting the political status quo from public assault at the ballot box. No innovative judicial logic was introduced, and the Court seemed content to give a rather literal reading to the expressed and implicit prohibitions contained in Article 75 of the Constitution, straying no further than its 1978 requirements that referendum proposals be clear, unified and comprehensible.

Six referendum requests were decided by the Court in early 1994. They included three involving unions and one each on pensions, the National Health Service and the sale of government property. All were announced in a single opinion. Three were the products of decrees issued by the Amato government in 1993 to modify pensions benefits, reorganize the National Health Service and sell some government assets, through share offerings and sale of government land. All were seen by the Court as budget and finance laws and were, as a consequence, inadmissible. At the same time, two involving union representation of non-union workers that called for opposite results and one on public sector unions were all upheld as within constitutional parameters.[69]

Parliament was dissolved in 1994, only two years after being invested, and new elections were called. The trade union referendum questions were, as a result, rolled-over to the following year, when they would be joined by a stack of others. In fact, 16 new requests were presented to the Constitutional Court for decision in early 1995. One set of proposals addressed the 1990 radio-television law, the so-called 'Mammì Law', and another was a hodge-podge collection jointly sponsored by the fringe left Radical Party and the separatist Northern League. The circuitous path of media pluralism is the subject of the next chapter, but the 1995 referendum questions targeted the most recent incarnation of enactments to regulate the airwaves. More specifically, they were challenges to the dominant position in television channels that had been acquired by the private holding company Finivest, owned by Silvio Berlusconi who had been prime minister in 1994.

The leftist parties sponsored the referendum proposals relating to the Mammì Law. One question would have repealed the limits on commercial advertising on television that were included in the 1990 law. The promoters of the request explained that their intent was to eliminate commercial advertising on public radio and television channels, making them more conducive to their public service mission. Laws dating from 1975 to 1990 and multiple amendments and decrees were involved in the abrogation proposal, which allowed the Court to reject the proposal on the grounds of 'absolute ambiguity'.[70] The other three referendums on the Mammì Law directly targeted Berlusconi: antitrust implications, advertising interruptions and publicity agencies. The Mammì Law's rather liberal limits on combined ownership of periodicals and televisions stations were the object of one, limiting the number and length of commercial interruptions permitted during programming was the subject of the second, and the third would limit television channel ownership in conjunction with public relations concessions. The Court declared all three admissible, finding them compatible with requirements of the European Union and the European convention on television transmissions and meeting the criteria of clarity, homogeneity and unifying theme.[71]

Of those proposed in the second packet, the reorganization of RAI (Radio-Televisione Italia), was admissible because it was 'inspired by a single unifying and rational matrix, clearly understandable by the elector and able to be implemented by a single law'.[72] Similarly, the proposal for regulating commercial licenses was found to be 'admissible under all profiles',[73] as were those for extending shop opening hours,[74] permitting internal exile for those charged with the crime of mafia association,[75] electing of communal councils,[76] and taking payroll deductions for union dues.[77] On the other side of the ledger, the Court found that initiatives to regulate advertising on public television were absolutely ambiguous,[78] to create a single national treasury was a budget law,[79] to modify withholding taxes was interconnected to other laws,[80] to reform unemployment benefits involved 35 different sections of laws and was incomprehensible,[81] and to stop obligatory membership in the National Health Service involved budget and state finance.[82] All were inadmissible. Finally, a proposal to alter elections for the both Chamber of Deputies and the Senate was found to fall into an area for which 'the only remedy was the legislator'.[83] Nine proposals were admitted, and seven were rejected.

Those nine were added to the three on unions held over from 1994 and presented to the voters on 11 June 1995. Despite the existence of some rather central issues of the almost monopoly power of the national unions and the oligopoly of Berlusconi's media empire, voter turnout only exceeded the 50 per cent threshold by a little; only one law, that on union dues deductions, was repealed through the process.

Even in light of lost public interest in the process, political gadfly Marco Pannella engineered another slate of proposals that would reach the Court and the public in 1997. Another 29 initiatives were laid at the door of the Court; 19 were rejected. The proposals deemed inadmissible ranged from challenging part of the system for electing both the Senate and the Chamber of Deputies, electing the membership of the Superior Council of Magistrates, and reorganizing the Financial Guard to eliminating the Ministries of Health and Industry, reconsidering abortion, legalizing hashish and marijuana, reforming secondary schools and regional–national government relations. The rationales for inadmissibility were, by this time, predictable: heterogeneous, ambiguous and unclear questions, linkages with others laws, and implication of international treaties or conventions. Reform of elections for both chambers of Parliament was rejected, in part, because their passage would create paralysis in the legislative branch. That, and the rejection of the abortion request on the grounds that it was entangled with constitutional norms dealing with health and life, were variations on earlier jurisprudential themes.[84] So repetitive was the language and so predictable the outcomes, that one major publisher of judicial decisions, *Il Foro Italiano*, only reprinted a synopsis of most and edited versions of what its editors deemed most important. More telling was the fact that there was not even an accompanying scholarly commentary in *Il Foro*.

The legal community found no surprises in the Court's rulings,[85] and the public was not moved to act. Seven of the proposals were finally on the ballot after legislative maneuvering to change some of the legislation in question. Headlines preceding the vote in mid-June 1997 heralded 'Referendum Overdose' and 'Growing Party of "We're Going to the Beach"'.[86] Less than one-third of Italian voters exercised their franchise in the 1997 balloting. None of the political parties actively supported or opposed any of the proposals, and voter interest was flat. The 1997 referendums were annulled for lack of participation.

Court's political agenda

The Constitutional Court's decisions evolved through four stages. Its initial response to proposed referendums was one of self-restraint, and it chose to read and apply only the literal words of Article 75 of the constitutional text. Then came expanding discretion, when in 1978 the Court creatively added other implicit criteria, those of clarity, homogeneity and unity, and the requirement that the proposal could not be entangled with other constitutional or legal provisions.[87] That began a period in which the Court moved steadily, using those rather elastic terms arbitrarily to admit some questions and block others. A new barrier that a proposed referendum would have to clear was 'discovered' in 1987, when the Court barred a referendum that would alter how members of the Superior Council of the Magistrature were chosen. What was a minor element in 1987 was later used to bar any challenge to electoral systems. From there, the step was small to the requirements that the processes of constitutional organs could not be impeded. A consistent expansion of the Court's original jurisprudence was obvious.[88]

The Court had appropriated the tools that it needed to maneuver around undesirable proposals, as it did most ably in 1991, when it denied serious challenges to the electoral system intended to impact the way in which politics were conducted. The constitutional judges reached the third phase of their jurisprudence governing admissibility of a referendum when what had been blocked came around through the door of criminal investigations. By 1993 the entire political system was quite literally under siege. Although members of the Constitutional Court were not directly implicated in any of the scandals, their image was nonetheless tarred by the brush. A 1993 survey found that 40 per cent of those interviewed were not supportive of the Constitutional Court.[89] The judges beat a hasty retreat and suddenly found that changes in the manner of electing senators, halted by a 1991 decision, was a valid subject for a referendum. The Court's admission of that vote opened the door to the transitions that would follow in Italian politics.[90] The Court found, thereafter, a flood of proposals, some trivial and some important, laid at its doorstep in 1993, 1995 and 1997. The Court limited, however, its choreography to a rote application of a non-controversial jurisprudence. The 'lost' amendment prohibiting electoral systems from change through referendums was not mentioned again. The Court's decisions on admissibility became so predictable that one wondered why the sponsors of the unsuccessful ones had not fashioned their questions to achieve conformity.

The referendum process and the Court's jurisprudence mirrored each other through every phase of development. Those factors that may have influenced the judges seem also to have varied. Clearly, the Court's initial reading of the constitutional limits to referendums fit a 'good law' explanation. The judges read the text of Article 75 and concluded that divorce was not a subject on the proscribed list. Their conclusion was coincidentally in agreement with prior legislative understandings and expectations that the divorce law would be repealed by the majority Roman Catholic electorate. It was also consistent with the wishes of the dominant Christian Democrats. Even though the Court's decision to permit the referendum was in keeping with dominant elite values, it was also unassailably correct from a legal perspective.

The Court's more elastic criteria adopted in 1978 gave it greater flexibility and discretion, and that discretion enabled it to deflect issues away from a popular vote and preserve dominant elite values. The seemingly arbitrary application of standards after 1978, and particularly from 1985 to 1991, suggests that the judges may have been acting less independently and playing to the audiences of the national elites, to whom they owed their positions and from whom they might receive future ones. The decision to 'discover' lost constitutional text and blunt the initiative to reform selection of members of the Superior Council of the Magistrature is the most compelling evidence to support that supposition. Policy goals were easily achieved through the guise of requiring clarity, homogeneity and a single unifying theme. That pliable judicially created standard served the judges – and others in the national elite – well by providing a vehicle to block proposed referendums in 1991 that would have restructured elections and threatened the status quo.

The Constitutional Court judges did not behave more independently as the existing political order began to unravel in 1992. Rather the audience from whom the judges sought approval shifted. Public sentiment and the political context seem to have driven the judges from 1993 forward. Prior jurisprudence was side-stepped and distinguished as electoral reforms were brought again before the judges as referendum proposals. All manner of initiatives were, in fact, approved if they were marginally comprehensible to the voters. The Court recast its structural role, moving from serving as the fulcrum of the referendum process to acting only as a passive filter. It chose to recede, leaving the center of the political scheme and bowing to public wishes. Oddly, by making a strategic political decision, the judges returned to a jurisprudential mode. Adherence to a clear, accurate and consistent legal policy dominated the Court's treatment of referendum proposals after 1993.

The referendum process had initially been embraced by the voters as a means of achieving reform, but every initiative from 1974 until 1987 resulted in upholding the existing laws. At the same time, a number of proposals that cleared the Constitutional Court proved to be catalysts for parliamentary action; legislation on the subjects of the referendums was passed before the voters could be asked.[91] The referendum may, in other words, have served to short-circuit the excessively cumbersome legislative machinery by raising the specter of voter rejection of existing laws. The process that was once a novelty and ignited voter interest had, after the momentous changes in 1993, become monotonous, and apathy replaced enthusiasm.

The evolution of the referendum institution proved those attending the Constitutent Assembly in 1947 prophetic. Mortati's arguments that the device allowed popular involvement in debates on public issues were validated in the 1970s, when divorce, crime prevention measures and public financing of political parties were brought to the voters. That was even true in the early 1980s, when abortion was the subject. Opponents had claimed that it could be used by small political parties to sabotage Parliament, and that is precisely what Pannella and the Radicals aimed to do with their rafts of proposals from the mid-1980s onward. The thin-edge-of-the-wedge argument against referendums also proved true. When some proposals were admitted after 1993, there was no stopping more and more and more, no matter how peripheral they might be.

The Court has been generally recognized as the 'censor' of potential referendums. That was justified as essential in light of the 'distorted use' into which they evolved and also in light of perennial legislative paralysis.[92] The referendum mechanism may have conflicted with parliamentary government, by allowing sponsors to go over the heads of elected representatives; that, too, argues for the role of the Court as a gatekeeper.[93] Even after permitting long lists of questions to reach the voters, the Court retained its position as the one limiting institution that has become essential to maintaining the process within the 'elementary exigencies of democracy'.[94]

Referendums have been further trivialized in the last few years. President of the Republic Oscar Luigi Scalfaro said, 'enough', and the voters echoed that sentiment in their 1997 shunning of the polls. But, as Paolo Barile said, speaking on behalf of the Court, 'if Parliament is empty, it is inevitable that some other power will fill the void; the fault is not ours [the judges]'.[95] Small parties and small groups replaced the major parties that once sponsored the plebiscites. The major parties had channeled and directed voters by offering meaningful cues. Referendums also proved useful as a prod to Parliament, which was too often inefficient and ineffective. The impact of that potentially useful device for asking the people directly has been diluted by too many referendums on too many subjects, too often. The Constitutional Court, whether motivated by political interests or simply applying even-handedly its now stable jurisprudence, has been the only institution acting as a gatekeeper, the 'great antagonist of referendums'.[96]

7
Protecting Individual Rights: Media Pluralism

Among the most common arguments for a constitutional court is the expectation that it can protect and preserve constitutionally guaranteed rights in the face of executive, legislative or popular tyranny. That proposition held considerable appeal in countries emerging from authoritarian rule, as Italy was at the close of the Second World War. The Constitution of the Republic of Italy declares respect for human rights in its fundamental principles, and then enumerates 16 articles of civil rights and 26 more of social, economic and political rights. The Constitutional Court was instrumental, primarily in its earliest years, in giving life to many of those guarantees, particularly ones abridged through the continuation of Fascist era criminal codes.

A seemingly basic prerequisite for democratic regimes is freedom of expression, the principle insuring exchange of opposing ideas. The Italian Constitution provides a broad mandate for its protection in Article 21, which says that 'all have the right to express freely their thoughts by word, in writing, and by all other means of communication'. It further prescribes that the press is to be free from prior authorization or censorship. However, it simultaneously stipulates that the government may interfere in times of emergency and to prohibit 'displays contrary to morality'. The blurry lines of protections and limitations in Article 21 gave rise to a substantial body of law, statutory and judge-made, under the heading of *'buon costume'* or public morality. That single article has been interpreted as it relates to religious expressions and sexual ones, preservation of the nation and interests of justice, and press and media in all of their forms.[1]

This chapter examines the Court's treatment of media pluralism, which falls under the rubric of freedom of expression. That the Italian Constitutional Court would have been involved in defining the lines of both public and private broadcast norms should not be surprising. The French Constitutional Council[2] and the German Constitutional Court[3] were central to setting the boundaries and arbitrating debates on radio and television within their respective nations. The irony in Italy lies in the fact that the media was not a political issue of notable consequence until the Court made it so in the 1970s. For more than two decades thereafter the Court tried, often futilely, to define and limit a political phenomenon of its own making.

The saga of media pluralism in Italy is particularly salient when discussing the policy role of the Constitutional Court, because the issue brought into play elements of other constitutional questions discussed in this book. It has involved at one point or another executive decree laws, referendums, an 'empty Parliament', alleged criminality and a leader of a major political party and former prime minister. The Court's forays into the political thicket of media pluralism resulted in decisions that are 'fragmented, contradictory and at times confused'.[4] The Court faced a choice between two different sets of constitutional values, those of freedom of expression and those of economic liberty. At times it tilted in favor of one over the other, as it tried to reconcile the two.[5]

Early political choices

Not long after the invention of radio, two conferences were held in Berlin, one in 1903 and another in 1906, to discuss ways of understanding and regulating the new technology. That led to the passage of the first law in Italy, in 1910, that regulated all forms of communication, including the mail, telephones, telegraph and radio. That all were not the same, not simply forms of communication, was recognized in 1923, and radio was legally designated as a state function for public service, but privatization remained possible. The inventor Guglielmo Marconi and a group of investors sought private access and were granted a state concession, a monopoly franchise that was state regulated. That arrangement was incorporated into law in 1936. Under the Fascist regime, the government, well aware of the potential power of the new technology, reserved the right to interrupt programming and to issue directives and proclamations and, thereby, retain control of the private concession. After the fall of Fascism, there was an interest in somehow infusing pluralism into the business of communication.[6]

The 1936 law had introduced a system, however, that would persist, one of monopoly, in the form of a private franchise under government control.[7] That was the general understanding of how the airwaves ought to be used when the Constituent Assembly met to write the postwar constitution. Radio was less of a concern at the constitution-writing gathering than were film and theater, which were discussed as exceptions to the otherwise broad understanding of freedom of expression. It was in this manner that 'public morality' and an acceptance of censorship of obscene materials was introduced into the debates. The media of radio and press were somehow merged with those of theater and film in discussions of appropriate limits on expression.

When the full Constituent Assembly met at the end of March to consider the draft article on freedom of expression, there was little dissension about the concept. Rather, the sticking point was how to limit it, how to require consistency with *'buon costume'*. Some amendments were proposed to guarantee that pornographic materials would not reach children. Not surprisingly, the Christian Democrat representatives were in the forefront of efforts to legislate public morality, but a few from other parties raised objections. One Liberal Party member complained that, while abhorring pornography, he could envision the police's sequestering objects of art that involved nudes or carnal scenes.[8] Two representatives of the Communist Party, Cavallari and Montagnana, asked if proposals for limitations 'by our Christian Democrat colleagues' might 'not retain also the ability to stop the distribution of other materials that are not pornographic and do not represent great danger, ... as for example materials that are anti-clerical'.[9] The Socialist Calasso wondered aloud if books like the *Decameron* and *Madame Bovary* or a very pornographic caricature drawn by a youth on the street or political writings and presentations might be suppressed under the proposed 'exception' to freedom of press.[10] When a final vote was taken on the last sentence of Article 21, near midnight on 14 April 1947, the words 'the law determines adequate preventive and repressive measures' were approved.[11]

Parliament I that convened in 1948 promptly confronted the need for a law to activate that last sentence. Law No. 958, 29 December 1949 attempted an implicit definition of proscribed films. Parliament II followed with another law, No. 897, 31 July 1956, that prohibited films from displaying subjects or scenes that were 'contrary to public morality and public order or that offend the nation, religious beliefs or public institutions'.[12] The Italian cinema faced twin threats, one from foreign competition and another from political pressures to control the content of films.[13]

The earliest decisions of the Court involving Article 21, freedom of expression, focused on reviewing applications of public morality.

Censorship, loss of a license or criminality were central to each of these decisions, all of which involved either film or theater.[14] Moreover, even in the earliest cases the judges succumbed to 'great oscillations'.[15] Television was not even mentioned, but the Court would be equally equivocal when it addressed that medium.

Television first reached Italy in 1939, with experimental transmissions from Monte Mario in Rome. In 1944 RAI (*Radio Audizioni Italiana*) was formed as a national agency under the Ministry of Post and Telegraph. After the war RAI was supervised by a commission of 30 parliamentarians, half named by the president of each parliamentary chamber. By virtue of a 1947 law, that parliamentary commission was charged with insuring the political independence of RAI and the objectivity of its transmissions. RAI began an experiment with television in 1949 with transmissions from Turin and assumed full national service in the autumn of 1953. On 10 April 1954, RAI's name was transformed to reflect its dual nature in radio and television. Retaining the acronym 'RAI', it was renamed Radio-televisione Italiana.[16] The state then held a monopoly of the airwaves, both radio and television, and proclaimed that RAI's operations were a public service.

Court enters

Some entrepreneurs presumed that Article 21 permitted private television networks alongside the state one, and in 1956 the owners of the magazine *Il Tempo* petitioned the Minister of Post and Telegraph for use of channels outside those allotted to RAI. Tempo-TV became the first alternative to RAI. Shortly thereafter, TVL (*Televisione Libra*) was also launched, but in 1958 its installation was seized. The two networks claimed that the seizure was unconstitutional, and the judge in Milan hearing criminal charges against the proprietors of Tempo-TV referred the case to the Constitutional Court.[17]

The Court rejected the constitutional challenge as unfounded, but its reasoning is instructive for how future analogous questions would be answered. Tempo-TV and TVL argued that the 1936 postal code that reserved a state monopoly violated not only Article 21 (freedom of expression), but also other articles of the Republican Constitution. The constitutional judges responded that the challenges were based not on an interest in freedom of expression, but on profit. The central element of the Court's logic was, however, that there were a 'limited number of usable channels'. Therefore, if there were to be free enterprise in the field of television, a potential for oligopoly at either the national or the local level existed. The private companies also argued against the monopoly of RAI on the basis of Article 41 of the Constitution which protected free enterprise and private economic initiative. The Court countered that Article 43, permitting state-owned monopolies of services, overcame that complaint. Freedom of expression was not infringed, the judges explained, by the inability to broadcast thoughts over the airwaves. Rather, television and radio were 'natural monopolies' or 'oligopolies' because of inherent limitations, and the state could reserve that monopoly status to itself 'on the conditions of objectivity and impartiality most favorable' in light of the 'natural limitations' of the medium. The Court, at the same time, urged the government to open the RAI airwaves to 'those who are interested in expressing their ideas'.[18]

Access to the most effective means of communication emerged as a major political question, and RAI responded within months of the Court's decision with a program called *Tribuna Elettorale* that permitted the airing of views of all candidates in the administrative elections.[19] That was insufficient, and the Court in 1965 acknowledged the 'interference and control' of the government in RAI and the special relationship that existed between those in political power and those who controlled the media.[20] The Court was not alone in recognizing the tremendous power of RAI, and the question of who controlled it grew in political importance. The Fanfani faction of the DCs dominated the state network, making it a source of intra- as well as inter-party feuds. The regional governments, newly established in 1970, were disgruntled at how little coverage they received, and their ire added yet another level of discontent. Ultimately, conflicts over control of RAI brought about the resignation of the government of Andreotti II in 1973.[21]

The following year the Constitutional Court changed its view of the state monopoly of RAI and in a pair of decisions prodded Parliament and the government into far-reaching changes. Roberto Zaccaria claimed that 'rarely...have the judges of the Consulta obtained an analogous result...for actual politics'.[22] Between May 1971 and June 1973, 16 lower court judges had referred questions of the compatibility of the state monopoly over radio and television with three articles of the Constitution: Article 21, freedom of expression; Article 41, insuring private economic initiative, and Article 43, allowing state ownership of certain enterprises. Numerous laws dating from 1923 were implicated as constitutionally invalid.

The Court's prologue to this decision included a restatement of the essential considerations in its 1960 decision and acknowledged that almost all of the referring judges had focused their attention on the earlier statement of 'limited usable channels'. Such limitations were, by 1974, no longer applicable, and, indeed, RAI left many frequencies unused. However, the existence of a state monopoly did not, in the Court's view, violate any of the constitutional provisions cited, nor necessarily preclude other legitimate operators. Since the number of channels was still limited and the cost of competing with RAI high, to allow private companies would lead, in the view of the judges, to an oligopoly that could violate constitutional requirements for freedom of expression. Permitting transmissions from outside the country would in some measure facilitate more sources of information without the threat of a domestic conglomerate. The Court called for retention of the state sponsored RAI, but with new regulations to insure that diversity of thought and expression would be preserved. The judges deferred, or so they said, to the legislature to choose the most appropriate method for achieving this end and continued by outlining quite specifically what legislative measures could achieve that goal: (a) regulation is essential, but to guarantee objectivity, the executive should not have primary or even majority control; (b) programming should be impartial and objective and represent many different cultural perspectives; (c) Parliament, as the elected representative body, should be controlling; (d) journalists should report news objectively, respecting their profession's ethical canons; (e) commercial interruptions should be limited because of 'the danger that financial control by advertisers could prejudice programming'; (f) access should be open and impartial with regard to politics, religion, culture and ideology; and (g) human rights should be respected.[23]

That decision had the effect of ending RAI's monopoly, but not of permitting private channels. The situation was confused even further by a second decision relating to cable television that was issued the same day. Cable was, unlike the airwaves, without limitations on the number of operating channels, but national cable was not financially feasible for any private company. The rise of an oligopoly situation was, in the view of the judges, unlikely. Therefore, the Court invalidated parts of a 1973 law that prohibited private *local* cable television networks.[24] These decisions were the direct causes for the 1975 law that reformed RAI.

At the time of the Court's decision, RAI was a fiefdom of the Christian Democrats and, more particularly, of a single faction within the DCs. RAI presented no debates or contrasting views, and only the government's line was reported. The Communist Party was completely blocked from airing its program on television and was restricted to the written press. The heretofore dominant DC party had seen much of its power base erode in 1974 with the divorce referendum, and Italian society was itself much more pluralistic than before. Against that background, the Court's 1974 decisions were well timed to spur the political forces into reforming RAI.[25]

The principles dictated by the Court, those of pluralism, independence, completeness and objectivity, were embodied in the 1975 law. Parliament assumed supervisory control of RAI, and the network was recast as an instrument of 'open monopoly', with open access and management.[26] Parliamentary oversight was lodged in a council of administration, staffed by parliamentarians, representatives of regional councils and representatives from the state holding company Industrial Reconstruction Institute. Local cable television provided by private companies was allowed, but none could have an audience of more than 150 000 viewers, and foreign transmissions were permitted.[27] What could not be anticipated in 1975 was that this law, following the dictates of the Constitutional Court's 1974 decisions, 'created the difficulties that would soon threaten to overwhelm the public radio and television system'.[28]

Parliament had tried to follow the dictates of the Constitutional Court, but just one year after the new law was passed, the Court invalidated four sections of it. The essence of the Court's decision was to completely open the airwaves to local stations, claiming that Article 21's freedom of expression (now referred to as 'freedom of information') required it. It also called for a national agency to assign frequencies and controls.[29] The Court's decision was a clear departure from its earlier rulings, even though it did not acknowledge the shift; it was a clear example of judicial legislation.[30] What was most surprising was the Court's returning some control over the medium to the executive by requiring a national regulator.[31] More importantly, as available technologies multiplied, this decision had the effect of muddying the situation even more.[32]

Liberty of the antennae

The Court's 1976 decision ignored the issue of oligopoly formation that had been central to its earlier pronouncements. Presumably, it could not envision how any local broadcaster could parley a single local market into one of national scale. That was, however, precisely what one entrepreneur, Silvio Berlusconi, managed to do. The 1975 law had distributed political control of RAI across party lines, with RAI 1 going to the Christian Democrats and RAI 2 to the Socialists. RAI 3, which took to the airwaves in 1978, was theoretically the 'property' of the Communists, though the smaller Social Democrats, Liberals and Republicans were given roles in it. The RAI corporation was now segmented, with separate governing boards and structures that were quickly competing with one another for resources and audiences. By 1980 there had also been an explosion of local and regional companies, the first step in what was eventually the rise of a bona fide duopoly.[33]

The Court's 1976 decision to permit private local companies had consequences that few could have anticipated. RAI was unprepared to compete, particularly since the 1975 law had shackled it financially by freezing both advertising and license fees. Parliament did nothing to regulate the loophole of local operators opened by the Constitutional Court or to enable RAI to compete effectively. Competition from private concerns had begun as early as 1974, but after the 1976 judicial decision, it proliferated aggressively. Publishing companies were among the first to enter the private side, with Rizzoli at the lead, followed by Mondadori and Rusconi. Another fledgling competitor was Telemilano, a local cable network created by Silvio Berlusconi. Whereas the Court had envisioned dozens or more local stations, large private networks appeared instead.

Berlusconi succeeded in rather short order in transforming Telemilano from a local cable operator to a local airwave company and then to a national network. Telemilano was part of the holding company Finivest that was expanding into other commercial ventures, beginning in 1979 with the launching of a public relations-advertising agency, Pubitalia. That was followed in 1980 by the Reteitalia network. Berlusconi was able to convert his local broadcasting company into a network by using videocassettes played simultaneously in different local markets. That was the basis for a complete broadcast network, Canale 5; by 1981 it had 18 transmitters and was challenging RAI directly.[34]

Obviously the situation that the Court had assumed in 1976 proved to be wrong by 1981 – neither the cost nor the logistics involved in broadcasting on a national scale was a bar to private companies' entering the market. Those changed circumstances formed the grounds for a lawsuit by RAI against the Rizzoli broadcast group. RAI contended that Rizzoli was not merely operating locally, but coordinating its local transmissions in such a way that they constituted a national network. That contention prompted a referral from the trial judge hearing the suit to the Constitutional Court for interpretation or reinterpretation of the partition of the airwaves between public and private. The judge *a quo* specifically drew the Court's attention to new technological advances and the absence of any regulations of 'local' broadcasting in the wake of the 1976 decision enabling local transmissions. The constitutional judges repeated their earlier pronouncements, underlining repeatedly the necessity of avoiding a private monopoly or oligopoly with 'potential influence incompatible with a democratic system'. Concentration of the means for forming public opinion in the hands of one or two companies could reduce freedom of expression. The Court's accusing finger pointed directly at Parliament: 'any different aspects of the phenomenon, regarding the means of transmission used, are matters that belong under legislative regulations and to which we urgently call the competent organ's attention'.[35] The Court rejected, with a strident declaration of self-restraint, the questions raised as unfounded or inadmissible. Those questions belonged before the political organs.

The ambiguity of the 1981 decision could be seen in the various interpretations it spawned. It was seen as overturning the 1976 case that recognized the legitimacy of the state monopoly[36] and, conversely, as reaffirming not only the constitutional legitimacy of that monopoly, but also its constitutional necessity.[37] Freedom of the antennae continued, but that liberty was quickly coming under the control of a single private company, Finivest. There were no rules for the private sector, which led Enzo Roppo to label the situation as one governed by 'natural selection', with evolution and dominance limited only by economics and technology.[38] From 1976 to 1979, there had been a rapid proliferation of local broadcasters both in radio and television, without government intervention or arbitration. Between 1980 and 1984, that changed dramatically, with the formation of a single concentration in Finivest that would later include three national television networks, along with one radio channel and ownership interests in newspapers, magazines, film, and European-wide television.[39]

'Duopoly' of the airwaves

In the absence of a regulatory scheme, the Finivest phenomenon was seemingly without limits. Berlusconi's friendship with Socialist Party leader Bettino Craxi, also from Milan, enhanced the media magnate's political fortunes, particularly when Craxi became prime minister in August 1983. In October of the following year, in an obviously partisan move, judges in Turin, Rome and Pescara ordered the videocassettes of Berlusconi's Canale 5 seized and transmissions blocked. Berlusconi met with Craxi, who voided the judicial actions with an executive decree law.[40] Though the decree was not converted within the required 60 days, it was eventually, and became Law No. 10, 10 February 1985. The so-called 'Berlusconi decree' not only helped Berlusconi with his immediate legal problem, but also made sweeping changes in the regulation of radio and television and conflicted with earlier pronouncements of the Court. It declared a mixed system of both public and private transmissions and referred to private transmissions both 'national and local'.[41] Although it gave lip service to prohibitions on oligopolies, it also limited RAI by curtailing the powers of the director general and the administrative council governing it.[42] This was the sole legislation since 1975 offering any regulation of radio and television and was transparently designed to benefit one private entity. RAI was even more hamstrung, and Berlusconi was acquiring the private companies that had been his competitors. Italy's mass communications were in the hands of a duopoly, Finivest and RAI.

The quest for a 'television pax' led to a proposal for new regulations by Antonio Gava, Minister of Post and Telegraph under Ciriaco DeMita, but that design went nowhere. Even without specific litigation pending before it, the President of the Constitutional Court Francesco Saja implored Parliament to regulate the airwaves. In his January 1987 press conference, Saja said, 'unfortunately, notwithstanding multiple solicitations, there has been no legislative intervention in the right to information, and some action is indispensable in light of the existing confusion'.[43] In June, the Council of Ministers approved a new series of regulations, proposed by Gava's successor Oscar Mammì, but they would not achieve final passage until 1990.

The Constitutional Court was approached in 1988 with a direct challenge to the Berlusconi Law of 1985. The Court, in an unusually long and carefully crafted opinion, reached a novel conclusion: the law was unconstitutional, but not so declared.[44] It was a 'decision not to decide'.[45] That rather novel conclusion was achieved by the Court's treatment of the 1985 Berlusconi decree as merely 'provisional', presumably to be replaced shortly with a version that would pass constitutional scrutiny.[46]

The case reached the Constitutional Court as a result of referrals by judges in Rome, Turin and Genoa. The case in Rome involved a suit brought by RAI against the three Finivest channels, Canale 5, Italia 1 and Rete 4, alleging that they were transmitting on a national scale through the interconnections among their so-called local stations. In Turin, a criminal case against Berlusconi and others involved violations of the 1985 law limiting 'bridge' radio transmissions or those with structural connections. The question from Genoa arose out of a criminal prosecution of a local station transmitting in conjunction with others on a national scale. The three referrals all focused on the antitrust implications of a cartel operated by the Berlusconi group. In the Court's statement of facts, rather startling statistical information was reported to demonstrate the level of control that the three Finivest channels held in comparison to RAI and to others. For example, RAI had only 3094 installations, whereas the Finivest channels jointly controlled 3800, and the remaining five private channels controlled a mere 2124. Similar data were presented comparing receiving households, radio listeners and advertising revenues.[47] The concentration Berlusconi had amassed was staggering.

The Court began its analysis of the law with five lengthy sections synthesizing and analyzing its previous jurisprudence and then tying it together into a coherent whole. The concepts of pluralism, private monopoly or oligopoly, dangerous concentrations and multiple sources of information for all citizens were the key unifying threads that ran through all of the prior decisions. Notably, the Court carefully clarified the intention of its 1981 decision to retreat from the requirement that a state monopoly on radio and television was reserved, but – and the conjunction is very important – with the expectation that Parliament would enact anti-trust provisions to prevent concentrations in the private sector. The 1985 law did not achieve that end. Yet, since that law was merely provisional, the questions challenging it were either unfounded or inadmissible. Its provisional status, the Court underlined, was already pushing the limits at three years.

The Court concluded its judgment with a clear set of prescriptions addressed to Parliament and the government. It acknowledged the Mammì design law already under discussion in Parliament and added that if the 1985 Berlusconi law's force remained for more than three years, the judges would be forced to see it as definitive and, thereby, constitutionally invalid. More to the point, new legislation must 'guarantee effective obstacles to monopolistic or oligopolistic concentrations' in real terms, not just technical ones, including control of advertising. It must 'effectively insure pluralism of information'. Barriers to concentrations, the Court added, were to reach beyond just television and radio to the other sectors of information. Anti-trust requirements were underscored as essential to any law that would avoid running afoul of Article 21. And, to guarantee that, the judges dictated a 'high level of openness about the assets, budgets, and associations of any private parties in the information business' to protect the constitutional value of pluralism.[48]

The Court was strong, clear and explicit about what would be necessary in a law regulating private radio and television, and the 1985 Berlusconi law did not meet those criteria. The obvious result of the case seemed to be declaring the law unconstitutional. Why did the Court choose to hang the challenged law on the provisional peg and allow it to escape the fate of invalidation? Borrello suggests that the answer lies in the larger political world, in which the Court did not wish to create 'a traumatic institutional rupture' between the government and the parliamentary majority.[49] Indeed, the brief government of Giovanni Goria had just ended in April, and the prime ministership had only recently passed to Ciriaco De Mita. The 1987 parliamentary elections had brought no changes to the increasingly contentious five-party coalition that had basically held power since 1981.[50]

Parliament remained notoriously slow in acting, as the Court remarked in virtually every decision it made on radio and television and freedom of information. That Parliament had only once amended its 1975 law governing the subject was indicative of the legislature's reluctance to re-enter the field. Private media had emerged in an *ad hoc* fashion, as might be expected in a climate of deregulation.[51] The judges in the Consulta may have calculated that they were on firmer ground by upholding the existing law and not allowing a vacuum while the legislature dallied. By carefully outlining requirements for a new law, they could direct negotiations and perhaps avoid having to invalidate portions of the replacement legislation later. The Court seemed intent on hanging a sword of Damocles over the collective head of Parliament by insisting that it act.[52]

The new regime: a mixed system

The Constitutional Court intended to provide a blueprint for Parliament to follow in redesigning its regulation of the mass media, but its overriding emphasis on the need for pluralism was subject to various interpretations. Was the desired pluralism an economic or an ideological one? The 1976 decision had alluded to economic pluralism, with private initiatives to counter the potential rise of monopoly or oligopoly situations; the 1988 decision had spoken of a 'plurality of concurrent voices'.[53] Two constitutionally protected rights were in collision, those of information and private initiative. The call for pluralism was, in Italian terms, a call for representation of the views of the parties, an adjunct to *partitocrazia*.[54] Perhaps that is how the 1988 Court decision was read, for in many ways that is what resulted when Parliament acted in 1990.

The Mammì Law was enacted on 6 August 1990 and provided a regulatory scheme for a mixed system of radio and television. Despite the guidelines proffered by the Court in advance, there were many doubts about the law's constitutionality.[55] One of its more dubious parts was that the law enabled Berlusconi to retain all three of his television networks, which seems to be the exact opposite of what a reading of the 1988 Court decision would require. Finivest was the clear beneficiary of the new enactment, which had come in the last phase of the Craxi-Andreotti-Forlani years. In gratitude to those three sponsors, Berlusconi announced that 'our news will reflect the view that Craxi, Forlani and Andreotti represent freedom'.[56]

Berlusconi was not relieved of any of his properties as a consequence of the Mammì Law, and, indeed, he had already added to his holdings by purchasing the Milan soccer team (AC Milano), the department and grocery store chain Standa, Mondadori publishers, pay television channels and, with another investor, Penta Film that produced and distributed motion pictures. He had effectively eliminated any serious competitors and secured his half of a relatively balanced duopoly.[57]

The Mammì Law's stated aim was to pass control of television and radio from the state monopoly to private hands and to set financial limits on the capitalization required. Advertising interruptions were limited, depending on the type of program being broadcast. For example, high culture, education and religious programs were to be aired without commercial breaks. It set a limit on the total proportion of all means of mass communications, including magazines and newspapers, that could be held by a single person or group, with percentage of distribution in one medium diminishing the amount that could be owned in another. For example, ownership of two radio-television networks operating on a national scale required ownership of no more than 8 per cent of newspaper distribution. And, to insure objective and impartial reporting, the law revised the manner of supervising RAI in a way that formally recognized *partitocrazia*. A commission of 40 members would be named by the presidents of the two chambers of Parliament according to relative party strength. That commission would literally parcel out, on the basis of relative partisan representation, hours of programming on the state networks.[58]

The law was criticized for incompatibility with judicial interpretations and constitutional requirements, but there was also another element to consider. On 6 August 1989, the Council of Ministers of the
European Community had passed the first Europe-wide directive on
television that was to be implemented by the member nations within
two years. Community directives require that member nations achieve
the ends specified, but are not restrictive as to the means used. The
intent of Directive No. 89/552 was to open borders within the Community to television programs, a form of services, and to eliminate state-
imposed barriers to transmission, reception and re-transmission. The
directive also included requirements for commercial advertising, the
number of interruptions and the proportion of broadcast time that can
be devoted to them. Other regulations addressed the content of commercial advertising, such as not offending human dignity, discriminat-
ing on the basis of sex, race or nationality or depicting behavior that
threatened national security.[59]

Since the Mammì Law came after the European directive, in certain
articles addressing advertising it simply stated that the Minister of Posts
and Telecommunications would issue the appropriate decrees to achieve
conformity with the directive. That language served as a compromise
device for getting certain sticky provisions through Parliament.[60] There
were a number of other areas, however, where the EC and Italian legislation were at variance. Parts of the EC directive would require additional
elaboration by Italian authorities, such as limitations and prohibitions
on depictions of alcohol and smoking, along with protection of minors
and prevention of political sponsorship of programming.[61]

That was not the only glitch in implementing the Mammì Law.
Parliament had established a series of time lines for actions to occur –
assignment of frequencies within six months, relaunching the concessions with 12 months – but none of the deadlines were met. A year and
a half after enactment, most had not been accomplished. One government had fallen during that time, and some parliamentary groups had
tried unsuccessfully to revisit some provisions. Issues of cable installations, whether by public or private concessions, were undetermined.
Issue after issue, application after application remained to be accomplished, because so much of the Mammì Law was not self-actuating.
Soon, it was clear that additional legislation would be required to clar-
ify, interpret and implement the 1990 law.[62] Radio frequencies were
assigned in August 1992, but a criminal investigation involving dis-
crepancies in assignments was initiated and all of the documents were
seized. Frequencies were finally assigned in 1993 through a decree law,

and private radio and television stations or networks were permitted to operate as before the 1990 law, but consistent with it, until 1996.[63]

The Constitutional Court's 1976 decision had opened the door to privatization of the airwaves and its 1988 judgment had attempted to set parameters for regulating what had become a free-for-all in the mass communications sector. The 1990 law that presumably responded to the Court's admonitions was challenged before the constitutional judges in 1993. Three separate references questioning different articles of the Mammì Law were decided together, as all were directed at the system of concessions, both private and public (RAI). The challenges addressed 'the central architecture' of the law, that of the concessions and government regulation of those in the private, as well as the public, sphere.[64] Despite the obvious failings of the 1990 law all of the challenges were rejected as unfounded, and the law was sustained. The Court repeated its commitment to the pluralism that it saw as basic to Article 21, calling it a 'constitutional imperative' that the legislature 'impede the formation of dominant positions and favor access to radio and television that insures the maximum possible number of different voices'.[65] This decision was made, as Leonardo Bianchi observed, 'at a particularly delicate moment in the regulation of radio and television'.[66] The new law had been operating for three years and, though not yet fully implemented, had included a measure of anti-trust protection. That had consistently been, in the words of the Court, the central factor that was essential to insure the plurality of sources of information required by Article 21.

By 1993 instability permeated all phases of political life in Italy, as the Clean Hands investigations took their toll on the old political parties and the political class. The government of Giuliano Amato, really the last of the old regime, was tottering and fell shortly after the Court's 1993 decision. A new government, a nonpartisan one, was invested in May 1993, under the premiership of the former head of the Bank of Italy, Carlo Azeglio Ciampi. One mini-reform law had been slowly working its way through Parliament for the last year and was passed on 25 June 1993. It completely overhauled the way top management for RAI was to be selected. The board of RAI was reduced to only five people, and they would be named by the presidents of the two chambers of Parliament. The law was described as severing 'the traditional and strong umbilical cord between the parties and RAI'.[67]

In an effort to stabilize the mass communications sector in the absence of real implementation of the Mammì Law, the Ciampi government offered another mini-reform. The government issued a decree, converted as Law No. 422 of 27 October 1993, that addressed pay television, licenses and advertising. Among other things, it limited the total number of private television network concessions to no more than 11 at the national level. That ceiling directly targeted Berlusconi and Finivest, since his ownership of three networks would transcend the 25 per cent limit imposed by the Mammì Law.[68]

Law, politics, television and Berlusconi

In December 1993, an administrative judge in Rome hearing a case involving the privileges that the 1990 law had given to Finivest, referred a series of constitutional questions to the Consulta, all questioning the constitutionality of parts of the Mammì Law. The Constitutional Court did not announce a decision until December 1994, but the political landscape in Italy had been dramatically altered in the course of that year. That interim period witnessed the rise of the 'media party', Berlusconi and his public relations agency Pubitalia's creation. It also ushered in the 'most tumultuous period in the history of Italian radio and television'.[69]

On 26 January 1994, Silvio Berlusconi had launched his new political party and his campaign for Parliament and the prime ministership. His new party was called *Forza Italia* (FI), a soccer chant meaning 'Let's Go Italy', with a style far slicker than Italians had previously known. From the moment Parliament was dissolved and new elections called, FI ran 14 major 'spots' or commercials on the three Finivest channels; the themes of all were 'saving Italy from Communism', which seemed a bit anachronistic five years after the demise of Communism in Europe, and creating 'the new economic miracle' through privatization in lieu of state control.[70] In the brief month regarded as pre-campaign – 25 January to 24 February – a total of 14052 minutes of television broadcasting were devoted to the political campaign, three-quarters of them on the Finivest channels. During the official campaign in the month following, however, there was a greater parity between RAI and Finivest, with the former carrying 54 per cent of campaign programming and the Berlusconi group only 40 percent. This was in part because of a reform law that applied equal time requirements to private broadcasters as well as to RAI.[71]

The glitz and glamour of the Berlusconi public relations were remarkable because they were so decidedly novel in Italian politics. The general perception was that Berlusconi's candidacy as leader of a center-right alliance added a new dimension of drama and polarization to the elections and contributed to the electoral success of his alliance.[72] However, analysis of actual voting shifts as a consequence of the media blitz found that most voters were not affected by it. Since all channels were under equal time requirements, the time allocated was symmetrical across RAI and Finivest channels. A panel study of 2500 voters from May 1993 until the March 1994 elections found only minor changes in preferences.[73]

Berlusconi's *Il Polo per la Libertà* or Freedom Pole consisted of a grouping of center-right parties, including *Forza Italia*, and was also allied under the label Pole for Good Government with Umberto Bossi's Northern League and Gianfranco Fini's National Alliance, self-labeled as the 'post-Fascist' party. That broad alliance succeeded in winning 360 seats in the Chamber of Deputies and 154 in the Senate, with Berlusconi's FI party in the lead.[74] Berlusconi assumed the position of prime minister at the end of March.[75]

Many of the conflicts that would color his brief nine-month premiership resulted from Berlusconi's dual roles as head of Finivest and prime minister, particularly when he attempted to purge RAI and declared war on the magistrates. That September Berlusconi's hand-picked RAI representative changed the heads and the news teams of all three state networks and installed two former Finivest employees at the top of RAI 1 and 2. Much was made of his efforts to cripple the state television and to discredit government prosecutors. On the latter score, he issued a decree in July releasing from detention hundreds of people charged in the Clean Hands investigation, including some of his own prominent supporters. The next day, the entire Milan Pool of prosecutors, in the forefront of the investigations, resigned. Berlusconi withdrew the decree in less than a week and the magistrates rescinded their resignations. In the concluding days of Berlusconi's short tenure as prime minister, his party also sustained major losses in local elections. In November, Berlusconi was called before the magistrates for interrogation about alleged bribes paid by Finivest to tax officials and Berlusconi's knowledge of them. He protested, but nonetheless appeared for a deposition on 13 December. On 19 December he went on 'his' state television channel and declared that Umberto Bossi of the Northern League, who had withdrawn his party's support from the coalition government, was a Judas and that the criminal investigation of Finivest was instigated because he refused to turn the country over to the Communists. He resigned two days later.[76]

In early November, the Constitutional Court heard arguments on the reference from the Roman judge a year earlier on privileges that the 1990 Mammì Law had conferred on Berlusconi and Finivest. It announced its opinion on 7 December, two weeks before Berlusconi was to resign as prime minister. The suit against the Minister of Post and Telecommunications had been initiated by TV International, whose Italian Telemontecarlo network had lost out in the allocations of national scale networks resulting from the 1990 Mammì Law and the mini-reforms that followed. Several other television groups joined TV International in its challenge before the Constitutional Court. The case centered on four issues. The first was the disparity of treatment among competing franchises to offer national service under the 1990 law; that was alleged to be contrary to Article 3 of the Constitution that guaranteed equality of treatment before the law. The next was a challenge to the excessive discretion granted to administrative authorities under the Mammì Law in setting criteria for allocating national frequencies; that violated, according to the challengers, freedom of expression. Both of these constitutional questions were disposed of by the Court rather quickly as unfounded, since the rights asserted, the Court said, must be balanced with the essential requirement of pluralism. The next question was that of the Mammì Law's limitation of ownership of three networks or 25 per cent of the market as contrary to requirements of pluralism in Article 21 and freedom of information. The Court declared that portion of the 1990 law unconstitutional, but upheld the transitory regimes that had been adopted pending full implementation of the Mammì Law. Finally, the part of the 1993 mini-reform that enabled prosecutions of national transmissions without authorization was also challenged as violating the principle of pluralism. The Court's response to this question was central to its entire approach. It argued in favor of the system of assigning frequencies used in the 1992 provisional law as essential in a sector in which technology was advancing so rapidly. But, it also highlighted its commitment to the goal of anti-trust in the mass communications sector and its three-year limit on achieving that objective.[77]

Invalidation of the Mammì Law's limitations on ownership might appear to conflict with the Court's commitment to anti-trust in the media sector. That is not the case, because the Court was actually urging more stringent regulations than those in the Mammì Law to thwart acquisition of a dominant position by any entity. The Mammì Law's restrictions had, in the Court's view, raised barriers to entry into the market and reinforced an already existing dominance in the sector. Opening frequencies to greater competition could preclude permanent domination.[78] The key to the Court's jurisprudence on media pluralism was consistently concern for anti-trust.[79] This decision's significance derived largely from its highlighting yet again the constitutional requirement of an anti-trust regime.[80]

Political reaction was immediate. The decision was characterized as 'rewriting' the law 'incoherently, irrationally and idiosyncratically' because it allowed Finivest to continue with three national networks, but only for three years.[81] Though Presidents of the Court often give press conferences to explain or justify decisions, President Francesco Paolo Casavola simply told journalists that the 66-page decision was at their disposal.[82] That was likely the easiest tactic since the judgment was a mixed one. On the one hand, the Court affirmed the transitory legislation of 1993, scheduled to lose effect at the end of 1996, and skirted the question of concentrations of all means of mass communications, not just television. That was counter-balanced by the Court's invalidation of the provision allowing any one company to hold one-quarter of 12 national networks, the core protection against dangerous control of the airwaves.[83] The decision was also consistent with its 1988 judgment that treated continuation of the dominant position of Finivest as merely provisional, with a definitive end point.[84]

The fate of the Finivest holdings was not yet determined, however. The highest ordinary court, in its capacity of verifying referendum signatures, was simultaneously certifying proposals for referendums on two questions of media pluralism. These were before the Constitutional Court within a month. In early January 1995, a stack of 16 referendum proposals were presented to the Court. Of these, several were directed at repeal of sections of the Mammì Law: limitations on television and periodical ownership, limitations on commercial interruptions, and a third on combined ownership of public relations agencies and television networks. The Court found all admissible, and parliamentary attempts to locate a political compromise and avert a referendum failed just weeks before the poll.[85] As discussed in Chapter 6, by this time, public interest in the now annual ritual of deciding multiple referendum questions was waning, and a bare 58 per cent voted in the June election that sustained the existing legislation on each radio-television question.

The Court's 1994 decision had set a three-year limit on reforms that centered on anti-trust protections within the mass communications industry. That item never seemed to move to the top of the agenda of the Dini government that succeeded Berlusconi and itself resigned in January 1996, within a year of its investiture. After lengthy squabbling over naming a successor, Parliament was dissolved and new elections held in May. Those elections ushered in a new government formula, a coalition of the center-left, including the reformed Communists, the Democratic Party of the Left. Addressing media pluralism was a high priority of the new Minister of Post and Telecommunications, Antonio Maccanico. Within weeks, he announced his 'big bang' proposal for a new law governing Italian telecommunications and emphasized its urgency in light of the Constitutional Court's rapidly approaching deadline for expiration of the 'provisional' nature of existing legislation. In the interim, the center-left government of Prime Minister Romano Prodi issued a decree that practically annulled the Court's 1996 decision. When not converted, that decree was reissued and eventually absorbed into a later law.[86] The decree was issued during negotiations over recommendations of the *Bicamerale* and was intended to buy Berlusconi's support. Finivest won, but the Bicameral Commission's proposals for constitutional reform died, largely because of opposition from Berlusconi and *Forza Italia*.

The Maccanico law in its design phase was closely tuned to requirements contained in the Court's 1994 decision. Anti-trust provisions were central to the design law, including limitations of ownership of no more than two television networks by a private group and no more than 20 per cent of the whole of the mass media market, including television, newspapers, films and other forms of mass communication. The industry would, according to the original design, be regulated in the future by a national agency along the lines of the US Federal Communications Commission. RAI would be transformed along regional lines, with consortiums of regional governments assuming control of some programming. It also provided for liberalization of access to other areas of mass communications, including telephones.[87] Nearly a year later, on 31 July 1997, the Maccanico design law was passed into law with the intent of ending more than two decades of confusion and chaos in the mass communications field that had begun as a consequence of the Court's 1974 decision allowing regional or local radio and television stations. The creation of an independent authority to regulate communications was not appointed until mid-November 1998, and a new regime was not projected to take effect until early in 1999.[88]

Assessing judicial intervention

The Constitutional Court was an important player as the politics of media pluralism evolved in Italy. It was involved in every phase in which access to the mass communications field was opened or closed.

Though players, the judges were repeatedly shown to be incapable of channeling the direction that the industry would take. The Court's actions over more than four decades of its mass communications jurisprudence have been described as 'schizophrenic',[89] but a series of false starts, based on excessively narrow premises may be a more appropriate description. The Court was the catalyst for what became a botched process of privatization, and when it attempted time and time again to hand the baton to Parliament, the pass-off went awry.

The Court's significance can be assessed in two ways: defining constitutional values and directing public policy, good law versus good policy. Its successes can be found in the former, where it seemed consciously to strive for legal clarity and legal accuracy. Article 21 of the Constitution referred to a liberty of thought and manifestation of thought, albeit with some limitations. From initial considerations of what materials could be prohibited on the grounds of public morality, the Court moved its agenda to transforming freedom of thought or expression to freedom of information and, then, freedom to receive information 'from a plurality of voices'. In other words, the Court simultaneously elevated both freedom of information and pluralism to the level of constitutional values.

The Court could not, however, read Article 21 in isolation, because two other, economic rights were also implicated. Article 41 protected private economic initiative, but Article 43 allowed for state-owned monopolies in which there was a general interest. From the Court's first holding that the state monopoly of radio and television under RAI was constitutional but that transmissions from external sources were also permitted, it consistently spoke of the public interest in information and the implied corollary of a plurality of sources for that information. Expression and the ability to convey it by any means, as prescribed by the Constitution, became the right to be informed. By 1988 that elevated right was read in tandem with Article 41 regarding private economic initiative as requiring that private transmissions provide citizens with the largest possible number of views, crossing all currents of thought.

This is the point where the Court began to oscillate, seeing two potential threats to pluralism, one from an oligopoly where a few groups dominated and another from a monopolistic situation in which a single conglomerate controlled the private sector. Early decisions focused on the former possibility, while the rise of Finivest made the latter a reality. Once the door to privatization was opened, only one constitutional provision was available to justify a requirement of pluralism: Article 42 which permits regulation of private property to insure its social function.[90] Using as a vehicle the 'value of pluralism', although only inferred from the constitutional text, the Court defined the reach of the freedom to information.[91] The judges were cognizant of the balancing act they were performing and acknowledged those difficulties as early as 1979. As a result a consistent jurisprudence was fashioned on the constitutional plane, with the themes of pluralism, rejection of monopolies, oligopolies or concentrations of power, and multiple voices running through the whole.

The Court's attempts to derive public policy from those values were, however, often contradictory and, too many times, counter-productive to the intended goals. That may be explained in part by a rapidly advancing technology that the judges were unable to foresee. The consequence was a wavering line of case development. In 1960 the reserved monopoly of state television was protected against challenges by private companies. The Court's miscalculation, and one that would plague its decisions for some time, was in the realm of technological capacity. In decisions in 1960, 1974 and 1976, the Court's reliance on estimates of technological limitations – number of useable channels, cost of national cable, technology for national airwave transmissions – were at the core of its decisions. Each time, the Court's predictions were short-sighted. In 1974, because of its inaccurate assessment of the potential of cable television, private cable channels were allowed. The same logic led the Court to authorize local airwave transmissions in 1976. In the latter case, the Court also erroneously argued that local transmissions would not develop into national oligopolies because of the cost and technologies involved. Berlusconi quickly proved the Court's evaluation wrong.

The rise of the Finivest-Berlusconi media conglomerate in the aftermath of the Court's 1976 decision clearly signaled that the Court might not be in the best position to make policy determinations. Parliament is the body better situated to regulate mass communications and to accommodate to new technologies, but in the Italian case, the legislature lacked the will or the ability to do so. The Court had opened the mass communications field to local broadcasting, but then Parliament took absolutely no action to regulate the field. Consequently, by 1981, Finivest had, through innovative manipulation of existing technologies, parlayed its local stations into a national network. That year, the Court deferred to the will of Parliament, but the legislators again did not act. The only legislation in this rapidly changing field since 1975 was the overtly partisan Berlusconi decree issued by Craxi in 1984 and converted into law in 1985. The President of the Court implored Parliament to act in 1987, and in 1988 declared central elements of the Berlusconi law unconstitutional, but allowed them to stand as provisional regulations.

The Court in 1988 adopted a new strategy: defer to Parliament, but provide clear instructions and set a deadline. That, too, was frustrated, since Parliament failed to meet the Court's timetable and, when it passed the 1990 Mammì Law, ignored the Court's dictates for replacement legislation. The subsequent mini-reforms were also upheld, but with the caveat that they, too, were merely provisional regulations with definitive end points. Even though the Court in these rulings sustained the status quo, part of which did not comport with constitutional requirements, it likely did so to avoid the advent of another legislative vacuum like the one that followed its 1976 decision.[92] Only in 1997 was a new regulatory regime passed by Parliament.

What explains the Court's activities in this field? Do the explanatory variables proposed offer any clues to the course the judges in the Consulta chose? Different explanations apply to the development of legal doctrine versus the evolution of public policy. Recruitment may be the factor that most illuminates the Court's approach to constitutionalizing values, in particular its emphasis on the need for a plurality of sources of information. The system of *lottizzazione* that governed appointments by Parliament and the President of the Republic that extended not only to the parties in power, but also to the major opposition forces, virtually insured that the Court at any point in time was itself representative of a variety of currents of thought. The cross-cutting division of judges named by three different political sectors enhanced that tendency. In other words, the judges themselves would likely be particularly sensitive to the need for pluralism, whether motivated by their own crass partisanship or by a more intellectual recognition of its virtues. The Court's 1965 decision, again upholding the validity of the state monopoly of radio and television, called for a break in the government's control of RAI. At that time, RAI was not only a fiefdom of the dominant Christian Democrats, but of a single faction within that party; opposition parties or factions were incapable of presenting their platforms. A heightened sensitivity to the one-sided perspective offered may well have resulted from the composition of the Court since a substantial proportion of its occupants' own ideological or political views were blocked from airing. Even as the Court's decisions were later mired in a bog created by its own dictates of privatization, adherence to pluralism as a constitutionally protected value remained.

This was true in its expressed apprehensions about the rise of oligopoly or dangerous concentrations of power, as well as in its calls for greater openness within the state-owned monopoly. There was a clear understanding by the judges of the media's 'power of persuasion' and its ability 'to mold public opinion, cultural and social norms'.[93]

The reach of the Court's legal competence can also shed some light on its policy-making on the issue of media pluralism. Legal competence does not refer to the type of review allowed or the means of access, but rather to the limits of the Court's competence. More precisely, the Court's inability to resolve the issue definitively was progressively more apparent in the aftermath of its 1976 decision that opened the airwaves to private local broadcasts. It could invalidate legislative, administrative and ordinary judicial actions, but it was incapable of orchestrating what would follow. Even when the Court prescribed very specific criteria for regulations to pass constitutional muster, Parliament could not be relied upon to follow them, if Parliament acted at all. The Court's reach was short; it could invalidate, but it could not propose.

That leads to an intimately related factor, that of the Court's place in the political scheme and more particularly its interest in institutional self-preservation. The Constitutional Court was not threatened by attacks from the legislative or executive branch at any time during the unfolding of the media pluralism saga. It was menaced by revelations of its own irrelevance in the process. When the Court invalidated portions of legislation, its dictates were accepted. However, when it attempted to prescribe the content of replacement norms, it was ignored. Its influence in directing the legislative process was minimal. Twice the Court enumerated what would be necessary in constitutionally accepted laws, and both times Parliament passed laws that did not conform. The Mammì Law served only to replicate by law the situation that the Court had earlier deemed unacceptable.[94] The Court seemingly recognized as early as 1981 that it was most effective when it upheld legislation, so it labeled unacceptable laws as 'provisional' and set timetables for replacement acts. The Court was more efficacious when it followed that route, as it did in 1981, in 1988, and again in 1994. At least the legislative and executive branches then responded with some kind of new legislation. Deference to the political branches of government also saved judicial face, and that strategy achieved more concrete results than had the Court's own failed attempts to dictate the policies to resolve the controversies.

The larger question remains, however, about the Italian Court's inability to channel change or even to serve as an effective catalyst prodding Parliament to act. The German Constitutional Court had, during the identical time period, been coping with similar questions, and its 1986 decision had 'proved to be a barrier against consequent deregulation and commercialization of broadcasting'.[95] The German court, far more than the legislature, set the parameters for privatization, by prescribing the rules. Similarly, the French Constitutional Council in three decisions in less than two years also effectively shaped the final legislation governing media pluralism in that country. In the face of Council rulings, the French Parliament essentially copied the terms dictated by the Council instead of even attempting other solutions.[96]

These sister courts in France and Germany were able to exert far more direct influence on legislative outcomes than was the Italian Constitutional Court. Why? One answer may lie in the particular importance that the mass media of television and radio have had in Italy. Luca Ricolfi suggests that television earned a place in Italian life that is different from other countries, for it served to homogenize Italians, who have learned 'to speak, to think and even to read and write through television'; the medium is almost 'an element of collective identity'. For this reason, he adds, regulating mass communications in Italy has been more delicate than elsewhere.[97] In other words, the extra-legal environment, the context of judicial action, has exerted strong modifying effects. This is most apparent in the diverse regulatory schemes that were ultimately adopted in Italy, France and Germany. Each was tailored to fit peculiar national interests, political and social. The lack of success on the part of the Italian Constitutional Court may be attributed, therefore, less to structural, political and legal factors than to environmental ones. At some point, probably 1981, the judges realized the futility of their attempting to write the legislation directly. Rather, they chose the path of institutional self-preservation and left the task of locating the delicate balance in the hands of ministers and parliamentarians, who were, alas, incapable of structuring a scheme that was constitutionally viable.

8
Good Law and Good Policy

Attributing political and policy motives to judges or courts is always tricky, whether at the empirical or theoretical level. It has been said of American judges that most 'would sooner admit to grand larceny than confess a political interest or motivation',[1] and rejection of any non-legal objective is even more strident on the opposite side of the Atlantic. Judges in the western legal tradition today are all trained in law and have advanced in their careers by relying on the language, traditions, trappings and logic of the law. They do not lightly admit that the law is not the only motif overlying and underpinning all their decisions. European lawyers are even more wed to the vision of law as a science than are their American brothers and sisters. There is a reverence for the syllogism, for the deductive logic that leads one from the legal rule to the correct judicial decision. 'Logic must win out.'[2] Even within the rigid deductive formula, however, often lurks the necessity that the legal principle be 'reworded in order to fit into the hypothesis of the case'.[3]

Subtle, even subconscious, rewording of the legal rule permits the intrusion of policy objectives. What is true of a judge acting alone is compounded when judges decide cases in their collective capacity as an institution and where presumably there is give and take about which is the 'right' principle from which to begin. The distinction between good law and good policy – and the two are not mutually exclusive – can only be isolated when attributing a purpose to why the principle is reworked. What triggers one over the other is the level of concern about the outcome of the case.[4]

In tracing lines of decisions by the Italian Constitutional Court, possible goals and motives have been imputed to the judges as explanations of why they chose to decide the way they did. That mode of analysis is not commonly accepted in continental legal circles, although even in Italy glimmers of the so-called 'legal realism' are penetrating conventional understanding of judicial decision making.[5] Part of the difficulty in assigning intent is that disentangling good law from good policy is complicated and requires no small measure of inference. Law and policy goals are intertwined, and both are announced and justified in the language of good law, of the legal model. Courts build legitimacy from and seek refuge in the rarified discourse of law. They stand in such a weak position vis-à-vis other political institutions that they must rely on 'the force of a principle'.[6]

All judicial decisions make policy in some sense, but where the judgment is broadly stated and has wider application, decisions are more akin to legislation. Rule adjudication results in policy even if only in the limited sense of eliminating some options from the repertoire of the legislator or the executive. The distinction between judicial decisions that are good policy and those that are good law goes to the intent that underlies the judgment, and there is always some theoretical ambiguity in attributing motives to behavior.[7] Moreover, legal considerations constitute relevant factors for either law or policy, jurisprudence or outcome.[8]

The thought processes of judges are certainly not always evident on any court, but are even more obscure for those serving on the Italian Constitutional Court, since not even individual votes are revealed. I can only suggest, in a paraphrase and modification of what Goldman and Jahnige said in their application of the attitudinal model, that the Italian Constitutional Court has behaved *as if* good policy or good law was its primary goal.[9] There are some markers that guided my analysis of the Italian Court. That Court is, after all, a new institution, and many of its decisions were those of first impression or the first instance in which a judicial interpretation was offered for a constitutional or other legal provision. The only 'law' in those instances from which the Court could derive its judgments was the constitutional text and deductive logic. In that sense, any deviation from a literal reading of the Constitution itself *might* be indicative of policy goals. Emphasis on the tentativeness of that indication is essential, because the Court also accepted a certain amount of the established jurisprudence that had evolved in the ordinary courts, at least to the extent that it was not transparently in contravention of the letter or the spirit of the Constitution. Moreover, legal scholarship that analyzed the Constitution, particularly in the eight-year lapse between its promulgation and the creation of the Constitutional Court, also carried some weight. Another juncture at which the choice between good law and good policy is evident is where more than one constitutional value is implicated in a case and the judges must choose between them or find a creative blend. When one constitutional value is elevated above others, good law is secondary to good policy. The likelihood is strong as well that the legal and the extra-legal jointly explain more decisions than either considered in isolation.[10]

There is, however, another, less fuzzy way to isolate some judgments whereby good policy obviously took priority over good law. When the Court created a clearly articulated jurisprudence – good law, if you will – on a particular subject, and then tacked off on a different course, good policy was primary. Repeatedly, in the lines of decisions analyzed here, the Court had a clearly articulated and legally clear doctrine in place, but then shifted away from it. When this occurred, even if the prior line of reasoning was not recanted, the Court chose good policy over good law. The logic is simple: if what had been treated as good law is repudiated, abandoned or significantly altered, then good policy must be trumping good law. Remember that a law-oriented court will always eschew a chance to make what it sees as good policy and prefer instead to make good law. When established law is abandoned, then good policy must be guiding the judges. A final reminder seems warranted when attributing a policy motive to the Court: the fact that the policy selected is not in fact the best one for the situation does not mean that the Court was not seeking what it thought was good policy. Sometimes what looks like irrational behavior or behavior that is driven by the imperative of good law 'may simply be rational errors' or bad strategy.[11]

Model of institutional decision making

The guiding assumption behind this analysis of the Italian Constitutional Court has been that judgments 'are a function of what they [judges] prefer to do, tempered by what they think they ought to do, but constrained by what they perceive as feasible to do'.[12] That statement captures the movement from individual judges' attitudes and values through the channels of institutional role orientations and structures to judicial policy. More specifically, the value preferences of the judges (what they prefer to do) are constrained by the Court as an institution (what they think they ought to do and what they believe is feasible) to result in a judgment of the Court. Each line of decisions has been analyzed separately, but ought to be considered jointly in light of the variables that were proposed to explain institutional-level decision making.

The threshold question must be about variation in the dependent variable, *judicial policies*. Did the Court vary its judicial response on any of the five subject areas examined in a way that would indicate a shift between good law and good policy? Plausibly any and all decisions may have been the result of a preference by the Court for good policy over good law, but to limit conjecture, only those instances where the Court had an established jurisprudence and then obviously departed from it will be treated as an indication of good policy's replacing good law. In its decree law jurisprudence, the Court in 1967 enunciated a clear and coherent statement of how it would treat executive decree laws. It held that since decree laws were only provisional measures and had no validity without parliamentary conversion, the Court would not entertain challenges to decree laws. Once decree laws had been converted, however, the Court would and did review their constitutional validity. Moreover, the Court refused to consider challenges to the urgency or emergency that gave rise to the decrees, reasoning that if Parliament passed the law, it must have concurred with the assertion of urgency.[13] The fervor with which the Court adhered to that jurisprudence was reflected in its 1994 exclamation that 'how many times must this Court affirm that, after conversion, the relevance of the decree law is gone!'[14] Likewise, the Court did not respond to challenges of the executive practice of reissuing unconverted decrees, except once, in 1988, when it invalidated a single decree on the grounds that its continual reissuance had jeopardized legal certainty.[15] Dramatically, then, in 1996 the Court sweepingly declared that all reissued decree laws were constitutionally unacceptable.[16] A choice of policy overcame that of legal accuracy and legal policy as established since the first decree was reissued more than 30 years earlier. Yet, the jurisprudential doctrines governing decree laws *per se* remained intact.

The jurisprudence of the Constitutional Court partitioning central and regional powers showed far less variation. The priority of Article 5's declaration of the unitary status of the Italian state was consistently followed, whether deciding conflicts of powers, priority of national interests, preventive control or international obligations. The Court turned constitutional somersaults to preserve its judgments on regional legislation and simultaneously to bring them in line with international obligations resulting from membership in the European Community/ Union.[17] More tolerance for regional prerogatives was apparent as jurisprudence on regions evolved, and the central government was required to justify its assertions of national interests; a measure of con-current jurisdiction was recognized in areas such as the National Health Service; and the national government was asked to provide spe-cific reasons, even political ones, for exercising preventive control over regional legislation.[18] Even so, the path taken in arbitrating between central and regional authorities was relatively straight. The supposition that the Court followed a path of good law seems warranted.

The Court has been perhaps its most creative in its approach to con-stitutionally acceptable proposals for referendums. It expanded its jurisprudence from merely checking the content of proposals against the four constitutionally prohibited categories to imposing criteria that were 'analogous': a referendum question must be homogeneous and ask a single question, must not implicate the constitution or other laws, and must not cause injury to other laws.[19] Though those criteria may have been applied arbitrarily in some cases, the underlying jurispruden-tial logic held. The prevalence of good policy goals over legal accuracy and clarity could be seen, however, when the issue of elections arose. What was constitutionally unacceptable under the lost constitutional text argument was suddenly wholly constitutional just two years later.[20] The goal of good law gave way to pursuit of good policy.

Trying accusations against the prime minister and other ministers is more difficult to dissect since there is no line of cases, but only a single experience. Even so, the Lockheed case required the Court to wear two different hats, one in its normal capacity deciding issues of constitu-tional interpretation and another as the integrated court with laypeo-ple judging guilt or innocence. There are no obvious signs that the Court did anything more than seek good law, even if its guiding lode-stone in the absence of constitutional guidance was pragmatism or fea-sibility, in its interpretation of the applicable law and constitutional requirements. The outcome of the actual trial, on the other hand, bears some fingerprints of partisanship that might justify a conclusion of a goal of good policy.

The Court's treatment of media pluralism presents perhaps the most complex scenario. Discerning clear goals of any sort in the torturous jurisprudential road from 1960 to 1996 is daunting. Assuming that the Court had no objective beyond articulating a clear statement of law and then of accurately applying it throughout, every decision made seemed to have consequences opposite to those that were intended. A regrouping and reappraisal of the 'law' then followed. The same themes are repeated consistently: the requirement of a plurality of voices, acceptance of a state monopoly so long as it responded to the necessity of pluralism, and the fear of unbridled economic initiative that could lead to oligopoly. Each judicial pronouncement was, however, manipulated in the bare-knuckled world of entrepreneurship and partisan politics, and results were unrecognizable. The Court appealed to Parliament to act, dictated what new legislation should look like, and granted provisional status to otherwise unconstitutional laws while setting deadlines for replacement legislation. Consistent judicial themes recur through the whole and might signal simply a quixotic quest for good law, but the shadings and emphases and even policy prescriptions that are likewise in the judgments suggest that the goal of feasible, if not necessarily good, policy was present as well. A definite turning point is not discernible.

There has, in other words, been something more present in the Italian Constitutional Court's handling of these five subject areas than a strict adherence to the objective of pronouncing clear, correct and coherent legal doctrine. Explaining deviations from the singular goal of achieving good law, warrants turning again to the model that describes judicial decisions as products of what the judges want to accomplish, filtered through beliefs about the institutional role and assumptions about what is institutionally feasible.

The absence of public explanations or even public records of votes limits analysis of what the judges individually might have preferred to do, their *values and ideologies*. These are treated in my model as antecedent variables that are structured by the institution of the Court. Nonetheless, certain conclusions are implicit. In the first 40 years of the Court's existence, the slightly more than 70 judges can likely be assumed to share the values of the dominant elite. Appointments by the President of the Republic and Parliament followed the dictates of the *lottizzazione* that parceled the positions among the six major parties, including the Communists. Though partisan affiliations were not relevant for the one-third of the Court named by their fellow judges on the ordinary and administrative courts, the judicial appointees were all at the pinnacles of their respective judicial hierarchies and presumably were also part of the national elite. Moreover, until 1994, when the old regime and old formulae collapsed, the majority of those appointed by the President and Parliament were also of the dominant Christian Democrat Party or one of its allies. Elite congruence has been demonstrated by linking all decisions of the Court from 1980 to 1991 for their consistency with parliamentary wishes, and considerable agreement (66 per cent) between Parliament and the Court was found.[21] Divided responsibility for naming the judges was intended by the framers of the Italian Constitution to bring cross-cutting allegiances to the Court. That, combined with the cycle of replacements and the dictates of the *lottizzazione*, insured some measure of pluralism on the Court at all times as well. Whatever biases, values or policy preferences the judges carried with them to the high bench are assumed, by the new institutionalist model, to have been constrained and directed thereafter by institutional features.

Pivotal elements of the *role orientation* of the Italian Constitutional Court are captured in the Guarnieri matrix of independence and authority,[22] and repeatedly that has emerged as a crucial determinant of whether the Court tilted toward good law or good policy in the lines of cases examined. The Court has occupied various places on the delegate, executor, guardian and politico taxonomy, depending on the subject and the political context. The Court pursued good law in its treatment of executive decree laws that bedeviled legislative–executive relations from 1967 when it decided the first challenge until 1996. The jurisprudential equation the judges had fashioned dictated that they stand aside and act as a delegate, exercising high levels of discretion, but lower levels of independence. They restricted themselves to reviewing the constitutional validity of decree laws only after their conversion by Parliament because of their consistent statements that decree laws have limited effects and that Parliament participated in the conversion process. That judicial self-effacement might have placed the Court in the position of a mere executor, with both low discretion and low autonomy, except for the fact that the judges were not reticent to invalidate decrees once enacted by the legislative branch. Independence was low until the demise of the old regime because of loyalty that may have been owed to the judges' appointers, but more relevant, to the audiences on whom they depended for their political or other careers after leaving the bench.

The Court's treatment of regions was consistent across issues of conflicts of power, the primacy of national interests, central government control of international dimensions, and preventive control of regional legislation by the central government. It has favored the central government in all but a handful of cases and, thereby, was never out of line with the wishes of its patrons. That translated into low autonomy and high discretion. Similarly, the actual trial of the Lockheed case indicates an absence of independence, although the Court's decisions on the guilt of the defendants were shared with 16 laypeople. Even so, the Christian Democrat office-holder was the only defendant completely exonerated, which would be consistent with the desires of the authority appointing most of the judges on the bench at that time. The Court acted similarly in its role as gatekeeper for the referendum process by deflecting challenges to laws not supported by the political office-holders to whom the judges owed their appointments and, perhaps, future. It fashioned a highly flexible set of requirements for homogeneity, injury to other laws and implications for constitution and constitutional organs that it could easily bend to admit or exclude referendum proposals. Exceptions to the trend of protecting the interests of the Court's past and future benefactors, at least before 1993, can be found in the Court's approval of the Communist Party sponsored challenge to reduction in the wage indexation scale and perhaps some of the 1987 referendums on nuclear energy, civil liability of judges and accusations of government ministers. In 1987 and again in 1993, the Court even found a lost constitutional text that it could use to block referendums that aimed at altering electoral mechanisms. In each of these instances, the Court acted as a delegate, exercising significant discretion, but with less independence.

The upheavals following the 1992 Clean Hands investigations and the rise in 1994 of new parties and new political configurations served to free the judges from prior allegiances to appointers and to future patrons. That was revealed regarding decree laws by the Court's firm 1996 repudiation of the practice of reissuing any decree law that had not been converted by the legislature within the constitutionally prescribed 60 days. Similarly, in its treatment of referendum requests, the Court made an about face in 1993 from its position only two years earlier on the ability of referendums to address questions of the electoral system, a system that had been central to maintenance of the regime of *partitocrazia*. The jurisprudence governing both decree laws and referendums altered dramatically in the years immediately following the breakdown of the old regime. The Court acted more in a politico mode, both highly independent and contrary to the wishes of the other powers of government, but at the same time with considerable authority.

Independence has, thus far, been treated as independence from appointing authorities and future patrons in political offices, but there are other audiences to which courts play and to which they may be accountable. Among these are the legal community, interest groups, the press and the public at large.[23] Normally, one would expect the governmental organs responsible for appointing judges to represent popular will, at least with reference to general policy directions. The Italian political system was traditionally, however, a *partitocrazia* in which parties drove public policies more than institutions did, and where only a tangential connection tied the mass public to elections and the government. Popular will was more likely exerted on policies through interest groups and the media.[24] Popular dissatisfaction with what had become politics as usual in Italy was instrumental in bringing down the old regime and destroying ties between judges and their partisan patrons. Simultaneously, the public was transformed into an extremely influential audience that the Court could not ignore. That is reflected most obviously in the Court's backtracking on its prohibition to allow the public to register its wishes through referendums on the form of elections. Proposals to reform Senate, Chamber of Deputies and communal council elections that were rejected by the Court in 1991 were validated by it in 1993 and passed by the voters by an overwhelming majority. The Court's 1993 decision is a clear example of a judicial bow to popular will, for that decision was a break with earlier jurisprudence and contrary to the interests of those occupying the other seats of national power. A different form of accountability was apparent, but it diminished independence as surely as any judgment designed to comport with the wishes of the other organs of government.

The Court's institutional structure also determines what goals and strategies are feasible for it to pursue. *Access, public debate* and *abstract versus concrete review* did not appear to be determinative of law or policy goals in the cases examined. These structural features of the Constitutional Court were largely invariable, since most access in the lines of cases examined here was through referrals from ordinary or administrative courts, but even those cases that came via direct access from another institution of government were treated neither more seriously nor frivolously than ones reaching the Court from the more common route. Indeed, the Court rejected most challenges of both types as unfounded or inadmissible. Type of review, whether abstract or concrete, was also irrelevant in the cases here considered, since most called for concrete review. And, with the exception of deliberations in chambers and the more recent practice of allowing promoters of referendum requests and the government to present their arguments in chambers, debate was always public. These features remain, however, defining of the very nature of the Court and are important in shaping how decisions are made, even if not directly affecting the law or policy inclinations of the judges in these specific cases.

A very important structural element of the Court is its *place in the political scheme*. This is where institutional self-preservation, public esteem, prestige and legitimacy all meet. The Italian Constitutional Court seemed determined to maintain or enhance its institutional standing in its handling of several issues. The Court tried, for example, to allow the executive and legislative branches to find their own accommodation in the area of executive decree laws and refused to intervene. It took refuge in adherence to a legal policy it had articulated as early as 1967. The Court liked to point to its invalidation of a single repeatedly reissued decree in 1988 as being the catalyst for parliamentary reforms in 1988 to regulate and expedite reception and disposition of executive decree laws. Those reforms were, unfortunately, undermined by Parliament's legendary inability to act in a timely fashion. Even so, the Court could rightly note that its decision which had spurred the ill-fated legislative reforms had been based on the jurisprudential doctrine of legal certainty. It could claim to pursue no goal beyond finding good law, which allowed it to remain outside the arena where the executive and legislative branches sparred. Once the old regime had been discredited and the first center-left coalition was in place in 1996, the Court was emboldened to inject itself and define the new rules of the game. Then, it sought to impose good policy and declared unconstitutional all reissued decree laws. Its standing was sufficient at that time that its dictate was accepted and followed scrupulously; not another decree was reissued.

Standing in the political scheme is also relevant to how the Constitutional Court approached the question of media pluralism. Although many of the Court's early decisions on the subject relied on flawed assumptions about technological limitations, there is no indication that the judges were not attempting to form a coherent and correct jurisprudence. The Court attempted, beginning in 1974, to dictate to Parliament what a constitutionally acceptable regulation should look like, and Parliament responded in 1975 with a law that largely ignored the Court's prescriptions. Moreover, loopholes relating to private local broadcasts that were created by the Court were not plugged by the legislature. The result was a Darwinian struggle for private control. The Court then assumed, perhaps correctly, that the technicalities of regulating radio and television were best left in parliamentary hands and so deferred to the legislature in 1981[25] and 1987.[26] What laws were passed, especially the notorious Berlusconi law of 1985, were contrary to the Court's earlier pronouncements. The Court then adopted a different institutional strategy that demonstrates its sensitivity to its weakened ability to define policy; it upheld unconstitutional laws on the grounds that they were provisional, but set deadlines for enactment of replacement regulations.[27] That strategy at least prevented the free-for-all situation that resulted earlier in the absence of regulation.

That course seemed no more successful that its earlier one of invalidating legislation, and the Court's outlines of what should be included in replacement legislation if it were to pass constitutional muster were largely ignored. Even when the Court acted with some measure of self-assurance, it was largely overruled by political compromises in the government-Parliament arena. The Court's standing – or more correctly, lack of standing – within the political scheme was underscored repeatedly in the saga of media pluralism, even as the Court tried different policy solutions.

The Constitutional Court's place in the political scheme may have influenced the law or policy decisions it pursued in its handling of central versus regional control. Even though that jurisprudence is relatively consistent throughout, the Court's position within the central government defined its selection of the constitutional principle, that of the unitary status of the state, on which all other decisions would hinge. The language of Article 5 allowed, had the judges been so inclined, a definition of the nation as more federal than unitary. That the Court was itself part of the central government predisposed it to preserve the pre-eminence of the national government.

The Court's institutional position was not implicated solely by the actions or wishes of Parliament and the executive. Differentiating itself and its prerogatives from those of the ordinary judiciary was also determinative. In many early decisions on referendum proposals, the Court's judgments were colored by its determination to limit activities of the highest ordinary court in its role as the Central Office for Referendum. The Constitutional Court stubbornly insisted that it alone could, under the Constitution, review the content of proposals, whereas the *Corte di Cassazione* was to do no more than verify signatures. Similarly, with reference to decree laws, there is certainly evidence that after one section of the *Corte di Cassazione* refused to apply reissued decree laws that affected criminal cases and that ruling was adopted by criminal judges in the ordinary court hierarchy, the Constitutional Court declared the practice of reissuance unconstitutional. Maintaining its position as the sole body able to rule on the constitutionality of laws or acts having force of law meant that the Court must regain the initiative from the ordinary court judges on the question of reissued decree laws.

A court's standing in the political scheme is determined not simply by its rapport with other organs of government, but also by its acceptance by the public. 'Trust and approval are especially important' for a body that is neither democratically selected nor democratically accountable.[28] The public is usually not knowledgeable of judicial decisions, but awareness can be quite high in the right situation.[29] That was the case when the Court first blocked in 1991 and then permitted in 1993 referendum initiatives to alter the electoral system. The anti-government sentiments of the public were high in those years, and a sense of betrayal by the Court found voice.[30] That is the only clear point for which there is evidence of heightened public awareness and public dissatisfaction to posit a direct influence on the Court's standing in relation to the public.

Context is never assumed to sway a court's pursuit of good law, but when it does affect judicial pronouncements, good policy is the obvious motive. The political context of decisions has been noted throughout my descriptions of how the Constitutional Court ruled on different issues. The influence of context might be debatable in some eras, but the period of 1992 to 1996 was a defining period in Italian political life that also coincides with more than one shift in judicial policy. At a time when the old political regime in Italy was crumbling and the transition to a new one began, many of the old precepts and practices fell away. In that context, the Court altered its treatment of referendums, not by creating a new set of criteria but by applying the existing legal doctrines differently. Only proposals that were very technically flawed or obviously contravened constitutional prohibitions were blocked by the Court after 1991.

The altered political context of the early 1990s had an emboldening effect on the Court in other areas, most clearly in its treatment of executive decree laws. The Constitutional Court not only changed its treatment of reissued decree laws, but it also announced its intention to carefully monitor the conditions of emergency and urgency that gave rise to executive decrees in the future. Also in this period of political upheaval, the Court gave its approval to the very questionable Mammì Law passed in 1990 to regulate public and private media[31] and, in a later case, extended its deadline for replacement legislation.[32]

The influence of the Court's institutional role orientation and structural role in directing some shifts from what had been embraced by the Court as good law to more strategic judgments that were good policy has been demonstrated in decisions on referendum proposals, executive decree laws and media pluralism. It is implicated, however, in a far more muted fashion in the Court's management of the Lockheed scandal and national–regional relations. No single variable standing alone can explain the Court's penchant for seeking good policy in lieu of good law or the reverse. Independence, authority, accountability, standing in the political scheme and political context are all interconnected and often mutually reinforcing. To attribute causality more directly would require a degree of conjecture than I am willing to risk. Rather, taken as a whole, the institutional role variables and those defining the structure of the Constitutional Court demonstrate the effect of extra-legal factors on the decisional processes of the Court as an institution. Those extra-legal factors intervened at the institutional level to incline the judges collectively to prefer good policy over simply good law in some instances. That is not to suggest that legal considerations and doctrine were not major considerations in any decision, but merely that coherent, consistent jurisprudence was at times manipulated toward a given end, where the principles were reworded or rejected entirely in a quest for a more viable or more acceptable policy.

Constitutional Court as a political institution

The overarching purpose of this study has been to demonstrate that the Italian Constitutional Court is a political institution, a political actor in Italian life. Some of the more controversial lines of decisions have been analyzed, but the Court's jurisprudence in other subject areas might have revealed fewer political influences, perhaps none at all, or plausibly even more. A court's political activities and political motivations are most obvious when it is deciding issues that define relationships among the centers of political power. The Italian Constitutional Court is relatively weak in the larger scheme of Italian politics. It has been described in this study as timid, restricted to the sidelines, submissive, dependent and with other terms that underscore its lack of strength vis-à-vis the other powers of government. That does not, however, mean that it is a marginal or irrelevant institutional actor. The best evidence of its importance can be found in the answer to the following question: Would the current law on executive decree laws, regional authority, accusations against ministers, referendums and media pluralism be the same had the Court not acted? The answer is no.

A brief description of the Court's impact in fashioning the current status of each of these subjects demonstrates its importance as a political institution. In the dispute over executive use of decree laws, the Court carefully crafted a jurisprudence that placed responsibility for monitoring executive actions in the hands of Parliament. Notably, the Court was not reluctant to slap down unconstitutional laws that may have begun as decrees once they had passed through the legislative gauntlet, but in advance of conversion it allowed Parliament alone to determine the fate of a decree. When the Court deviated from that course in 1988, its single decision was sufficient motivation for the legislators to enact a reform to resolve the problem for the future. That reform was totally ineffective in modifying how the government used decrees, but had the side benefit of altering other stumbling blocks in legislative–executive relations, particularly regarding secret ballots used to defeat government programs. The Court's position of not reviewing the constitutionality of decree laws, either for process or for content, enabled the other two branches to define their own equilibrium. That basic position never changed, even when the Court finally struck down the practice of reissuing decree laws.

The Court's clear articulation, as early as 1957, of the primacy of Italy's status as a unitary state, regardless of whose interests were served by that pronouncement, steered central–regional relations thereafter. The judges set a high barrier for the regions to clear whenever they claimed a conflict of power. That prevented regions from successfully challenging national actions and limited the transformation of regional–central disputes into litigation. That barrier and the Court's recognition of the reserve power of the central government to act exclusively in fields in which there was particular national interest and when the regions failed to act in a timely fashion reinforced the unitary nature of the nation. The same was true of the Court's decisions on national prerogatives when any international dimension was touched and on the central government's use of preventive control. The Court consistently emphasized the subordinate position of the regions and thereby limited the scope for confrontations between the two levels of government. Having chosen that course, the Court was able in 1992 to define concurrent jurisdiction in certain domains, such as the National Health Service, and in 1989 to insist on fair treatment of the regional governments by the central authorities when asserting national interests or rejecting regional laws. The Court was not the catalyst for the regional devolution that began in the 1970s, but its jurisprudence defined the parameters and limited the constitutional contours for regional development.

The Court's work in trying government officials also influenced how the process would work in the future. No one was pleased, except perhaps the exonerated Christian Democrat Luigi Gui, with how the system worked. The judges themselves decried the process as it stood in 1979, and when no reforms were forthcoming, they permitted a referendum proposal in 1987 that required Parliament to institute changes.

Their handling of the Lockheed case, with non-political defendants, military personnel and government ministers highlighted the ambiguity of the existing rules, and their vindication of the only Christian Democrat who was accused illustrated how partisan sentiments could intrude. All ministers and parliamentarians, as well as any non-political people, were thereafter subject to regular investigations and trials before judges trained in criminal prosecutions. That change was a reaction to the procedures and outcome of the Lockheed case.

The Court's role as a gatekeeper in the referendum process is one where there is little doubt that the judges of the Consulta were instrumental players, blocking or facilitating all manner of referendums from 1972 until 1993. Even the most sympathetic observers would call the Court's jurisprudence highly creative in the field of constitutionally acceptable referendum subjects. Proposals of both major and minor importance were adjudicated using flexible judicially created criteria, and most that challenged the status quo of existing power relationships were rejected. The 1985 wage indexation scale question is the obvious exception to that inclination on the part of the Court. That changed in 1993, and the Court faded into a more objective filter, but it still relied on the judicial gloss on Article 75 that it had made in 1978. The torrent of referendum questions reaching the Court in 1993, 1994, 1995 and 1997 were still expected to adhere to the requirements that they not involve multiple and heterogeneous questions, implicate the Constitution and other laws or cause injury to other laws. The Court more than any other political institution shaped the referendum process.

The Court's interpretation of Article 21 and other related constitutional provisions touching on media pluralism is where the Court too often seemed ineffectual. Yet, even there, the law governing radio and television would not look the same had the Court not had its hand in the subject. The Court initially upheld the state monopoly, and then enunciated the constitutional imperative of facilitating a plurality of voices, created the right of citizens to receive information, opened the Pandora's box that led to private enterprise in the media industry, and tried in different ways to force the government and Parliament to enact constitutionally valid regulations. Even if the Court's lead was usually ineffective, it had a major role – if largely unintended – in shaping the contours of radio and television in Italy.

The Court's effects on Italian political life are also discernible in a number of more subtle ways. Often, when the Court failed to invalidate a law or practice or refused to hear a case challenging a law or act having the force of law, it granted legitimacy to the activity in question. This is readily apparent in the case of decree laws, where urgency and emergency were never questioned, although the Court promised in 1996 that it might commence review of those circumstances, and where missing the 60-day limits for parliamentary conversion were overlooked. By placing priority on the fact of conversion or rejection by Parliament, the Court sanctioned many deviations, so long as neither Parliament nor the executive was dissatisfied with the eventual outcome. National dominance over the regions was also approved and, thereby, regional governments were denied grounds for challenges. Most notably, in the Court's handling of media pluralism questions, it validated, from 1988 until 1994, regulatory schemes that it admitted could not pass constitutional muster. Those decisions avoided the opening of a legislative vacuum that might be exploited pending passage of a new regime. Those decisions were, whether one chooses to view them as a quest for good law or for good policy, politically relevant policies that drove how issues would ultimately be resolved.

Other times, the Court's invalidation of acts by the government, Parliament or referendum promoters removed some options from the play book. The Court acted also to fill an otherwise vacuum in power, usually a void left by the inability of Parliament to act. Indeed, 'if Parliament is empty, it is inevitable that some other power will fill the void'.[33] That simple political truism justified executive incursions into the parliamentary sphere through decree laws, much of the national government's activity in the realm of regional competencies, and the rise of Berlusconi and Finivest as a media conglomerate that potentially threatened both the state broadcasting company and pluralism in any real sense. The Court's pragmatism in fashioning strategies to avoid lacunae of power made it instrumental in eliminating some options for the other institutional players.

Conclusion

Constitutional courts in Europe are still relatively young institutions, and each has worked to define its own political space in a rather short span of time. Both the German Federal Constitutional Court and the French Constitutional Council have solidified constellations of authority for themselves within their national frameworks. The Italian Constitutional Court has been more tentative, more cautious, in locating its precise orbit, but that is somewhat in keeping with the development of democracy in Italy. The vision of what democracy in Italy should look like has been consistent, but the route to achieving it has not been linear. As the old system crumbled under the weight of its own corruption in the early 1990s, Italians spoke optimistically of a Second Republic. As the new millennium approaches, that possibility appears more remote. Even so, there have been some reconfigurations of power, and the Constitutional Court appears to have stepped more boldly into the spotlight.

The Italian Constitutional Court will not likely ever be, in terms of sheer political power, on a par with Parliament, the executive, or even the President of the Republic. But that is the nature of courts and what distinguishes them institutionally from other political institutions. Rule adjudication is what courts do, and that is always a passive activity. Courts can only react to events that have already occurred and must rely on some rule or norm to justify their conclusion in the case.[34] American political scientists often overstate court effectiveness, wishing to attribute more power and influence to courts than is warranted and to ascribe to them the ability to instigate broad social reforms. That view must be balanced by a realization of the essential traits of courts that limit their power but define their essence. Yet, a view of courts that oversimplifies and understates their political and social relevance – the perspective more common in Europe – yields an equally inaccurate and incomplete description.[35]

Constitutional courts were embraced in Italy and in other countries in postwar Europe in part because of the assumption that 'if parliaments cannot keep an effective check on governments, then maybe courts can'.[36] That expectation may or may not be borne out in all situations, as the Italian experience demonstrates. Constitutional courts are dynamic institutions, not wholly wed to past jurisprudence, as the legal model and assertions of legal policy would suggest. Each decision that a court makes influences future circumstances that will give rise to new conflicts and require more decisions. 'Law and office are comprised of social practice, the same aspects of social life from which conflict stems and to which it must appeal.'[37] That necessary and essential connection to the social and political life of a country requires that courts, particularly those exercising constitutional review, mirror the changes that occur in society and thereby periodically reinvent themselves and their policies.

The Italian Constitutional Court evolved from a disputed entity, tied in political knots in Parliament until 1956, to a self-aware and respected player in Italian political life. It now has an institutional personality and history that transcend links to its past through precedent and legal doctrine. Italian legal scholars have long referred to their Republican Constitution as the *costituzione vivente* or living constitution,[38] and part of the oxygen that keeps the Constitution alive comes from the Constitutional Court. The Court is a political institution that shapes the values and beliefs of those who serve on it, and through judgments that combine a quest for good law and good policy, influences how the political game is played.

Notes

1   Courts as Political Institutions

1. Donald Sassoon, *Contemporary Italy: Politics, Economy and Society since 1945* (London: Longman, 1986), p. 207.
2. Frederic Spotts and Theodor Wieser, *Italy: a Difficult Democracy* (Cambridge: Cambridge University Press, 1986), p. 152.
3. David Hine, *Governing Italy: the Politics of Bargained Pluralism* (Oxford: Clarendon Press, 1993), p. 162.
4. See, for example, Joseph LaPalombara, *Democracy Italian Style* (New Haven: Yale University Press, 1987); Paul Furlong, *Modern Italy: Representation and Reform* (London: Routledge, 1994); and Robert D. Putnam, *Making Democracy Work: Civic Traditions in Modern Italy* (Princeton: Princeton University Press, 1993).
5. For examples, see Gino Pallotta, *Dizionario della Politica Italiana* (Rome: Newton Compton Editori, 1985), p. 394.
6. James G. March and Johan P. Olsen, 'The New Institutionalism: Organizational Factors in Political Life', *American Political Science Review*, 78 (1984), 734.
7. See Donald P. Kommers, *The Constitutional Jurisprudence of the Federal Republic of Germany* (Durham: Duke University Press, 1997); Christine Landfried, 'Constitutional Review and Legislation in the Federal Republic of Germany', in Christine Landfried, ed., *Constitutional Review and Legislation: an International Comparison* (Baden-Baden: Nomos Verlagsgesellschaft, 1988), pp. 147–67; Alec Stone, *The Birth of Judicial Politics in France: the Constitutional Council in Comparative Perspective* (New York: Oxford University Press, 1992); António Araújo, *O Tribunal Constitucional (1989–1996)* (Lisbon: Coimbra Editora, 1997); and Rodriguez Piniero, *La Jurisdiccion Constitucional en España* (Madrid: Centro de Estudios Constitucional, 1996).
8. Yves Mény, *Government and Politics in Western Europe: Britain, France, Italy, West Germany* (Oxford: Oxford University Press, 1990), p. 299.
9. James L. Gibson, 'From Simplicity to Complexity: the Development of Theory in the Study of Judicial Behavior', *Political Behavior*, 5 (1983), 9.
10. Jeffrey A. Segal and Harold J. Spaeth, *The Supreme Court and the Attitudinal Model* (Cambridge: Cambridge University Press, 1993), p. 359.
11. Jean Edward Smith, *John Marshall: Definer of a Nation* (New York: Henry Holt and Company, 1996), p. 293.
12. John Brigham, *The Cult of the Court* (Philadelphia: Temple University Press, 1987), p. 6.
13. Ibid., p. 13.
14. Herbert Jacob, 'Decision Making in Trial Courts', in John B. Gates and Charles A. Johnson, eds, *The American Courts: a Critical Assessment* (Washington, DC: CQ Press, 1991), p. 223.
15. Donald R. Songer, Charles M. Cameron and Jeffrey A. Segal, 'An Empirical Test of the Rational-Actor Theory of Litigation', *Journal of Politics*, 57 (1995), 1119–29.

16. Paul Brace and Melinda Gann Hall, 'Studying Courts Comparatively: the View from the American States', *Political Research Quarterly*, 48 (1995), 24–5.
17. Rogers M. Smith, 'Political Jurisprudence, the "New Institutionalism" and the Future of Public Law', *American Political Science Review*, 82 (1988), 100.
18. Jean Blondel, *Comparative Government: an Introduction* (New York: Philip Allan, 1990), p. 16.
19. Daniela Giannetti, 'Il Neo-Istituzionalismo in Scienza Politica: Il Contributo della Teoria della Scelta Razionale', *Rivista Italiana di Scienza Politica*, 23 (1993), 174.
20. Michael Laver and Norman Schofield, *Multiparty Government: the Politics of Coalition in Europe* (Oxford: Oxford University Press, 1990), p. 197.
21. Ibid., p. 214.
22. Richard Rose, 'Prime Ministers in Parliamentary Democracies', in G. W. Jones, ed., *West European Prime Ministers* (London: Frank Cass, 1991), p. 9.
23. Blondel, *Comparative Government*, p. 323.
24. Yves Mény and Andrew Knapp, *Government and Politics in Western Europe: Britain, France, Italy, Germany* (Oxford: Oxford University Press, 1998), p. 350.
25. Bradley C. Canon and Charles A. Johnson, *Judicial Policies: Implementation and Impact*, 2nd edn (Washington, DC: CQ Press, 1999), p. 2.
26. Renaud Dehousse, *The European Court of Justice: the Politics of Legal Integration* (London: Macmillan, 1998), Chapter 3.
27. James L. Gibson, 'Decision Making in Appellate Courts', in John B. Gates and Charles A. Johnson, eds, *The American Courts: a Critical Assessment* (Washington, DC: CQ Press, 1991), p. 255.
28. Ibid., p. 256.
29. Montesquieu, *L'Esprit des Lois* (1748), Book XI, p. 49.
30. Lawrence Baum, *The Puzzle of Judicial Behavior* (Ann Arbor: University of Michigan Press, 1997), p. 58.
31. See, for example, the discussion in P. S. Atiyah and R. S. Summers, *Form and Substance in Anglo-American Law* (Oxford: Clarendon Press, 1987), Chapter 3.
32. C. Herman Pritchett, *The Roosevelt Court: a Study in Judicial Values and Votes, 1937–1947* (New York: Macmillan, 1948).
33. Segal and Spaeth, *The Supreme Court and the Attitudinal Model*, p. 64.
34. Tracey E. George and Lee Epstein, 'On the Nature of Supreme Court Decision Making', *American Political Science Review*, 86 (1992), 325.
35. Baum, *The Puzzle of Judicial Behavior*, p. 60.
36. H. W. Perry, Jr, *Deciding to Decide: Agenda-Setting in the United States Supreme Court* (Cambridge: Harvard University Press, 1991), p. 275.
37. George and Epstein, 'On the Nature of Supreme Court Decision Making', 332–4.
38. Gibson, 'From Simplicity to Complexity', 9.
39. Baum, *The Puzzle of Judicial Behavior*, p. 84.
40. S. F. Nadel, *The Theory of Social Structure* (Glencoe: Free Press, 1956), pp. 31–2.
41. Martin Shapiro, *Courts: a Comparative and Political Analysis* (Chicago: University of Chicago Press, 1981), p. 21; and J. Mark Ramseyer, 'The Puzzling (In)Dependence of Courts: a Comparative Approach', *Journal of Legal Studies*, 23 (1994), 721–48.

42. Theodore L. Becker, *Comparative Judicial Politics* (Chicago: Rand McNally, 1972), p. 167; William M. Landes and Richard A. Posner, 'The Independent Judiciary in an Interest Group Perspective', *Journal of Law and Economics*, 18 (1975), 875–905; and Gerald N. Rosenberg, 'Judicial Independence and the Reality of Political Power', *Review of Politics*, 54 (1992), 372.

43. John R. Schmidhauser, 'Introduction: the Impact of Political Change upon Law, Courts and Judicial Elites', *International Political Science Review*, 13 (1992), 231.

44. Robert Dahl, 'Decision Making in a Democracy: the Supreme Court as a National Policy Maker', *Journal of Public Law*, 6 (1957), 279–95.

45. Baum, *The Puzzle of Judicial Behavior*, pp. 42–3.

46. Carlo Guarnieri, *Magistratura e Politica* (Bologna: Il Mulino, 1992), p. 27; and Carlo Guarnieri and Patrizia Pederzoli, *La Democrazia Giudiziaria* (Bologna: Il Mulino, 1997), pp. 56–7.

47. R. Kent Weaver and Bert A. Rockman, 'When and How Do Institutions Matter?', in R. Kent Weaver and Bert A. Rockman, eds, *Do Institutions Matter? Government Capabilities in the United States and Abroad* (Washington, DC: Brookings Institute, 1993), p. 446.

48. Baum, *The Puzzle of Judicial Behavior*, p. 47.

49. Canon and Johnson, *Judicial Policies*, pp. 115–16.

50. Baum, *The Puzzle of Judicial Behavior*, pp. 48–9.

51. Mény, *Government and Politics in Western Europe*, p. 306.

52. Carlo Guarnieri, 'Change and Continuity in the Bureaucratic Setting of European Judiciaries', presented at 'Judges: Selection and Evaluation', Oñati International Institute for the Sociology of Law (1997), p. 19.

53. Alec Stone, *The Birth of Judicial Politics in France*, pp. 212–21.

54. Charles H. Franklin and Liane C. Kosaki, 'Media, Knowledge, and Public Evaluations of the Supreme Court', in Lee Epstein, ed., *Contemplating Courts* (Washington, DC: CQ Press, 1995), p. 370.

55. Lee Epstein and Jack Knight, *The Choices Justices Make* (Washington, DC: CQ Press, 1997), pp. 137–8.

56. Canon and Johnson, *Judicial Policies*, p. 191.

57. James L. Gibson, Gregory A. Caldeira and Vanessa A. Baird, 'On the Legitimacy of National High Courts', *American Political Science Review*, 92 (1998), 353.

58. William Mishler and Reginald S. Sheehan, 'The Supreme Court as a Countermajoritarian Institution? The Impact of Public Opinion on Supreme Court Decisions', *American Political Science Review*, 87 (1993), 87–101; Helmut Norpoth and Jefferey A. Segal, 'Popular Influence on Supreme Court Decisions', *American Political Science Review*, 88 (1994), 711–16; William Mishler and Reginald S. Sheehan, 'Response', *American Political Science Review*, 88 (1994), 716–24; Timothy R. Johnson and Andrew D. Martin, 'The Public's Conditional Response to Supreme Court Decisions', *American Political Science Review*, 92 (1998), 299–309; and John M. Scheb II and William Lyons, 'Public Perception of the Supreme Court in the 1990s', *Judicature*, 82 (1998), 66–9.

59. Franklin and Kosaki, 'Media, Knowledge and Public Evaluations of the Supreme Court', p. 373.

60. Canon and Johnson, *Judicial Policies*, pp. 180–3.

61. Jack Knight and Lee Epstein, 'On the Struggle for Judicial Supremacy', *Law and Society Review*, 30 (1996), 91.
62. Mény, *Government and Politics in Western Europe*, pp. 318–22.
63. Ibid., pp. 322–5.
64. Ibid., p. 318.
65. March and Olsen, 'The New Institutionalism', 742.
66. Smith, 'Political Jurisprudence', 102.
67. Guglielmo Negri, *Il Quadro Costituzionale: Tempi e Istituti della Libertà* (Varese: Giuffré Editore, 1984), p. 6.
68. Ibid., p. 11.
69. Carlo Ghisalberti, *Storia Costituzionale d'Italia, 1848/1948* (Rome: Editori Laterza, 1977), I, pp. 26–33.
70. 'Statuto Albertino', in Niccoló Rodolico, ed., *Storia del Parlamento Italiano* (Palermo: S. F. Flaccovio Editore, 1963), pp. 421–8.
71. Negri, *Il Quadro*, p. 3.
72. Guglielmo Negri, 'The Rise and Fall of the Fascist Constitution', *Il Politico*, 47 (1982), 450–1.
73. As quoted in Negri, 'The Rise and Fall of the Fascist Constitution', 451.
74. Ghisalberti, *Storia Costituzionale*, II, pp. 381–2.
75. Ibid., II, pp. 395–408.
76. Decree law, Luogotenenziale, 25 June 1944, No. 151.
77. Philip V. Cannistraro, ed., *Historical Dictionary of Fascist Italy* (Westport, CT: Greenwood Press, 1982), pp. 143–4.
78. Carla Rodotà, *La Corte Costituzionale: Come e Chi Garantisce il Pieno Rispetto della Nostra Costituzione* (Rome: Editori Riuniti, 1986), p. 13.
79. Hans Kelsen, *Pure Theory of Law*, trans. by Max Knight (Berkeley: University of California Press, 1967), p. 22.
80. Hans Kelsen, *General Theory of Law and State*, trans. by Anders Wedberg (New York: Russell and Russell, 1961), p. 157.
81. Ibid., p. 269.
82. Stefano Maria Cicconetti, Maurizio Cortese, Giuseppe Torcolini and Silvio Traversa, eds, *La Costituzione della Repubblica: Nei Lavori Preparatori della Assemblea Costituente* (Rome: Camera dei Deputati, 1970), p. I-304.
83. Ibid., p. I-305.
84. Ibid., p. I-329.
85. Ibid., p. I-331.
86. Ibid., p. V-4202.
87. Ibid., p. V-4228.
88. Guido Neppi Modena, 'The Courts and the Difficult Road to Independence', *Italian Journal*, 3 (1989), 23.
89. Cicconetti *et al.*, *La Costituzione*, pp. V-4212–13.
90. Ibid., pp. V-4215–16.
91. Ibid., pp. V-4223–4.
92. Ibid., p. V-4236.
93. Ibid., p. V-4600.
94. Paul Ginsborg, *A History of Contemporary Italy: Society and Politics 1943–1988* (London: Penguin, 1990), p. 72.
95. ISTAT, *45 Anni di Elezioni in Italia, 1946–1990* (Rome: Istituto Nazionale di Statistica, 1990), p. 18.

96. Ettore Laurenzano, *Corte Costituzionale e Parlamento* (Rome: Bulzoni Editore, 1983), pp. 27–8.
97. Unlike a regular law or statute, a constitutional law is essentially a constitutional amendment. It requires passage twice by each chamber at intervals of at least three months. An absolute majority of each house is required on the second vote. The procedure is outlined in Constitution Article 138.
98. Pallotta, *Dizionario della Politica Italiana*, pp. 271–4.
99. ISTAT, *45 Anni di Elezioni in Italia, 1946–90*, p. 26.
100. Hughes Portelli, 'Les Deux Constitutions', *Il Veltro*, 23 (1989), 6; Carla Rodotà, *Corte Costituzionale*, p. 19.
101. The government argued that the abrogation of anterior or pre-existing laws was the exclusive prerogative of the ordinary courts. See Judgment No. 1/1956.
102. Judgment No. 1/1956.

2 Institutional Properties

1. Law No. 87, 11 March 1953, Title I, 2.
2. Mario Chiavario (ed.), *Codice della Giustizia Costituzionale* (Milan: Dott. A. Giuffré Editore, 1985), p. 60.
3. Constitutional Law No. 2, 22 November 1967, Article 4.
4. Law No. 87, 11 March 1953, Title I, 3.
5. Carla Rodotà, *La Corte Costituzionale: Come e Chi Garantisce il Pieno Rispetto della Nostra Costituzione* (Rome: Editori Riuniti, 1986), p. 20.
6. Serio Galeotti, *Il Presidente della Repubblica Garante della Costituzione* (Milan: Dott. A. Giuffré Editore, 1992), p. 104.
7. Alessandro Pizzorusso, *Sistema Istituzionale del Diritto Pubblico Italiano* (Naples: Jovene Editore, 1988), p. 250.
8. Gustavo Zagrebelsky, *La Giustizia Costituzionale* (Milan: Il Mulino, 1988), p. 74.
9. Nino Valentino, *Il Presidente della Repubblica: Maestro di Corte o Tribuno del Popolo?* (Rome: Editalia, 1992), p. 79.
10. Zagrebelsky, *La Giustizia Costituzionale*, p. 75.
11. See, for example, the 1982 selection of the Socialist Party nominee. Francesco Bonini, *Storia della Corte Costituzionale* (Rome: La Nuova Italia Scientifica, 1996), p. 273.
12. For an excellent discussion of the so-called 'clean hands' investigations, see Alessandro Pizzorusso, *La Costituzione: i Valori da Conservare, le Regole da Cambiare* (Turin: Einaudi, 1995), pp. 35–40; and Patrick McCarthy, *The Crisis of the Italian State: From the Origins of the Cold War to the Fall of Berlusconi and Beyond* (New York: St. Martin's Press, 1997), pp. 139–67.
13. 'Something New in Italy', *The Economist* (27 April 1996), 31.
14. Bonini, *Storia della Corte Costituzionale*, pp. 337–8.
15. Carlo Guarnieri, *Magistratura e Politica in Italia* (Bologna: Il Mulino, 1992), pp. 105–8.
16. Alessandro Pizzorusso, 'Italian and American Models of the Judiciary and of Judicial Review of Legislation: a Comparison of Recent Tendencies', *American Journal of Comparative Law*, 38 (1993), 384.

17. Constitutional Law No. 1, 11 March 1953, Articles 5 and 6.
18. Law No. 87, 11 March 1953, Article 7.
19. Lawrence Baum, *The Puzzle of Judicial Behavior* (Ann Arbor: University of Michigan Press, 1997), pp. 42–3.
20. Gino Pallotta, *Dizionario della Politica Italiana* (Rome: Newton Compton Editori, 1985), p. 394.
21. 'Se il Giudice Va in Politica', *Corriere della Sera* (12 December 1992), 1.
22. Baum, *The Puzzle of Judicial Behavior*, p. 29.
23. Constitutional Law No. 1, 16 January 1989.
24. Pizzorusso, 'Italian and American Models of the Judiciary and of Judicial Review of Legislation', 381.
25. Pizzorusso, *Sistema Istituzionale*, p. 253.
26. Law No. 87, 11 March 1953, Articles 31–35.
27. Constitutional Law No. 1, 11 March 1953, Article 2.
28. 'Norme Integrative per i Giudizi Davanti all Corte Costituzionale, Article 18', in Chiavario (ed.), *Codice della Giustizia Costituzionale*, p. 137.
29. Judgment No. 164/1980.
30. Giuseppe Borre, 'Verso la Realtà dell'Dissenting Opinion', *Questione Giustizia*, 13 (1994), 583.
31. Judgment No. 18/1989.
32. 'Indice Cronologico delle Disposizioni di Legge e di Atti con Forza di Legge Dichiarate Costituzionalmente Illegittime dalla Entrata in Funzione della Corte a Tutto il 1966', *Giurisprudenza Costituzionale*, 11 (1966), cxlvi–cxc.
33. 'Indice delle Disposizioni di Legge Dichiarate Incostituzionali a Seguito di Guidizi Incidentali nel 1967', *Sentenze e Ordinanze delle Corte Costituzionale*, 6 (1967), lxiv–lxx.
34. 'Indice Cronologico delle Questioni Decise', *Giurisprudenza Costituzionale*, 40 (1995), xi–xxviii.
35. Alec Stone, *The Birth of Judicial Politics in France: the Constitutional Council in Comparative Perspective* (New York: Oxford University Press, 1992), p. 238.
36. Christine Landfried, 'Judicial Policy-Making in Germany: the Federal Constitutional Court', *West European Politics*, 15 (1992), 50.
37. Henry J. Abraham, *The Judicial Process* (New York: Oxford University Press, 1998), p. 301.
38. Rudolfo Pagano, 'Il Riordino della Legislazione in Italia', *Nuovi Studi Politici*, 24 (April–June, 1994), 31.
39. Presidenza del Consiglio dei Ministri, Dipartimento per la Funzione Pubblica, *Rapporto sulle Condizioni delle Pubbliche Amministrazione* (Rome: Presidenza del Consiglio dei Ministri, 1993), pp. 23–4.
40. Pagano, 'Riordino della Legislazione', 31.
41. Frederic Spotts and Theodor Wieser, *Italy: a Difficult Democracy* (Cambridge: Cambridge University Press, 1986), pp. 151–2.
42. Giuseppe Di Palma, *Surviving without Governing: the Italian Parties in Parliament* (Berkeley: University of California Press, 1977), pp. 75–6.
43. Ibid., p. 69.
44. Enzo Cheli, 'Giustizia Costituzionale e Sfera Parlamentare', *Quaderni Costituzionali*, 13 (1993), 265.

45. Christine Landfried, 'Constitutional Review and Legislation in the Federal Republic of Germany', in Christine Landfried, ed., *Constitutional Review and Legislation: an International Comparison* (Baden-Baden: Nomos Verlagsgesellschaft, 1988), p. 154.
46. Mario Montella, *Tipologia delle Sentenze della Corte Costituzionale* (Rimini: Maggioli Editore, 1992), p. 94.
47. Ibid., p. 100.
48. Ibid., p. 105.
49. Cheli, 'Giustizia Costituzionale e Sfera Parlamentare', 269.
50. Francesca Curi, 'L'Attività "Paralegislativa" della Corte Costituzionale in Ambito Penale: Cambia la Pena dell'Oltraggio a Pubblico Ufficiale', *Giurisprudenza Costituzionale*, 40 (1995), 1091.
51. Franco Modugno, 'Ancora sui Controversi Rapporti tra Corte Costituzionale e Potere Legislativo', *Giurisprudenza Costituzionale*, 33 (1988), 24.
52. Alessandro Pizzorusso, 'Constitutional Review and Legislation in Italy', in Christine Landfried, ed., *Constitutional Review and Legislation: an International Comparison* (Baden-Baden: Nomos Verlagsgesellschaft, 1988), p. 119.
53. Stefano Rodotà, 'Del Ceto dei Giuristi e di Alcune sue Politiche del Diritto', *Politica del Diritto*, 17 (1986), 5.
54. Raffaele De Mucci, *Giudici e Sistema Politico: Alte Corti e Cittadinanza* (Messina: Rubbettino, 1995).
55. Guarnieri, *Magistratura e Politica in Italia*, p. 27.
56. Jack Knight and Lee Epstein, 'On the Struggle for Judicial Supremacy', *Law and Society Review*, 30 (1996), 113.

3 Executive–Legislative Relations: Decree Laws

1. Thomas M. Franck, *Political Questions, Judicial Answers: Does the Rule of Law Apply to Foreign Affairs?* (Princeton: Princeton University Press, 1992), p. 30.
2. Jeffrey A. Segal, 'Separation-of-Powers Games in the Positive Theory of Congress and the Courts', *American Political Science Review*, 91 (1997), 42–3; and Joseph Ignagni and James Meernik, 'Explaining Congressional Attempts to Reverse Supreme Court Decisions', *Political Research Quarterly*, 47 (1994), 353–72.
3. Carlo Guarnieri and Patrizia Pederzoli, *La Democrazia Giudiziaria* (Bologna: Il Mulino, 1997), p. 105.
4. 'Statuto Albertino', in M. Bassani, V. Italia and C. E. Traverso, eds, *Leggi Fondamentali del Diritto Pubblico e Costituzionale* (Milan: Dott. A. Giuffrè, 1995), pp. 1277–8.
5. Livio Paladin, 'Art. 76–77', in Giuseppe Branca, ed., *Commentario della Costituzione: La Formazione delle Leggi, Art. 76–82* (Bologna: Nicolà Zanichelli Editore, 1979), p. 45.
6. Gustavo Zagrebelsky, *Manuale di Diritto Costituzionale: il Sistema delle Fonti del Diritto* (Turin: UTET, 1990), p. 175.
7. Paladin, 'Art. 76–77', p. 45.
8. Zagrebelsky, *Manuale di Diritto Costituzionale*, p. 175.
9. Paladin, 'Art. 76–77', p. 48.

10. Andrea Manzella, *Il Parlamento* (Bologna: Il Mulino, 1977), p. 272.
11. Joseph LaPalombara, *Democracy Italian Style* (New Haven: Yale University Press, 1987), p. 215.
12. Annarita Criscitiello, 'The Political Role of Cabinet Ministers in Italy', in Michael Laver and Kenneth A. Shepsle, eds, *Cabinet Ministers and Parliamentary Government* (Cambridge: Cambridge University Press, 1994), p. 187.
13. Judgment No. 75/1967.
14. See, for example, Judgment No. 113/1967.
15. Alberto Predieri, 'Il Governo Colegislatore', in Franco Cazzola, Alberto Predieri and Grazia Priulla, eds, *Il Decreto Legge fra Governo e Parlamento* (Milan: Giuffrè Editore, 1975), pp. xv–xvi.
16. G. D'Orazio, 'Nota Minima sul Vuoto Legislativo quale Caso di Necessità e di Urgenza', *Giurisprudenza Italiana*, 123 (1971), IV-113.
17. Maurizio Cotta, 'The Rise and Fall of the "Centrality" of the Italian Parliament: Transformations of the Executive–Legislative Subsystem after the Second World War', in Gary W. Copeland and Samuel C. Patterson, eds, *Parliaments in the Modern World: Changing Institutions* (Ann Arbor: University of Michigan Press, 1994), p. 67.
18. Ibid., p. 72.
19. Alfonso Celotto, 'Gli Atti Legislativi del Governo e i Rapporti fra i Poteri' (Unpublished paper presented at the Annual Meeting of Associazione Italiana dei Costituzionalisti, Parma, 24–25 November 1995), 3.
20. ISTAT, *45 Anni di Elezioni in Italia, 1946–90* (Rome: Istituto Nazionale di Statistica, 1990), p. 45.
21. Norman Kogan, *A Political History of Italy: the Postwar Years* (New York: Praeger, 1983), p. 298.
22. David Hine, *Governing Italy: the Politics of Bargained Pluralism* (Oxford: Clarendon Press, 1993), p. 176.
23. Judgment No. 55/1977.
24. Predieri, 'Il Governo Colegislatore', p. xii.
25. Celotto, 'Gli Atti Legislativi del Governo', 3.
26. Criscitiello, 'The Political Role of Cabinet Ministers', p. 195.
27. Cotta, 'The Rise and Fall of the "Centrality" of the Italian Parliament', p. 67.
28. Celotto, 'Gli Atti Legislativi del Governo', 3.
29. Judgment No. 59/1982.
30. Massimo Morisi and Franco Cazzola, 'La Decisione Urgente: Usi e Funzioni dei Decreto Legge nel Sistema Politico Italiano', *Rivista Italiana di Scienza Politica*, 11 (1981), 452.
31. Stefano Rodotà, 'Fenomenologia dei Decreti', *Politica del Diritto*, 11 (1980), 379.
32. Ibid., 380.
33. Antonio Baldassarre and Cesare Salvi, 'Contro l'Irrigidimento Autoritario del Sistema Politico', *Politica del Diritto*, 11 (1980), 387.
34. Morisi and Cazzola, 'La Decisione Urgente', 447.
35. Ibid., 457.
36. Giorgio Berti, *Interpretazione Costituzionale* (Padua: CEDAM, 1988), p. 158.
37. David Hine, *Governing Italy*, p. 346.
38. Vincenzo Lippolis, 'Il Procedimento di Esame dei Disegni di Legge di Conversione dei Decreti-Leggi', *Quaderni Costituzionali*, 11 (1982), 227.

39. Giovanni Bertolini, 'Le Istituzioni in Italia: Parlamento', *Quaderni Costituzionali*, 11 (1982), 450.
40. Judgment No. 304/1983.
41. Celotto, 'Gli Atti Legislativi del Governo', 3.
42. Zagrebelsky, *Manuale di Diritto Costituzionale*, p. 178.
43. Vincent della Sala, 'Government by Decree: the Craxi Government and the Use of Decree Legislation in the Italian Parliament', in Rafaella Y. Nanetti, Robert Leonardi and Piergiorgio Corbetta, eds, *Italian Politics: a Review, Vol. 2* (London: Francis Pinter, 1988), p. 20.
44. Temistocle Martines, *Diritto Costituzionale* (Milan: Giuffrè Editore, 1994), p. 452.
45. Zagrebelsky, *Manuale di Diritto Costituzionale*, p. 178.
46. Martines, *Diritto Costituzionale*, pp. 454–5.
47. Rolando Tarchi, 'Incompetenza Legislativa del Governo, Interposizione del Parlamento e Sindacato della Corte Costituzionale', *Giurisprudenza Costituzionale*, 33 (1985), I-248.
48. Judgment No. 51/1985.
49. Giuliano Vassalli, 'Decreti-Leggi Favorevoli a Reo non Convertiti, Emendati or Decaduti: Una Prima Tappa verso la Chiarezza su un Controverso Tema di Diritto Transitorio', *Giurisprudenza Costituzionale*, 16 (1985), I-248–9.
50. Celotto, 'Gli Atti Legislativi del Governo', 3.
51. Giovanni Pitruzzella, *La Legge di Conversione del Decreto Legge* (Padua: CEDAM, 1989), p. 154.
52. Judgment No. 302/1988.
53. Pitruzzella, *La Legge di Conversione del Decreto Legge*, p. 154.
54. Mauro Ferri, 'Quarantesimo Anniversario della Corte Costituzionale', *Giurisprudenza Costituzionale*, 41 (1996), 2067.
55. Cotta, 'The Rise and Fall of the "Centrality" of the Italian Parliament', p. 67.
56. Hine, *Governing Italy*, p. 192.
57. Law No. 400, 23 August 1988, published in *Gazzetta Ufficiale*, Ordinary Supplement No. 86 (12 September 1988).
58. Enzo Cheli, 'Ruolo dell'Esecutivo e Sviluppi Recenti del Potere Regolamentare', *Quaderni Costituzionale*, 10 (1990), 73.
59. Angelamaria Scuderi, 'La Nuova Disciplina della Decretazione d'Urgenza', *Nuovi Studi Politici*, 20 (1990), 133–42.
60. Ibid., 133.
61. Martines, *Diritto Costituzionale*, p. 453.
62. Ibid., p. 455.
63. Judgment No. 544/1989.
64. Judgment No. 40/1994.
65. Judgment No. 263/1994.
66. Judgment No. 29/1995.
67. Judgment No. 360/1996.
68. Judgment No. 310/1988.
69. Tarchi, 'Incompetenza Legislativa del Governo', 977.
70. Claudia Nasi, 'Sul Controllo da Parte della Corte Costituzionale dei Presupposti Giurisficativi della Decretazione d'Urgenza', *Giurisprudenza Italiana*, 147 (1995), 392.

71. Stefano Maria Cicconetti, 'La Reiterazione dei Decreti Legge', *Politica del Diritto*, 16 (1995), 387.
72. Alessandro Pizzorusso, *Sistema Istituzionale del Diritto Pubblico Italiano* (Naples: Jovene Editore, 1988), p. 231.
73. Luciano Gallino, *Della Ingovernabilità* (Milan: Edizioni di Communità, 1987); Joseph LaPalombara, *Democracy Italian Style*, pp. 144–65; and Paul Furlong, *Modern Italy: Representation and Reform* (London: Routledge, 1994), pp. 4–6.
74. 'Nuovi Giudici alla Consulta, il Polo Accusa', *Corriere della Sera* (5 November 1996), 8.
75. Court of Cassation, Section I Criminal, Judgment No. 5209, 15 January 1994.
76. Celotto, 'Gli Atti Legislativi del Governo', 19–24.
77. Data furnished by Services of the Chamber of Deputies (Rome: Unpublished document, March 1998).

4   Arbitrating National–Regional Conflicts

1. Alexander Hamilton, *The Federalist, No. 80* (New York: Everyman's Library, 1969), p. 516.
2. Alec Stone, *The Birth of Judicial Politics in France: the Constitutional Council in Comparative Perspective* (New York: Oxford University Press, 1992), p. 230.
3. Stefano Maria Cicconetti, Maurizio Cortese, Giuseppe Torcolini and Silvio Traversa, eds, *La Costituzione della Repubblica nei Lavori Preparatori della Assemblea Costituente* (Rome: Camera dei Deputati, 1970), p. V-4217.
4. Robert D. Putnam, *Making Democracy Work: Civic Traditions in Modern Italy* (Princeton: Princeton University Press, 1993), p. 18.
5. Antonio Cantaro and Federico Petrangeli, *Guida all Costituzione e alla sua Riforma* (Rome: Editori Riuniti, 1997), p. 85.
6. Sergio Bartole, 'Art. 114–117', in S. Bartole, G. Falcon, L. Vandelli, U. Allegretti and A. Pubusa, eds, *Commentario della Costituzione a Cura di G. Branca: Art. 114–120* (Bologna: Nicolò Zanichelli Editore, 1985), p. 1.
7. P. A. Allum, *Italy – Republic without Government?* (New York: W. W. Norton and Company, 1973), p. 212.
8. Putnam, *Making Democracy Work*, p. 19.
9. Allum, *Italy*, p. 213.
10. Cicconetti *et al.*, *La Costituzione della Repubblica*, p. III-2396.
11. Ibid., p. III-2501.
12. Ibid., p. III-2397.
13. Gian Franco Ciaurro, 'Regioni: Che Fare?' *Nuovi Studi Politici*, 16 (1986), 20.
14. Constitutional Law No. 3, 27 December 1963.
15. Livio Paladin, *Diritto Costituzionale* (Padua: CEDAM, 1991), p. 211.
16. Ettore Rotelli, 'Regionalismo', in Norberto Bobbio, Nicola Matteucci and Gianfranco Pasquino, eds, *Dizionario di Politica* (Turin: UTET, 1983), p. 945.
17. Vittorio Angiolini, 'L'Obbligatorietà della Legge Regionale nei Rapporti con lo Stato', *Le Regioni*, 25 (1997), 13.

18. See Vezio Crisafulli and Livio Paladin, *Commentario Breve all Costituzione* (Padua: CEDAM, 1990), pp. 41–2.
19. Fausto Cuocolo, 'Diritto e Politica nella Giurisprudenza Costituzionale in Materia di Regioni', in F. Cuocolo, L. Carlassare, U. De Siervo, M. Bertolissi, M. Scudiero and F. Sorrentino, eds, *Corte Costituzionale e Regioni* (Naples: Edizioni Scientifiche Italiane, 1988), p. 31.
20. Judgment No. 9/1957.
21. Judgments No. 4/1956; No. 4/1964; No. 13/1964; No. 79/1966.
22. Judgments No. 7/1956; No. 18/1957; No. 105/1965.
23. Putman, *Making Democracy Work*, p. 20.
24. 'L'Istituzione delle Regioni a Statuto Ordinario', in Francseco Bonini, ed., *Storia Costituzionale della Repubblica: Profilo e Documenti (1948–1992)* (Rome: La Nuova Italia Scientifica, 1993), pp. 189–93.
25. Law No. 281, 16 May 1970.
26. Gianfranco Cerea, 'Regionalismo Possible e Regionalismo Auspicabile', *Le Regioni*, 25 (1997), 107–12.
27. Alessandro Pizzorusso, *Sistema Istituzionale del Diritto Pubblico Italiano* (Naples: Jovene Editore, 1988), pp. 110–11.
28. Allum, *Italy – Republic without Government?*, pp. 228–9.
29. Putnam, *Making Democracy Work*, p. 21.
30. Ibid., pp. 22–3.
31. Federico Sorrentino, 'I Rapporti tra lo Stato e le Regioni nella Giurisprudenza della Corte Costituzionale sui Conflitti di Attribuzione', in F. Cuocolo, L. Carlassare, U. De Siervo, M. Bertolissi, M. Scudiero and F. Sorrentino, eds, *Corte Costituzionale e Regioni* (Naples: Edizioni Scientifiche Italiane, 1988), p. 127.
32. Sergio Bartole and Franco Mastragostino, *Le Regioni* (Bologna: Il Mulino, 1997), p. 286.
33. D. Law No. 112, 31 March 1998.
34. Livio Paladin, 'Corte Costituzionale ed Autonomie Locali: gli Orientamenti Giurisprudenziali dell'Ultimo Quinquennio', in Paolo Barile, Enzo Cheli and Stefano Grassi, eds, *Corte Costituzionale e Sviluppo della Forma di Governo in Italia* (Milan: Società Editrice il Mulino, 1982), p. 335.
35. Francesco Rimoli, 'Il Principio di Cooperazione tra Stato e Regioni nella Giurisprudenza della Corte Costituzionale: Riflessioni su una Prospettiva', *Diritto e Società* (1988), 367.
36. Franco Bassanini, 'Autonomie Locali', in Nicola Occhiocupo, ed., *La Corte Costituzionale tra Norma Giuridica e Realtà Sociale: Bilancio di Vent'Anni di Attitività* (Padua: CEDAM, 1984), p. 190.
37. Judgment No. 18/1970.
38. Stefano Grassi, 'La Competenza in Tema di Conflitti di Attribuzione tra Stato e Regioni: "Disinteresse" o Nuovo "Ruolo" della Corte?' *Quaderni Costituzionali*, 5 (1985), 165.
39. Fausto Cuocolo, 'Diritto e Politica nella Giurisprudenza Costituzionale in Materia di Regioni,' *Giurisprudenza Costituzionale*, 32 (1987), 350.
40. Judgment No. 307/1983.
41. Judgment No. 219/1984.
42. Judgment No. 215/1988.
43. Judgment No. 214/1988.

44. Ordinance of 22 November, 1988.
45. Judgment No. 473/1992.
46. Mario Bassani, 'Il Conflitto di Attribuzioni nella Giurisprudenza', in CIDIS, *Il Controllo dello Stato sulle Regioni* (Padua: CEDAM, 1987), p. 24.
47. Giorgio Berti, *Interpretazione Costituzionale* (Padua: CEDAM, 1987), p. 162.
48. Livio Paladin, *Diritto Regionale* (Padua: CEDAM, 1985), p. 104.
49. Judgment No. 20/1970.
50. Judgments No. 171/1971; No. 220/1972; No. 145/1975; No. 78/1978.
51. Judgment No. 39/1971.
52. Judgment No. 203/1974.
53. Judgment No. 175/1975.
54. Judgment No. 175/1976.
55. Judgment No. 138/1972.
56. Judgments Nos 139, 140, 141, 142/1972.
57. Judgment No. 70/1981.
58. Judgment No. 223/1984.
59. Judgment No. 245/1985.
60. Judgment No. 8/1985.
61. Judgment No. 151/1986.
62. Judgment No. 271/1986.
63. Judgments No. 204/1987 and No. 214/1987.
64. Judgment No. 168/1987.
65. Judgment No. 157/1990.
66. Angelo Costanzo, 'Paradigmi e Sussunzioni nel Giudizio di Costituzionalità', *Giurisprudenza Costituzionale*, 39 (1994), II-2598.
67. Judgment No. 355/1993.
68. Judgment No. 302/1994.
69. Angelo Costanzo, 'Paradigmi e Sussunzioni nel Giudizio dei Costituzionalità', II-2599.
70. Paladin, *Diritto Costituzionale*, p. 214.
71. Maurizio Pedetta, 'Riserva allo Stato dei "Rapporti Internazionale" e Regime della "Previa Intesa" in Ordine alle Attività delle Regioni all'Estero', *Giurisprudenza Costituzionale*, (1985), I-1797.
72. Judgment No. 142/1972.
73. Judgments No. 182/1976 and No. 81/1979.
74. Beniamino Caravita, 'I "Poteri Sostitutivi" dopo le Sentenze della Corte Costituzionale', *Politica del Diritto*, 18 (1987), 317.
75. Paul Craig and Gráinne de Búrca, *EC Law: Text, Cases, & Materials* (Oxford: Clarendon Press, 1995), pp. 166–7.
76. Judgment No. 183/1973.
77. Judgment No. 232/1975.
78. Judgment No. 170/1984.
79. Judgment No. 115/1993.
80. Federico Sorrentino, 'Una Svolta Apparente nel "Cammino Comunitario" della Corte: l'Impugnativa Statale delle Leggi Regionali per Contrasto con il Diritto Communitario', *Giurisprudenza Costituzionale*, 39 (1994), 3458.
81. Judgments No. 384/1994 and No. 94/1995.
82. Judgments No. 187/1985 and No. 179/1987.
83. Paladin, *Diritto Costituzionale*, p. 525.

84. Franco Bassanni, 'Untitled', in Nicola Occhiocupo, ed., *La Corte Costituzionale tra Norma Giuridica e Realtà Sociale: Bilancio di Vent'Anni di Attività* (Padua: CEDAM, 1984), p. 196.
85. Judgment No. 2/1972.
86. Judgment No. 147/1972.
87. Judgment No. 40/1977.
88. Judgment No. 158/1988.
89. Judgment No. 496/1993.
90. Valerio Onida, 'Sindacato di Legittimità Costituzionale e Regioni', in E. Spagna Musso, ed., *Giustizia e Regioni* (Padua: CEDAM, 1990), p. 25.
91. Carla Rodotà, *La Corte Costituzionale: Come e Chi Garantisce il Pieno Rispetto della Nostra Costituzione* (Rome: Editori Riuniti, 1986), p. 90.
92. Temistocle Martines, *Diritto Costituzionale* (Milan: Giuffrè Editore, 1994), p. 797.
93. Sabino Cassese and Donatello Serrani, 'Regionalismo Moderno: Cooperazione tra Stato e Regioni e tra Regioni in Italia', *Le Regioni*, 8 (1980), 398–418.
94. Maria Teresa Serra, 'Il Neoregionalismo nei Lavori della Commissione Parlamentare per le Riforme Istituzionale', *Studi Parlamentari e di Politica Costituzionale*, 26 (1993), 65–83.
95. Putnam, *Making Democracy Work*, p. 81.
96. Grassi, 'La Competenza in Tema di Conflitti di Attribuzione tra Stato e Regioni', 165–75.
97. Onida, 'Sindicato di Legittimità Costituzionale e Regioni', 26.
98. 'Bossi sul Po, un Rito per la Secessione,' *Corriere della Sera* (13 September 1996), 2.
99. See Fulvio Mastropaolo, 'Revisione della Costituzione e Autonomia Regionale', *Giurisprudenza Italiana*, 149 (1997), IV-52–66; and Cantaro and Petrangeli, *Guida all Costituzione e alla sua Riforma*, pp. 85–93.
100. Cuocolo, 'Diritto e Politica nella Giurisprudenza Costituzionale in Materia di Regioni', 361–2.

5 Impeachment: the Lockheed Corruption Trial

1. Stefano Maria Cicconetti, Maurizio Cortese, Giuseppe Torcolini and Silvio Traversa, eds, *La Costituzione della Repubblica: Nei Lavori Preparatori della Assemblea Costituente* (Rome: Chamber of Deputies, 1970), p. V-4313.
2. Gustavo Zagrebelsky, *La Giustizia Costituzionale* (Bologna: Il Mulino, 1977), p. 394.
3. 'Statuto Albertino', in Niccolò Rodolico, ed., *Storia del Parlamento Italiano* (Palermo: S. F. Flaccovio Editore, 1963), pp. 424–5.
4. Zagrebelsky, *La Giustizia Costituzionale*, p. 397.
5. Carlo Ghisalberti, *Storia Costituzionale d'Italia, 1848–1948* (Rome: Editori Laterza, 1977), p. 241.
6. Cicconetti *et al.*, *La Costituzione della Repubblica*, p. IV-3492.
7. Ibid., p. IV-3497.
8. Ibid., pp. IV-3493–5.
9. Ibid., p. IV-3497.

10. Ibid., pp. IV-3501–2.
11. Ibid., p. IV-3559.
12. Ibid., p. IV-3569.
13. Ibid., p. V-4313.
14. Ibid., pp. V-4313–14.
15. Ibid., p. V-4321.
16. Constitutional Law No. 1, 11 March 1953.
17. Law No. 20, 25 January 1962.
18. Giorgio Berti, *Interpretazione Costituzionale* (Padua: CEDAM, 1988), p. 540.
19. Ibid., pp. 540–1.
20. Norman Kogan, *A Political History of Italy: the Postwar Years* (New York: Praeger, 1983), p. 219.
21. Vezio Crisafulli and Livio Paladin, *Commentario Breve all Costituzione* (Padua: CEDAM, 1990), p. 603.
22. Carla Rodotà, *La Corte Costituzionale: Come e Chi Garantisce il Pieno Rispetto della Nostra Costituzione* (Bari: Editori Riuniti, 1986), pp. 99–100.
23. Ibid., pp. 101–2.
24. Gino Pallotta, *Dizionario della Politica Italiana* (Rome: Newton Compton Editori, 1985), p. 279.
25. Presidential Decree, 14 March 1977, 'Notificazione dell'Atto di Accusa agli Imputati'.
26. Ordinance 18 March 1977 and Ordinance 28 March 1977.
27. Giustino D'Orazio, 'Giudizio Penale-Costituzionale e Legittimo Impedimento del Giudice', *Giurisprudenza Costituzionale*, 24 (1979), 370–1.
28. Presidential Decree, 30 March 1977, 'Convocazione della Corte Integrata per il Giorno 21 Aprile 1977'.
29. Ordinance No. 2, 7 May 1977.
30. Ordinance Nos 1–3, 7 May 1977.
31. Decree No. 1, 5 July 1977 and Decree No. 99, 20 July 1977.
32. Judgment No. 125/1977.
33. Mario Chiavario, 'Spunti di Tematica Processualistica nelle Pronunce Interlocutori sull'Affare Lockheed', *Giurisprudenza Costituzionale*, 24 (1979), 306.
34. 'Legge 10 Maggio 1978, n. 170 – Nuove Norme sui Procedimenti d'Accusa di cui all Legge 25 Gennaio 1962, n. 20 (annotato)', in Mario Chiavario, ed., *Codice della Giustizia Costituzionale* (Milan: Dott. A. Giuffrè Editore, 1985), pp. 107–14.
35. Rodotà, *La Corte Costituzionale*, pp. 98–9.
36. Ibid., pp. 101–3.
37. Pallotta, *Dizionario della Politica Italiana*, p. 279; and Rodotà, *La Corte Costituzionale*, p. 98.
38. Judgment, 1 March 1979; Explanation of Judgment, Deposited in the Cancelleria, 2 August 1979.
39. Ibid.
40. Ibid.
41. Raffaele Brunette, 'Anacronismi Legislativi e Processo Lokheed', *Il Nuovo Diritto*, 102 (1979), 102.
42. Andrea Manzella, *Il Parlamento* (Bologna: Il Mulino, 1977), p. 371.
43. Judgment No. 27/1987.

44. Giacomo Arezzo di Trifeletti, *Il Referendum Abrogativo e gli Istituti di Democrazia Diretta* (Rimini: Maggioli Editore, 1988), p. 200.
45. ISTAT, *45 Anni di Elezioni in Italia, 1946–90* (Rome: Istituto Nazionale di Statistica, 1990), p. 219.
46. Constitutional Law No. 1, 16 January 1989.
47. Law No. 219, 5 June 1989.
48. M. Bassani, V. Italia and C. D. Traverso, *Legge Fondamentali del Diritto Pubblico e Costituzionale* (Milan: Giuffrè Editore, 1995), p. 713.
49. Crisafulli and Paladin, *Commentario Breve*, p. 607.
50. Alessandro Massai, *Dentro il Parlamento: Come Funzionano le Camere* (Milan: Sole 24 Ore Società Editoriale Media Economici, 1992), p. 37.
51. Temistocle Martines, *Diritto Costituzionale* (Milan: Giuffrè Editore, 1994), pp. 613–15.
52. Livio Paladin, *Diritto Costituzionale* (Padua: CEDAM, 1991), pp. 797–9.
53. Manzella, *Il Parlamento*, p. 370.
54. David Hine, *Governing Italy: the Politics of Bargained Pluralism* (Oxford: Clarendon Press, 1993), p. 162.
55. Manzella, *Il Parlamento*, pp. 365–7.
56. 'La Difficile Via dell'Impeachment, 2 Agosto 1991', in Cesare Dell'Acqua, ed. *La Costituzione Vivente* (Turin: G. Giappichelli Editore, 1993), pp. 254–5.
57. Francesco Bonini, ed., *Storia della Costituzione della Repubblica* (Rome: La Nuova Italia Scientifica, 1993), p. 339.
58. Constitutional Law No. 3, 29 October 1993.
59. Orlando Roselli, 'Legge Costituzionale, 29 Ottobre 1993, n. 3 – Modifica dell'Art. 68 della Costituzione', in Alessandro Pizzorusso, ed., *Disposizioni Transitorie e Finali I-VIII, Leggi Costituzionali e di Revisione Costituzionale (1948–1993).* (Bologna: Zanichelli Editore, 1995), pp. 650–1.
60. Judgment No. 1150/1988.
61. Antonio Gialanella, 'La Corruzione Italiana e la Questione "Politica" della Legalità', *Questione Giustizia*, 12 (1993), 766.
62. Alessandro Pizzorusso, *La Costituzione: I Valori da Conservare, le Regole da Cambiare* (Turin: Einaudi, 1996), pp. 35–40.
63. Luca Ricolfi, *L'Ultimo Parlamento* (Rome: La Nuova Italia Scientifica, 1993), p. 156.
64. Roberto Pinardi, 'L'Autorizzazione a Procedere per i Giudici della Corte Costituzionale dopo la Riforma delle Immunità Parlamentari', *Giurisprudenza Costituzionale*, 40 (1995), 1161.

6 Gatekeeper to the Public: Referendums

1. Vernon Bogdanor, 'Western Europe', in David Butler and Austin Ranney, eds, *Referendums around the World* (Washington, DC: AEI, 1994), p. 27.
2. David Butler and Austin Ranney, 'Practice', in David Butler and Austin Ranney, eds, *Referendums around the World* (Washington, DC: AEI, 1994), p. 1.
3. Pier Vincenzo Uleri, 'Introduction', in Michael Gallagher and Pier Vincenzo Uleri, eds, *The Referendum Experience in Europe* (London: Macmillan, 1996), p. 7.
4. Butler and Ranney, 'Practice', p. 3.

5. ISTAT, *45 Anni di Elezioni in Italia, 1946–90* (Rome: Istituto Nazionale di Statistica, 1990), p. 80.
6. Quoted in Camera dei Deputati, *Il Referendum Abrogativo in Italia* (Rome: CD, 1981), pp. 7–8.
7. Ibid., pp. 10–11.
8. Ibid., p. 115.
9. Paul Ginsborg, *A History of Contemporary Italy: Society and Politics, 1943–1988* (London: Penguin, 1990), pp. 326–7.
10. Law No. 352, 25 May 1970.
11. As quoted in Maria Elisabetta de Franciscis, *Italy and the Vatican: the 1984 Concordat between Church and State* (New York: Peter Lang, 1989), p. 80.
12. Ginsborg, *A History of Contemporary Italy*, p. 328.
13. De Franciscis, *Italy and the Vatican*, p. 80.
14. Judgment No. 10/1972.
15. Judgment No. 251/1975.
16. Giacomo Arezzo di Trifiletti, *Il Referendum Abrogativo e gli Istituti di Democrazia Diretta* (Rimini: Maggioli Editore, 1988), p. 188.
17. Salvatore Bellomia, 'Legittimità e Ammissibilità del Referendum sull'Aborto tra Corte Costituzionale e Corte di Cassazione', *Giurisprudenza Costituzionale*, 20 (1975), III-3046.
18. Judgment No. 16/1978.
19. Ibid.
20. Ibid.
21. Di Trifiletti, *Il Referendum Abrogativo*, pp. 190–1.
22. Judgment No. 68/1978.
23. Judgment No. 69/1978.
24. Judgment No. 22/1981.
25. Judgment No. 23/1981.
26. Judgment No. 24/1981.
27. Judgment No. 25/1981.
28. Judgment No. 26/1981.
29. Judgment No. 27/1981.
30. Judgment No. 28/1981.
31. Judgment No. 29/1981.
32. Judgment No. 30/1981.
33. Judgment No. 31/1981.
34. Judgment No. 27/1982.
35. Judgment No. 26/1982.
36. Di Trifeletti, *Il Referendum Abbrogativo*, pp. 197–8.
37. Judgment No. 35/1985.
38. Ibid.
39. 'Referendum, le Otto Facce della Discordia', *Corriere della Sera* (18 January 1987), 2.
40. Judgment No. 29/1987.
41. Judgment No. 28/1987.
42. Francesco Crisafulli, 'Vecchi e Nuove Incertezze della Giurisprudenza Costituzionale in Tema di Referendum Abbrogativo', *Giurisprudenza Costituzionale*, 33 (1988), 122–3.

43. Ibid., 114.
44. Mauro Volpi, 'Il Referendum tra Rinnovamento e Declino', *Politica del Diritto*, 19 (1988), 50–1.
45. Judgment No. 63/1990.
46. Judgment No. 64/1990.
47. Judgment No. 65/1990.
48. Ordinance No. 273, 30 May 1990.
49. Nicolò Zanon, 'Procedimento di Referendum, Rilevanza della Volontà dei Promotori e Oggetto del Conflitto di Attribuzioni in una Vicenda Problematica', *Quaderni Costituzionale*, 10 (1990), 513.
50. 'Richio di Fuga dai Referendum', *Corriere della Sera* (17 May 1990), 2.
51. Judgment No. 47/1991.
52. Ibid.
53. Sebastiano Messina, 'Passa Soltanto un Referendum: la Corte Dichiara Inammissibili le Due Domande Più Importanti', *La Repubblica* (18 January 1991), 19.
54. 'Occhetto Rilancia la Sfida del Sì', *La Repubblica* (27 May 1991), 11.
55. Judgment No. 26/1993.
56. Judgment No. 35/1993.
57. Judgment No. 34/1993.
58. Judgment No. 36/1993.
59. Judgment No. 29/1993.
60. Judgment No. 28/1993.
61. Judgment No. 27/1993.
62. Judgment No. 30/1993.
63. Judgment No. 37/1993.
64. Judgment No. 38/1993.
65. Judgment No. 31/1993.
66. Judgment No. 137/1993.
67. Judgment No. 32/1993.
68. Judgment No. 33/1993.
69. Judgment No. 1/1994.
70. Judgment No. 1/1995.
71. Judgment No. 8/1995.
72. Judgment No. 7/1995.
73. Judgment No. 3/1995.
74. Judgment No. 4/1995.
75. Judgment No. 9/1995.
76. Judgment No. 10/1995.
77. Judgment No. 13/1995.
78. Judgment No. 1/1995.
79. Judgement No. 12/1995.
80. Judgment No. 11/1995.
81. Judgment No. 6/1995.
82. Judgment No. 2/1995.
83. Judgment No. 5/1995.
84. Judgments No. 14–42/1997.
85. Andrea Giorgis, 'Referendum Elettorali: la Corte Costituzionale Ribadisce la Propria Giurisprudenza', *Il Foro Italiano*, 120 (1995), I-441.

86. 'Overdose Referendum per Quasi Mezza Italia', *La Repubblica* (14 June 1997), 19; 'Cresce il Partito dell "Andiamo al Mare"', *La Repubblica* (8 June 1997), 19.
87. Anna Chimenti, *Storia dei Referendum: Dal Divorzio alla Riforma Elettorale* (Rome: Editore Laterza, 1993), p. 59.
88. Paolo Carnevale, 'Inabbrogabilità di Leggi "Costituzionalmente Obbligatorie" ed Inammissibilità di Referendum "Puramente" Abbrogativi: Ancora una "Svolta" nella Giurisprudenza Costituzionale in Materia Referendaria', *Giurisprudenza Costituzionale*, 32 (1987), 308–9.
89. James L. Gibson, Gregory A. Caldeira and Vanessa A. Baird, 'On the Legitimacy of National High Courts', *American Political Science Review*, 92 (1998), 360.
90. Francesco Bonini, *Storia della Corte Costituzionale* (Rome: La Nuova Italia Scientifica, 1996), p. 335.
91. Marcello Fedele, *Democrazia Referendaria* (Rome: Donzelli Editore, 1994), p. 152.
92. Roberto Pinardi, 'Corte Costituzionale e Referendum sulla Caccia: una Questione ancora Aperta', *Giurisprudenza Costituzionale*, 32 (1987), 297.
93. Eugenio De Marco, 'Referendum e Indirizzo Politico', *Giurisprudenza Costituzionale*, 39 (1994), I-1421–3.
94. Giuseppe G. Florida, 'Partita a Tre: La Disciplina Elettorale tra Corte, Referendum e Legislatore', *Giurisprudenza Costituzionale*, 40 (1995), 118–19.
95. As quoted in Chimenti, *Storia dei Referendum*, p. 69.
96. Ibid., p. 58.

7   Protecting Individual Rights

1. See Vizio Crisafulli and Livio Paladin, *Commentario Breve alla Costituzione* (Padua: CEDAM, 1990), pp. 129–63.
2. Alec Stone, *The Birth of Judicial Politics in France* (New York: Oxford University Press, 1992), pp. 173–208.
3. Christine Landfried, 'Judicial Policy-Making in Germany: the Federal Constitutional Court', *West European Politics*, 15 (July 1993), 52–3.
4. Livio Paladin, 'Libertà di Pensiero e Libertà d'Informazione: Le Problematiche Attuali', *Quaderni Costituzionali*, 7 (1987), 13.
5. Enzo Roppo, 'Il Servizio Radiotelevisivo fra Giudici, Legislatore e Sistema Politico', *Giurisprudenza Costituzionale*, 33 (1988), I-3945.
6. Guido Alpa, 'La Posizione degli Utenti nella Legislazione sulle Radiotelediffusioni', *Il Diritto dell'Informazione e dell'Informatica*, 9 (1995), 555–6.
7. Roberto Zaccaria, *Radiotelevisione e Costituzione* (Milan: Dott. A. Giuffrè Editore, 1977), p. 1.
8. Stefano Cicconetti, Maurizio Cortese, Giuseppe Tocolini and Silvio Traversa, eds, *La Costituzione della Repubblica nei Lavori Preparatori della Assemblea Costituente* (Rome: Camera dei Deputati, 1970), p. I-2626.
9. Ibid., p. I-2808.
10. Ibid., p. I-2818.
11. Ibid., p. I-2860.
12. *Orientamenti Giurisprudenziali in Tema di Buon Costume* (Rome: Servizio Studi Legislazione e Inchieste Parlamentari, 1972), p. 59.

13. Peter Bondanella, *Italian Cinema: From Neorealism to the Present* (New York: Continuum, 1998), p. 87.
14. See Judgments No. 2/1956; No. 121/1957; No. 11/1963.
15. Paladin, 'Libertà di Pensiero e Libertà d'Informazione', 7.
16. Franco Monteleone, *Storia della Radio e della Televisione in Italia* (Venice: Tascabili Marsilio, 1995), pp. 269–75.
17. Ibid., pp. 328–9.
18. Judgment No. 59/1960.
19. Monteleone, *Storia della Radio e della Televisione in Italia*, pp. 333–4.
20. Alessandro Pace, 'La Televisione Pubblica in Italia', *Il Foro Italiano*, 120 (1995), V-246.
21. Norman Kogan, *A Political History of Italy: the Postwar Years* (New York: Praeger Publishers, 1983), pp. 278–9.
22. Roberto Zaccaria, 'L'Alternativa Posta dalla Corte: Monopolio "Pluralistico" della Radiotelevisione o Liberalizzazione del Servizio', *Giurisprudenza Costituzionale*, 19 (1974), II-2169.
23. Judgment No. 225/1974.
24. Judgment No. 226/1974.
25. Carlo Marletti, 'Parties and Mass Communication: the RAI Controversy', in Raffaella Nanetti, Robert Leonardi and Piergiorgio Corbetta, eds, *Italian Politics: a Review* (London: Pinter Publishers, 1988), pp. 170–1.
26. Roberto Zaccaria, *Radiotelevisione e Costituzione*, pp. 4–5.
27. Monteleone, *Storia della Radio e della Televisione in Italia*, pp. 388–90.
28. Gianpietro Mazzoleni, 'The RAI: Restructuring and Reform', in Carol Mershon and Gianfranco Pasquino, eds, *Italian Politics: Ending the First Republic* (Boulder: Westview Press, 1995), p. 159.
29. Judgment No. 202/1976.
30. Francesco D'Onoforio, 'Groviglio nell'Etere: la Corte "Apre" ai Privati "Locali"', *Giurisprudenza Costituzionale*, 21 (1976), I-1424.
31. Claudio Chiola, 'Il Pluralismo Spontaneo per la Radiotelevisione Locale', *Giurisprudenza Costituzionale*, 21 (1974), I-1424.
32. Francesco Bonini, *Storia della Corte Costituzionale* (Rome: La Nuova Italia Scientifica, 1996), p. 243.
33. Marletti, 'Parties and Mass Communication', pp. 171–2.
34. Philip Schlesinger, 'The Berlusconi Phenomenon', in Zygmunt G. Baranski and Robert Lumley, eds, *Culture and Conflict in Postwar Italy* (London: Macmillan, 1990), pp. 273–4.
35. Judgment No. 148/1981.
36. Massimo Luciani, 'La Libertà d'Informazione nella Giurisprudenza Costituzionale Italiana', *Politica del Diritto*, 20 (1989), 626.
37. Enzo Roppo, 'Il Servizio Radiotelevisivo', I-3947–8.
38. Ibid., I-3946.
39. Monteleone, *Storia della Radio e della Televisione in Italia*, p. 429.
40. Schlesinger, 'The Berlusconi Phenomenon', pp. 277–8.
41. As quoted in Maria Adalgisa Caruso, *Le Emissioni Radiotelevisive nella Direttiva Comunitaria e nella sua Applicazione in Italia* (Milan: Dott. A. Giuffrè, 1993), p. 12.
42. Monteleone, *Storia della Radio e della Televisione in Italia*, p. 468.

43. Francesco Saja, 'La Giustizia Costituzionale nel 1987', *Giurisprudenza Costituzionale*, 33 (1988), 181.
44. Roberto Borrello, 'Cronaca di una Inconstituzionalità Annunciata (ma non...Dichiarata)', *Giurisprudenza Costituzionale*, 33 (1988), I-3950.
45. Monteleone, *Storia della Radio e della Televisione in Italia*, p. 472.
46. Borrello, 'Cronaca di una Inconstitutionalità Annunciata', I-3956.
47. Judgment No. 826/1988.
48. Ibid.
49. Borrello, 'Cronaca di una Inconstitutionalità Annunciata', I-3956.
50. Piero Calandra, *I Governi della Repubblica* (Bologna: Il Mulino, 1996), pp. 601–7.
51. Schlesinger, 'The Berlusconi Phenomenon', p. 282.
52. Monteleone, *Storia della Radio e della Televisione in Italia*, p. 472.
53. Sergio Fois, 'Profili Costituzionali e Disciplina Radiotelevisiva', *Giurisprudenza Costituzionale*, 34 (1989), II-2148.
54. Ibid., I-2155.
55. Pace, 'La Televisione Pubblica in Italia', V-248.
56. As quoted in Patrick McCarthy, *The Crisis of the Italian State* (New York: St. Martin's Press, 1997), p. 82.
57. Monteleone, *Storia della Radio e della Televisione in Italia*, p. 473.
58. Temistocle Martines, *Diritto Costituzionale* (Milan: Giuffrè Editore, 1994), pp. 678–80.
59. Raffaella Niro, 'La TV senza Frontiere', *Studi Parlamentari e di Politica Costituzionale*, 23 (1990), 65.
60. Caruso, *Le Emissioni Radiotelvisive nella Direttiva Communitaria*, p. 15.
61. Giovanna Savorani, 'Le Legge sul Sistema Radiotelevisivo e la "Catena Normativa"Appunti', *Politica del Diritto*, 23 (1992), 63–73.
62. Roberto Zaccaria, 'La Difficile Attuazione della Legge N. 223 del 1990 (C.D. "Mammì")', *Quaderni Costituzionali*, 11 (1992), 65–93.
63. Pace, 'La Televisione Pubblica in Italia', V-248.
64. Piero Alberto Capotosti, 'L'Emittenza Radiotelevisiva Privata tra Concessione e Autorizzazione', *Giurisprudenza Costituzionale*, 38 (1993), I-2118.
65. Judgment No. 112/1993.
66. Leonardo Bianchi, 'La Concessione Radiotelevisiva tra Riserva di Legge e Situazioni dei Concessionari', *Giurisprudenza Costituzionale*, 38 (1993), II-2122.
67. Mazzoleni, 'The RAI', 154.
68. Pace, 'La Televisione Pubblica in Italia', V-249.
69. Monteleone, *La Storia della Radio e della Televisione in Italia*, p. 535.
70. Ibid., p. 537.
71. Paolo Segatti, 'I Programmi Elettorali e il Ruolo dei Mass Media', in Stefano Bartolini and Roberto D'Alimonte, eds, *Maggioritario ma non Troppo* (Bologna: Il Mulino, 1995), pp. 165–9.
72. Ibid., 172.
73. Luca Ricolfi, 'Elezioni e Mass Media: Quanti Voti Ha Spostato la TV', *Il Mulino*, 43 (1994), 1031–46.
74. 'Vince Berlusconi, Sinistra Sconfitta', *Corriere della Sera* (29 March 1994), 1.
75. 'La Carico dei Nuovi Ministri', *Corriere della Sera* (30 March 1994), 1.
76. McCarthy, *The Crisis of the Italian State*, pp. 167–88.

77. Judgment No. 420/1994.
78. Stefano Ambrosini, 'Antitrust e Informazione Radiotelevisiva: Incostituzionalità della Norma sulle Concentrazioni', *Giurisprudenza Italiana*, 147 (1995), 130.
79. Roberto Pardolesi, 'Pluralismo Esterno (Non Più d'Una Rete a Testa?) Per l'Etere Privato', *Il Foro Italiano*, 120 (1995), I-6.
80. Roberto Zaccaria, 'La Corte Costituzionale Applica Direttamente il Principio Pluralistico in Materia Radiotelevisiva e ... "Non Fa il Vuoto"', *Giurisprudenza Costituzionale*, 39 (1994), III-3748.
81. 'La Consulta: Illegittime Tre Reti alla Finivest', *Corriere della Sera* (8 December 1994), 1.
82. 'Arrivano le "Ricette" per l'Assetto TV', *Corriere della Sera* (9 December 1994), 7.
83. Ottavio Grandinetti, 'Risorse Pubblicitarie, Stampa, Emittenza Locale e "Pay-TV": le Grandi Assenti nella Decisione che ha Dichiarato l'Inconstituzionalità dell'Art. 15 Comma 4 l.n. 223 del 1990', *Giurisprudenza Costituzionale*, 39 (1994), III-3758–65.
84. Pace, 'La Televisione Pubblica in Italia', 49.
85. 'Referendum TV, Fatale l'Ultimo Passo', *Corriere della Sera* (25 May 1995), 3.
86. Decree Law No. 444, 28 August 1996.
87. 'La Rivoluzione di Maccanico per TV e Telecomunicazioni', *La Repubblica* (26 June 1996), 7.
88. 'Frequenze, Rivoluzionato il Pianeta TV', *Corriere della Sera* (31 October 1998), 4.
89. Vincenzo Cuffaro, 'La Direttiva CEE sulla TV: un Primo Passo Verso la Disciplina del "Caos nell'Etere" Italiano', *Il Diritto dell'Informazione e dell'Informatica*, 6 (1990), 291.
90. Massimo Luciani, 'La Libertà di Informazione', 629.
91. Franco Modugno, *Il "Nuove Diritti" nella Giurisprudenza Costituzionale* (Turin: G. Giappichelli Editore, 1995), pp. 80–1.
92. Francesco Bonini, *Storia della Corte Costituzionale*, p. 332.
93. Pace, 'La Televisione Pubblica in Italia', V-262.
94. Luca Ricolfi, 'Politics and the Mass Media in Italy', *West European Politics*, 20 (January 1997), 136.
95. Landfried, 'Judicial Policy-Making in Germany', 53.
96. Stone, *The Birth of Judicial Politics in France*, p. 203.
97. Ricolfi, 'Politics and the Mass Media in Italy', 152.

8   Good Law and Good Policy

1. Donald Dale Jackson, *Judges* (New York: Atheneum, 1974), p. 18.
2. Michel Villey, 'Questions of Legal Logic in the History of the Philosophy of Law', in Volkmar Gessner, Armin Hoeland and Csaba Varga, eds, *European Legal Cultures* (Aldershot: Dartmouth, 1996), p. 113.
3. Jean Louis Goutal, 'Characteristics of Judicial Style in France, Britain and the USA', in Volkmar Gessner, Armin Hoeland and Csaba Varga, eds, *European Legal Cultures* (Aldershot: Dartmouth, 1996), p. 117.
4. H. W. Perry, Jr, *Deciding to Decide: Agenda Setting in the United States Supreme Court* (Cambridge: Harvard University Press, 1991), p. 275.

5. Raffaele De Mucci, *Giudici e Sistema Politico* (Messina: Rubbettino Editore, 1996), p. 109.
6. Yves Mény and Andrew Knapp, *Government and Politics in Western Europe: Britain, France, Italy and Germany* (Oxford: Oxford University Press, 1996), p. 350.
7. Lawrence Baum, *The Puzzle of Judicial Behavior* (Ann Arbor: University of Michigan Press, 1997), p. 102.
8. Perry, *Deciding to Decide*, p. 281.
9. Sheldon Goldman and Thomas P. Jahnige, *The Federal Courts as a Political System* (New York: Harper and Row, 1985), p. 137.
10. Tracey E. George and Lee Epstein, 'On the Nature of Supreme Court Decision Making', *American Political Science Review*, 86 (1992), 325.
11. Baum, *Puzzle of Judicial Behavior*, p. 103.
12. James L. Gibson, 'From Simplicity to Complexity: the Development of Theory in the Study of Judicial Behavior', *Political Behavior*, 5 (1983), 9.
13. Judgment No. 75/1967.
14. Judgment No. 263/1994.
15. Judgment No. 302/1988.
16. Judgment No. 360/1996.
17. Judgment No. 232/1975.
18. Franco Bassanni, 'Untitled', in Nicola Occhiocupo, ed., *La Corte Costituzionale tra Norma Giuridica e Realtà Sociale: Bilancio di Vent'Anni di Attitità* (Padua: CEDAM, 1984), p. 196.
19. Judgment No. 16/1978.
20. Judgments No. 47/1991 and No. 33/1993.
21. De Mucci, *Giudici e Sistema Politico*, p. 109.
22. Carlo Guarnieri, *Magistratura e Politica in Italia* (Bologna: Il Mulino, 1992), p. 27.
23. Bradley C. Canon and Charles A. Johnson, *Judicial Policies: Impact and Implementation*, 2nd edition (Washington, DC: CQ Press, 1999), pp. 115–16.
24. Joseph La Palombara, *Democracy Italian Style* (New Haven: Yale University Press, 1987), p. 217.
25. Judgment No. 148/1981.
26. Francesco Saja, 'La Giustizia Costituzionale nel 1987', *Giurisprudenza Costituzionale*, 33 (1988), 181.
27. Judgment No. 826/1988.
28. Charles H. Franklin and Liane C. Kosaki, 'Media, Knowledge, and Public Evaluations of the Supreme Court', in Lee Epstein, ed., *Contemplating Courts* (Washington, DC: CQ Press, 1995), p. 370.
29. Ibid., p. 373.
30. Maria Elisabetta de Franciscis and Rosella Zannini, 'Judicial Policy Making in Italy: the Constitutional Court', *West European Politics*, 15 (1992), 77.
31. Judgment No. 112/1993.
32. Judgment No. 420/1994.
33. Paolo Barile, as quoted in Anna Chimenti, *Storia dei Referendum: Dal Divorzio alla Riforma Elettorale* (Rome: Editori Laterza, 1993), p. 69.
34. Jean Blondel, *Comparative Government: an Introduction* (New York: Philip Allan, 1990), pp. 323–4.

35. Gerald N. Rosenberg, *The Hollow Hope: Can Courts Bring about Social Change?* (Chicago: University of Chicago Press, 1991), p. 30.
36. Michael Gallagher, Michael Laver and Peter Mair, *Representative Government in Modern Europe* (New York: McGraw-Hill, 1992), p. 4.
37. John Brigham, *The Cult of the Court* (Philadelphia: Temple University Press, 1987), p. 13.
38. Franco Modguno, 'Ancora sui Controversi Rapporti tra Corte Costituzionale e Potere Legislativo', *Giurisprudenza Costituzionale*, 33 (1988), 22.

Bibliography

Abraham, Henry J. *The Judicial Process*. New York: Oxford University Press, 1998.

Allum, P. A. *Italy – Republic without Government?* New York: W. W. Norton and Company, 1973.

Alpa, Guido. 'La Posizione degli Utenti nella Legislazione sulle Radioteledifussioni', *Il Diritto dell'Informazione e dell'Informatica*, 9 (1995), 555–78.

Ambrosini, Stefano. 'Antitrust e Informazione Radiotelevisiva: Incostituzionalità della Norma sulle Concentrazioni', *Giurisprudenza Italiana*, 147 (1995), 129–40.

Angiolini, Vittorio. 'L'Obbigatorietà della Legge Regionale nei Rapporti con lo Stato', *Le Regioni*, 25 (1997), 9–30.

Araùjo, António. *O Tribunal Constitucional (1989–1996)*. Lisbon: Coimbra Editora, 1997.

Atiyah, P. S. and R. S. Summers. *Form and Substance in Anglo-American Law*. Oxford: Clarendon Press, 1987.

Baldasarre, Antonio and Cesare Salvi. 'Contro l'Irrigidimento Authoritario del Sistema Politico', *Politica del Diritto*, 11 (1980), 386–90.

Baranski, Zygmunt G. and Robert Lumley, eds. *Culture and Conflict in Postwar Italy*. London: Macmillan, 1990.

Barile, Paolo, Enzo Cheli and Stefano Grassi, eds. *Corte Costituzionale e Sviluppo della Forma di Governo in Italia*. Milan: Società Editrice il Mulino, 1982.

Bartole, S., G. Falcon, L. Vandellin, U. Allegretti and A. Pubusa, eds. *Commentario della Costituzione a Cura di G. Branca: Art. 114–120*. Bologna: Nicolò Zanichelli Editore, 1985.

Bartolini, Stefano and Roberto D'Alimonte, eds. *Maggioritario ma non Troppo*. Bologna: Il Mulino, 1995.

—— and Franco Mastragostino. *Le Regioni*. Bologna: Il Mulino, 1997.

Bassanni, M., V. Italia and C. E. Traverso, eds. *Leggi Fondamentali del Diritto Pubblico e Costituzionale*. Milan: Dott. A. Giuffrè, 1995.

Baum, Lawrence. *The Puzzle of Judicial Behavior*. Ann Arbor: University of Michigan Press, 1997.

Becker, Theodore. *Comparative Judicial Politics*. Chicago: Rand McNally, 1972.

Bellomia, Salvatore. 'Legittimità e Ammissibilità del Referendum sull'Aborto tra Corte Costituzionale e Corte di Cassazione', *Giurisprudenza Costituzionale*, 20 (1975), III-3046–58.

Berti, Giorgio. *Interpretazione Costituzionale*. Padua: CEDAM, 1988.

Bertolini, Giovanni. 'Le Istituzioni in Italia: Parlamento', *Quaderni Costituzionali*, 11 (1982), 449–63.

Bianchi, Leonardo. 'La Concessione Radiotelevisiva tra Riserva di Legge e Situazioni dei Concessionari', *Giurisprudenza Costituzionale*, 38 (1993), II-2122–38.

Blondel, Jean. *Comparative Government: An Introduction*. New York: Philip Allan, 1990.

Bobbio, Norberto, Nicola Matteucci and Gianfranco Pasquino, eds. *Dizionario di Politica*. Turin: UTET, 1983.

Bondanella, Peter. *Italian Cinema: From Neorealism to the Present*. New York: Continuum, 1998.

Bonini, Francesco. *Storia della Corte Costituzionale*. Rome: La Nuova Italia Scientifica, 1996.

——, ed. *Storia della Costituzione della Repubblica: Profilo e Documenti (1948–1992)*. Rome: La Nuovo Italia Scientifica, 1993.

Borre, Giuseppe. 'Verso la Realtà dell "Dissenting Opinion"', *Questione Giustizia*, 13 (1994), 581–93.

Borrello, Roberto. 'Cronaca di una Incostituzionalità Annunciata (ma non ... Dichiarata)', *Giurisprudenza Costituzionale*, 33 (1988), 3950–61.

Brace, Paul and Melinda Gann Hall. 'Neo-Institutionalism and Dissent in State Supreme Courts', *Journal of Politics*, 52 (1990), 54–70.

——. 'Studying Courts Comparatively: the View from the American States', *Political Research Quarterly*, 48 (1995), 5–29.

Branca, Giuseppe, ed. *Commentario della Costituzione: la Formazione delle Leggi, Art. 76–82*. Bologna: Nicolò Zanichelli Editore, 1979.

Brigham, John. *The Cult of the Robe*. Philadelphia: Temple University Press, 1987.

Brunette, Raffaele, 'Anacronismi Legislativi e Processo Lokheed', *Il Nuovo Diritto*, 102 (1979), 97–102.

Butler, David and Austin Ranney, eds. *Referendums around the World*. Washington, DC: AEI, 1994.

Calandra, Piero. *I Governi della Repubblica*. Bologna: Il Mulino, 1996.

Camera dei Deputati. *Il Referendum Abbrogativo in Italia*. Rome: CD, 1981.

Cannistraro, Philip V., ed. *Historical Dictionary of Fascist Italy*. Westport, CT: Greenwood Press, 1982.

Canon, Bradley C. and Charles A. Johnson. *Judicial Policies: Implementation and Impact*. Washington, DC: CQ Press, 1999.

Cantaro, Antonio and Federico Petrangeli. *Guida all Costituzione e alla sua Riforma*. Rome: Editori Riuniti, 1997.

Capotosi, Piero Alberto. 'L'Emittenza Radiotelevisiva Privata tra Concesione e Autorizzazione', *Giurisprudenza Costituzionale*, 38 (1993), 2118–22.

Caravita, Beniamino. 'I "Poteri Sostitutivi" Dopo le Sentenze della Corte Costituzionale', *Politica del Diritto*, 18 (1987), 315–25.

Carnevale, Paolo. 'Inabbrogabilità di Leggi "Costituzionalmente Obbligatoria" ed Inaddmissibilità di Referendum "Puramente" Abbrogativi: Ancora una "Svolta" nella Giurisprudenza Costituzionale in Materia Referendaria', *Giurisprudenza Costituzionale*, 32 (1987), 308–33.

Caruso, Maria Adalgisa. *Le Emissioni Radiotelevisive nella Direttiva Comunitaria e nella sua Applicazione in Italia*. Milan: Dott. A. Giuffrè, 1993.

Cassese, Sabino and Donatello Serrani. 'Regionalismo Moderno: Cooperazione tra Stato e Regioni e tra Regioni in Italia', *Le Regioni*, 8 (1980), 398–418.

Cazzola, Franco, Alberto Predieri and Grazia Priulla, eds. *Il Decreto Legge fra Governo e Parlamento*. Milan: Giuffrè, 1975.

Celotto, Alfonso, 'Gli Atti Legislativi del Governo e i Rapporti fra i Poteri'. Parma: Unpublished paper presented at Associazione Italiana dei Costituzionalisti, 1995.

Cerea, Gianfranco. 'Regionalismo Possibile e Regionalismo Auspicabile', *Le Regioni*, 25 (1997), 107–12.

Cheli, Enzo. 'Giustizia Costituzionale e Sfera Parlamentare', *Quaderni Costituzionali*, 13 (1993), 263–77.

Cheli, Enzo. 'Ruolo dell'Esecutivo e Sviluppi Recenti del Potere Regolamentare', *Quaderni Costituzionali*, 10 (1990), 53–73.

Chiavario, Mario, ed. *Codice della Giustizia Costituzionale*. Milan: Dott. A. Giuffrè Editore, 1985.

——. 'Spunti di Tematica Processualistica nelle Pronunce Interlocutori sull'Affare Lockheed', *Giurisprudenza Costituzionale*, 24 (1979), 293–329.

Chimenti, Anna. *Storia dei Referendum: Dal Divorzio all Riforma Elettorale*. Rome: Editore Laterza, 1993.

Chiola, Claudio. 'Il Pluralismo Spontaneo per la Radiotelevisione Locale', *Giurisprudenza Costituzionale*, 21 (1974), I-1424–6.

Ciaurro, Gian Franco. 'Regioni: Che Fare?' *Nuovi Studi Politici*, 16 (1986), 19–34.

Cicconetti, Stefano Maria. 'La Reiterazione dei Decreti Legge', *Politica del Diritto*, 26 (1995), 383–92.

——, Maurizio Cortese, Giuseppe Torcolini and Silvio Traversa, eds. *La Costituzione della Repubblica: Nei Lavori Preparatori della Assemblea Costituente*. Rome: Camera dei Deputati, 1970.

CIDIS. *Il Controllo dello Stato sulle Regioni*. Padua: CEDAM, 1987.

Copeland, Gary W. and Samuel Patterson, eds. *Parliaments in the Modern World: Changing Institutions*. Ann Arbor: University of Michigan Press, 1994.

Costanzo, Angelo. 'Paradimi e Sussunzioni nel Giudizio di Costituzionalità', *Giurisprudenza Costituzionale*, 19 (1994), II-2598–630.

Craig, Paul and Gráinne de Búrca. *EC Law: Text, Cases, & Materials*. Oxford: Clarendon Press, 1995.

Crisafulli, Vezio. 'Vecchie e Nuove Incertezze della Giurisprudenza Costituzionale in Tema di Referendum Abbrogativo', *Giurisprudenza Costituzionale*, 33 (1988), 114–43.

—— and Livio Paladin. *Commentario Breve all Costituzione*. Padua: CEDAM, 1990.

Cuffaro, Vincenzo. 'La Direttiva CEE sulla TV: un Primo Passo Verso la Disciplina del "Caos" nell'Etere Italiano', *Il Diritto dell'Informazione e dell'Informatica*, 6 (1990), 291–9.

Cuocolo, Fausto. 'Diritto e Politica nella Giurisprudenza Costituzionale in Materia di Regioni', *Giurisprudenza Costituzionale*, 32 (1987), 334–62.

——, L. Carlassare, U. De Siervo, M. Bertolissi, M. Scudiero and F. Sorrentino, eds. *Corte Costituzionale e Regioni*. Naples: Edizioni Scientifiche Italiane, 1988.

Curi, Francesca. 'L'Attivita "Paralegislativa" della Corte Costituzionale in Ambito Penale: Cambia la Pena dell'Oltraggio a Pubblico Ufficiale', *Giurisprudenza Costituzionale*, 40 (1995), 1091–101.

Dahl, Robert. 'Decision Making in a Democracy: the Supreme Court as a National Policy Maker', *Journal of Public Law*, 6 (1957), 279–95.

De Franciscis, Maria Elisabetta. *Italy and the Vatican: the 1984 Concordat between Church and State*. New York: Peter Lang, 1989.

—— and Rosella Zannini. 'Judicial Policy-Making in Italy: the Constitutional Court', *West European Politics*, 15 (1992), 68–79.

Dehousse, Renaud. *The European Court of Justice: the Politics of Legal Integration*. London: Macmillan, 1998.

Dell'Acqua, Cesare, ed. *La Costituzione Vivente*. Turin: G. Giappichelli Editore, 1993.

De Marco, Eugenio. 'Referendum e Indirizzo Politico', *Giurisprudenza Costituzionale*, 39 (1994), 1401–27.

De Mucci, Raffaele. *Giudici e Sistema Politico: Alte Corti e Cittadinanza*. Messina: Rubbettino, 1995.

Di Palma, Giuseppe. *Surviving without Governing: the Italian Parties in Parliament*. Berkeley: University of California Press, 1977.

Di Trifeletti, Giacomo Arezzo. *Il Referendum Abbrogativo e gli Istituti de Democrazia Diretta*. Rimini: Maggioli Editore, 1988.

D'Onoforio, Francesco. 'Groviglio nel Etere: La Corte "Apre" a Privati "Locali"', *Giurisprudenza Costituzionale*, 21 (1976), I-1424.

D'Orazio, Giustino. 'Giudizio Penale-Costituzionale e Legittimo Impedimento del Giudice', *Giurisprudenza Costituzionale*, 24 (1979), 367–71.

———. 'Nota Minima sul Vuoto Legislativo quale Caso di Necessità e di Urgenza', *Giurisprudenza Italiana*, 123 (1971), IV-113.

Epstein, Lee, ed. *Contemplating Courts*. Washington, DC: CQ Press, 1995.

——— and Jack Knight. *Choices Justices Make*. Washington, DC: CQ Press, 1997.

Fedele, Marcello. *Democrazia Referendaria*. Rome: Donzelli Editore, 1994.

Ferri, Mauro. 'Quarantesimo Anniversario della Corte Costituzionale', *Giurisprudenza Costituzionale*, 41 (1996), 2061–70.

Florida, Giuseppe G. 'Partita a Tre: La Disciplina Elettorale tra Corte, Referendum e Legislatore', *Giurisprudenza Costituzionale*, 40 (1995), 103–19.

Fois, Sergio. 'Profili Costituzionali e Disciplina Radiotelevisiva', *Giurisprudenza Costituzionale*, 34 (1989), II-2148–57.

Franck, Thomas M. *Political Questions, Judicial Answers: Does the Rule of Law Apply to Foreign Affairs?* Princeton: Princeton University Press, 1992.

Furlong, Paul. *Modern Italy: Representation and Reform*. London: Routledge, 1994.

Galeotti, Serio. *Il Presidente della Repubblica: Maestro di Corte or Garante della Costituzione*. Milan: Dott. A. Giuffrè Editore, 1992.

Gallagher, Michael, Michael Laver and Peter Mair. *Representative Government in Modern Europe*. New York: McGraw-Hill, 1992.

——— and Pier Vincenzo Uleri, eds. *The Referendum Experience in Europe*. London: Macmillan, 1996.

Gallino, Luciano. *Della Ingovernabilità*. Milan: Edizioni di Comunità, 1987.

Gates, John B. and Charles A. Johnson, eds. *The American Courts: a Critical Assessment*. Washington, DC: CQ Press, 1991.

George, Tracey E. and Lee Epstein. 'On the Nature of Supreme Court Decision Making', *American Political Science Review*, 86 (1992), 323–37.

Gessner, Volkmar, Armin Hoeland and Csaba Varga, eds. *European Legal Cultures*. Aldershot: Dartmouth, 1996.

Ghisalberti, Carlo. *Storia Costituzionale d'Italia, 1848/1948*. Rome: Editori Laterza, 1977.

Gialanella, Antonio. 'La Corruzione Italiana e la Questione "Politica" della Legalità', *Questione Giustizia*, 12 (1993), 765–76.

Giannetti, Daniela. 'Il Neo-Istituzionalismo in Scienza Politica: il Contributo della Teoria della Scelta Razionale', *Rivista Italiana di Scienza Politica*, 23 (1993), 151–83.

Gibson, James L. 'From Simplicity to Complexity: the Development of Theory in the Study of Judicial Behavior', *Political Behavior*, 5 (1983), 7–49.

———, Gregory A. Caldeira and Vanessa A. Baird. 'On the Legitimacy of National High Courts', *American Political Science Review*, 92 (1998), 343–58.

Giorgis, Andrea. 'Referendum Elettorali: la Corte Costituzionale Ribadisce la Propria Giurisprudenza', *Il Foro Italiano*, 120 (1995), 441–4.

Goldman, Sheldon and Thomas P. Jahnige. *The Federal Courts as a Political System*. New York: Harper and Row, 1985.

Grandinetti, Ottavio. 'Risorse Pubblicitarie, Stampa, Emittenza Locale e "Pay-TV": Le Grandi Assenti nella Decisione che ha Dichiarato l'Inconstituzionalità dell'Art. 15 Comma 4 l.n. 223 del 1990', *Giurisprudenza Costituzionale*, 39 (1994), 3758–65.

Grassi, Stefano. 'La Competenza in Tema di Conflitti di Attribuzione tra Stato e Regioni: "Disinteresse" o Nuovo "Ruolo" della Corte?', *Quaderni Costituzionali*, 5 (1985), 165–75.

Guarnieri, Carlo. 'Change and Continuity in the Bureaucratic Setting of Europe'. Paper presented at 'Judges: Selection and Evaluation,' Oñati International Institute for the Sociology of Law, 1997.

——. *Magistratura e Politica*. Bologna: Il Mulino, 1992.

—— and Patrizia Pederzoli. *La Democrazia Giudiziaria*. Bologna: Il Mulino, 1997.

Hamilton, Alexander. *The Federalist, No. 80*. New York: Everyman's Library, 1969.

Hine, David. *Governing Italy: the Politics of Bargained Pluarlism*. Oxford: Clarendon Press, 1993.

Ignagni, Joseph and James Meernick. 'Explaining Congressional Attempts to Reverse Supreme Court Decisions', *Political Research Quarterly*, 47 (1994), 353–72.

'Indice Cronologico delle Disposizioni di Legge e di Atti con Forza di Legge Dichiarate Costituzionalmente Illegittime dalla Entrata in Funzione della Corte a Tutto il 1966', *Giurisprudenza Costituzionale*, 11 (1966), cxlvi–cxc.

'Indice Cronologico delle Questioni Decise', *Giurisprudenza Costituzionale*, 40 (1995), xi–xxviii.

'Indice delle Disposizioni di Legge Dichiarate Inconstituzionali a Seguito di Giudizi Incidentali nel 1967', *Sentenze e Ordinanze delle Corte Costituzionale*, 6 (1967), lxiv–lxx.

ISTAT. *45 Anni di Elezioni in Italia, 1946–90*. Rome: Istituto Nazionale di Statistica, 1990.

Jackson, Donald Dale. *Judges*. New York: Atheneum, 1974.

Johnson, Timothy R. and Andrew D. Martin. 'The Public's Conditional Response to Supreme Court Decisions', *American Political Science Review*, 92 (1998), 299–309.

Jones, G. W., ed. *West European Prime Ministers*. London: Frank Cass & Co., 1991.

Kelsen, Hans. *General Theory of Law and State*. Trans. by Anders Wedberg. New York: Russell and Russell, 1961.

——. *Pure Theory of Law*. Trans. by Max Knight. Berkeley: University of California Press, 1967.

Knight, Jack and Lee Epstein. 'On the Struggle for Judicial Supremacy', *Law and Society Review*, 30 (1996), 87–120.

Kogan, Norman. *A Political History of Italy: the Postwar Years*. New York: Praeger, 1983.

Kommers, Donald P. *The Constitutional Jurisprudence of the Federal Republic of Germany*. Durham: Duke University Press, 1997.

Landes, William M. and Richard A. Posner, 'The Independent Judiciary in an Interest Group Perspective', *Journal of Law and Economics*, 18 (1975), 875–905.

Landfried, Christine, ed. *Constitutional Review and Legislation: an International Comparison.* Baden-Baden: Nomos Verlagsgesellschaft, 1988.

——. 'Judicial Policy-Making in Germany: The Federal Constitutional Court', *West European Politics*, 15 (1992), 50–67.

LaPalombara, Joseph. *Democracy Italian Style.* New Haven: Yale University Press, 1987.

Laver, Michael and Norman Schofield. *Multiparty Government: the Politics of Coalition in Europe.* Oxford: Oxford University Press, 1990.

—— and Kenneth A. Shepsle, eds. *Cabinet Ministers and Parliamentary Government.* Cambridge: Cambridge University Press, 1994.

Lippolis, Vincenzo. 'Il Procedimento di Esame dei Disegni di Legge di Conversione dei Decreti-Legge', *Quaderni Costituzionali*, 2 (1982), 227–37.

Luciani, Massimo. 'La Libertà di Informazione nella Giurisprudenza Costituzionale Italiana', *Politica del Diritto*, 20 (1989), 605–37.

McCarthy, Patrick. *The Crisis of the Italian State: From the Origins of the Cold War to the Fall of Berlusconi and Beyond.* New York: St. Martin's Press, 1997.

Manzella, Andrea. *Il Parlamento.* Bologna: Il Mulino, 1977.

March, James G. and Johan P. Olsen. 'The New Institutionalism: Organizational Factors in Political Life', *American Political Science Review*, 78 (1984), 734–49.

Martines, Temistocle. *Diritto Costituzionale.* Milan: Giuffrè Editore, 1994.

Massai, Alessandro. *Dentro il Parlamento: Come Funzionano le Camere.* Milan: Sole 24 Ore Società Editoriale Media Economici, 1992.

Mastropaolo, Fulvio. 'Revisione della Costituzione e Autonomia Regionale', *Giurisprudenza Italiana*, 149 (1997), IV-52–66.

Mèny, Yves. *Government and Politics in Western Europe: Britain, France, Italy, West Germany.* Oxford: Oxford University Press, 1990.

—— and Andrew Knapp. *Government and Politics in Western Europe: Britain, France, Italy, Germany.* Oxford: Oxford University Press, 1998.

Mershon, Carol and Gianfranco Pasquino, eds. *Italian Politics: Ending the First Republic.* Boulder, CO: Westview Press, 1995.

Mishler, William and Reginald S. Sheehan. 'Response', *American Political Science Review*, 88 (1994), 716–24.

——. 'The Supreme Court as a Countermajoritarian Institution? The Impact of Public Opinion on Supreme Court Decisions', *American Political Science Review*, 87 (1993), 87–101.

Modugno, Franco. 'Ancora sui Controversi Rapporti tra Corte Costituzionale e Potere Legislativo', *Giurisprudenza Costituzionale*, 33 (1988), 16–25.

——. *Il "Nuove Diritti" nella Giurisprudenza Costituzionale.* Turin: G. Giappichelli Editore, 1995.

Monteleone, Franco. *Storia della Radio e della Televisione in Italia.* Venice: Tascabili Marsilio, 1995.

Montella, Mario. *Tipologia della Sentenze della Corte Costituzionale.* Rimini: Maggioli Editore, 1992.

Montesquieu, Baron. *L'Esprit des Lois* (1748).

Morisi, Massimo and Franco Cazzola. 'La Decisione Urgente, Usi e Funzioni del Decreto Legge nel Sistema Politico Italiano', *Rivista Italiana di Scienza Politica*, 11 (1981), 447–81.

Nadel, S. F. *The Theory of Social Structure.* Glencoe: Free Press, 1956.

Nanetti, Rafaella Y., Robert Leonardi and Piergiorgio Corbetta, eds. *Italian Politics: a Review, Vol. 2*. London: Francis Pinter, 1988.

Nasi, Claudia. 'Sul Controllo da Parte della Corte Costituzionale dei Presupposti Giustificativi della Decretazione d'Urgenza', *Giurisprudenza Italiana*, 147 (1995), 391–3.

Negri, Guglielmo. *Il Quadro Costituzionale: Tempi e Istituti della Libertà*. Varese: Giuffrè Editore, 1984.

——. 'The Rise and Fall of the Fascist Constitution', *Il Politico*, 47 (1982), 449–78.

Neppi Modena, Guido. 'Courts and the Difficult Road to Independence', *Italian Journal*, 3 (1989), 23–7.

Niro, Raffaella. 'La TV Senza Frontiere', *Studi Parlamentari e di Politica Costituzionale*, 23 (1990), 65.

Norpoth, Helmut and Jeffrey A. Segal, 'Popular Influence on Supreme Court Decisions', *American Political Science Review*, 88 (1994), 711–16.

Occhiocupo, Nicola, ed. *La Corte Costituzionale tra Norma Giuridica e Realtà Sociale: Bilancio di Vent'Anni di Attitività*. Padua: CEDAM, 1985.

Orientamenti Giurisprudenziali in Tema di Buon Costume. Rome: Servizio Studi Legislazione e Inchieste Parlamentari, 1972.

Pace, Alessandro. 'La Televisione Pubblica in Italia', *Il Foro Italiano*, 120 (1995), V-245–62.

Pagano, Rudolfo. 'Il Riordino della Legislazioni in Italia', *Nuovi Studi Politici*, 24 (1994), 31–40.

Paladin, Livio. *Diritto Costituzionale*. Padua: CEDAM, 1991.

——. *Diritto Regionale*. Padua: CEDAM, 1985.

——. 'Libertà di Pensiero e Libertà d'Informazione: le Problematiche Attuali', *Quaderni Costituzionali*, 7 (1987), 5–27.

Pallotta, Gino. *Dizionario della Politica Italiana*. Rome: Newton Compton Editori, 1985.

Pardolesi, Roberto. 'Pluralismo Esterno (Non Più d'Una Rete a Testa?) Per l'Etere Privato', *Il Foro Italiano*, 120 (1995), I-5–18.

Pedetta, Maurizio. 'Riserva allo Stato dei "Rapporti Internazionale" e Regime della "Previa Intesa" in Ordine alla Attività delle Regioni all'Estero', *Giurisprudenza Costituzionale*, 30 (1985), I-1797.

Perry, H. W. *Deciding to Decide: Agenda Setting in the United States Supreme Court*. Cambridge: Harvard University Press, 1991.

Pinardi, Roberto. 'L'Autorizzazione a Procedere per i Giudici della Corte Costituzionale dopo la Riforma delle Immunità Parlamentari', *Giurisprudenza Costituzionale*, 40 (1995), 1161–79.

——. 'Corte Costituzionale e Referendum sulla Caccia: una Questione ancora Aperta', *Giurisprudenza Costituzionale*, 32 (1987), 293–307.

Piniero, Rodriguez. *La Jurisdiccion Constitucional en España*. Madrid: Centro de Estudios Constitucional, 1996.

Pitruzzella, Giovanni. *La Legge di Conversione del Decreto Legge*. Padua: CEDAM, 1989.

Pizzorusso, Alessandro. *La Costituzione: i Valori da Conservare, le Regole da Cambiare*. Turin: Einaudi, 1995.

——, ed. *Disposizioni Transitorie e Finali I–VIII, Leggi Costituzionali e di Revisione Costituzionale (1948–1993)*. Bologna: Zanichelli Editore, 1995.

——. 'Italian and American Models of the Judiciary and of Judicial Review of Legislation: a Comparison of Recent Tendencies', *American Journal of Comparative Law*, 38 (1993), 373–86.

——. *Sistema Istituzionale del Diritto Pubblico Italiano*. Naples: Jovene Editore, 1988.

Portelli, Hughes. 'Les Deux Constitutions', *Il Veltro*, 23 (1989), 5–13.

Presidenza del Consiglio dei Ministri, Dipartimento per la Funzione Pubblica, *Rapporto sulle Condizioni delle Pubbliche Amministrazione*. Rome: Presidenza del Consiglio dei Ministri, 1993.

Pritchett, C. Herman. *The Roosevelt Court: a Study in Judicial Politics and Values, 1937–1947*. New York: Macmillan, 1948.

Putnam, Robert D. *Making Democracy Work: Civic Traditions in Modern Italy*. Princeton: Princeton University Press, 1993.

Ramseyer, J. Mark. 'The Puzzing (In)Dependence of Courts: a Comparative Approach', *Journal of Legal Studies*, 23 (1994), 721–48.

Ricolfi, Luca. 'Elezioni e Mass Media: Quanti Voti ha Spostato la TV', *Il Mulino*, 43 (1994), 1031–46.

——. 'Politics and the Mass Media in Italy', *West European Politics*, 20 (1997), 133–56.

——. *L'Ultimo Parlamento*. Rome: La Nuova Italia Scientifica, 1993.

Rimoli, Francesco. 'Il Principio di Cooperazione tra Stato e Regioni nella Giurisprudenza della Corte Costituzionale: Riflessioni su una Prospettiva', *Diritto e Società*, (1988), 361–99.

Rodolico, Niccolò, ed. *Storia del Parlamento Italiano*. Palermo: S. F. Flaccovio Editore, 1963.

Rodotà, Carla. *La Corte Costituzionale: Come e Chi Garantisce il Pieno Rispetto della Nostra Costituzione*. Rome: Editore Riuniti, 1986.

Rodotà, Stefano. 'Del Ceto dei Giuristi e di Alcune sue Politiche del Diritto', *Politica del Diritto*, 17 (1986), 3–12.

——. 'Fenomenolgia dei Decreti', *Politica del Diritto*, 11 (1980), 379–89.

Roppo, Enzo. 'Il Servizio Radiotelevisivo fra Giudici, Legislatore e Sistema Politico', *Giurisprudenza Costituzionale*, 33 (1988), I-3945–50.

Rosenberg, Gerald N. *The Hollow Hope: Can Courts Bring about Social Change?* Chicago: University of Chicago Press, 1991.

——. 'Judicial Independence and the Reality of Political Power', *Review of Politics*, 54 (1992), 369–97.

Saja, Francesco. 'La Giustizia Costituzionale nel 1987', *Giurisprudenza Costituzionale*, 33 (1988), 175–88.

Sassoon, Donald. *Contemporary Italy: Politics, Economy and Society since 1945*. London: Longman, 1986.

Savorani, Giovanna. 'La Legge sul Sistema Radiotelevisivo e la "Catena Normativa". Appunti', *Politica del Diritto*, 23 (1992), 63–73.

Scheb, John M., III and William A. Lyons, 'Public Perception of the Supreme Court in the 1990s', *Judicature*, 82 (1998), 67–9.

Schmidhauser, John R. 'Introduction: the Impact of Political Change upon Law, Courts and Judicial Elites', *International Political Science Review*, 13 (1992), 231.

Scuderi, Angelamaria. 'La Nuova Disciplina della Decretazione d'Urgenza', *Nuovi Studi Politici*, 20 (1990), 133–42.

Segal, Jeffrey A. 'Separation-of-Powers Games in the Positive Theory of Congress and the Courts', *American Political Science Review*, 91 (1997), 28–44.

Segal, Jeffrey A. and Harold J. Spaeth. *The Supreme Court and the Attitudinal Model*. Cambridge: Cambridge University Press, 1993.

Serra, Maria Teresa. 'Il Neoregionalismo nei Lavori della Commissione Parlamentare per le Riforme Istituzionale', *Studi Parlamentari e di Politica Costituzionale*, 26 (1993), 65–83.

Shapiro, Martin. *Courts: a Comparative and Political Analysis*. Chicago: University of Chicago Press, 1981.

Smith, Jean Edward. *John Marshall: Definer of a Nation*. New York: Henry Holt and Company, 1996.

Smith, Rogers M. 'Political Jurisprudence, the "New Institutionalism", and the Future of Public Law', *American Political Science Review*, 82 (1988), 89–108.

Songer, Donald R., Charles M. Cameron and Jeffrey A. Segal. 'An Empirical Test of the Rational-Actor Theory of Litigation', *Journal of Politics*, 57 (1995), 1119–29.

Sorrentino, Federico. 'Una Svolta Apparente nel "Cammino Comunitario" della Corte: L'Impugnativa Statale delle Leggi Regionali per Contrasto con il Diritto Communitario', *Giurisprudenza Costituzionale*, 39 (1994), 3456–8.

Spagna Musso, E., ed. *Giustizia e Regioni*. Padua: CEDAM, 1990.

Spotts, Frederic and Theodore Wieser. *Italy: a Difficult Democracy*. Cambridge: Cambridge University Press, 1986.

Stone, Alec. *The Birth of Judicial Politics in France: the Constitutional Council in Comparative Perspective*. New York: Oxford University Press, 1992.

Tarchi, Rolando. 'Incompetenza Legislativa del Governo, Interposizione del Parlamento e Sindacato della Corte Costituzionale', *Giurisprudenza Costituzionale*, 33 (1988), 941–78.

Vassalli, Giuliano. 'Decreti-Legge Favorevoli al Reo non Convertiti, Emendati o Decaduti: una Prima Tappa verso la Chiarezza su un Controverso Tema di Diritto Transitorio', *Giurisprudenza Costituzionale*, 16 (1985), I-242–53.

Volpi, Mauro. 'Il Referendum tra Rinnovamento e Declino', *Politica del Diritto*, 19 (1988), 439–53.

Weaver, R. Kent and Bert A. Rockman, eds. *Do Institutions Matter? Government Capabilities in the United States and Abroad*. Washington, DC: Brookings Institution, 1993.

Zaccaria, Roberto. 'L'Alternativa Posta dalla Porte: Monopolio "Pluralistico" della Radiotelevisione o Liberalizzazione del Servizio', *Giurisprudenza Costituzionale*, 19 (1974), II-2169–74.

———. 'La Corte Costituzionale Applica Direttamente il Principio Pluralistico in Materia Radiotelevisiva e ... "Non Fa il Vuoto"', *Giurisprudenza Costituzionale*, 39 (1994), 3748–58.

———. 'La Dificile Attuazione della Legge N. 223 del 1990 (C. D. "Mammì")', *Quaderni Costituzionali*, 11 (1992), 65–73.

———. *Radiotelevisione e Costituzione*. Milan: Dott. A. Giuffrè Editore, 1997.

Zagrebelsky, Gustavo. *La Giustizia Costituzionale*. Milan: Il Mulino, 1988.

———. *Manuale di Diritto Costituzionale*. Turin: UTET, 1990.

Zanon, Nicolò. 'Procedimento di Referendum, Rilevanza della Volontà dei Promotori e Oggetto del Conflitto di Attribuzioni in una Vicenda Problematica', *Quaderni Costituzionali*, 10 (1990), 508–22.

Index